"With Éclat"

THE BOSTON ATHENÆUM
AND THE ORIGIN OF
THE MUSEUM OF FINE ARTS,
BOSTON

First published 1981 in the USA by
ST MARTIN'S PRESS INC.
175 FIFTH AVENUE
NEW YORK, NY10010

© PHILIP ALLAN PUBLISHERS LIMITED 1981, 1985

Reprinted 1983
Second edition 1985
Perfect Bound edition 1988

Library of Congress Cataloging-in-Publication Data
Main entry under title:

Comparative international accounting.

   Includes bibliographies and index.
   1. Comparative accounting.   I. Nobes, Christopher.
II. Parker, R. H. (Robert Henry)
HF5625.C74   1985   657   85-26110
ISBN 0-312-15347-3 (St. Martin's)

Comparative International Accounting

SECOND EDITION

Edited by

CHRISTOPHER NOBES

University of Strathclyde

ROBERT PARKER

University of Exeter

Foreword by Professor Edward Stamp

St Martin's Press

"With Éclat"

THE BOSTON ATHENÆUM
AND THE ORIGIN OF
THE MUSEUM OF FINE ARTS,
BOSTON

HINA HIRAYAMA

The Boston Athenæum

DISTRIBUTED BY UNIVERSITY PRESS OF NEW ENGLAND

© 2013 The Boston Athenæum

Published in the United States of America by The Boston Athenæum

10½ Beacon Street, Boston, Massachusetts 02108

LIBRARY OF CONGRESS CATALOGING-IN-PUBLICATION DATA

Hirayama, Hina

"With éclat" : the Boston Athenæum and the origin of

the Museum of Fine Arts, Boston / Hina Hirayama.

pages cm

Includes bibliographical references and index.

ISBN 978-0-934552-82-0 (alk. paper) — ISBN 978-0-934552-83-7 (ebook)

1. Boston Athenæum—History.   2. Museum of Fine Arts, Boston—History.

3. Art museums—Massachusetts—Boston—History—19th century.   I. Title.

N521.A8H57 2013

708.144'61—dc23

2012026620

Design & typography by Howard I. Gralla

Copyedited by Fronia W. Simpson

Proofread by Phil Freshman · Indexed by Karla Knight

Printed by GHP, West Haven, Connecticut

Bound by The Riverside Group, Rochester, New York

Distributed by University Press of New England,

One Court Street, Lebanon, New Hampshire 03766

Except figures 2, 4, 8, 9, and 10, images of objects in the

Boston Athenæum's collection are by Boston Photo Imaging.

COVER ILLUSTRATION

Enrico Meneghelli, *Picture Gallery of the Boston Athenæum*, 1876. Oil on canvas, 33.2 × 53.7 cm.

Collection of the Boston Athenæum, Purchase, 1876 (fig. 58, detail)

FRONTISPIECE

Enrico Meneghelli, *Hall of the Maidens, Museum of Fine Arts, Boston,*

at Copley Square, with Casts from the Boston Athenæum, 1899. Oil on canvas, 35.9 × 23.5 cm.

Collection of the Boston Athenæum, Purchase, 1998

CONTENTS

ACKNOWLEDGMENTS

$\mathcal{D}$URING THE MANY YEARS I have been working on this book, I have incurred numerous debts of gratitude to those who have made its creation possible. At the Boston Athenæum, David B. Dearinger, Susan Morse Hilles Curator of Paintings and Sculpture, has been an ideal mentor and supervisor, always a fount of steadfast encouragement and timely advice. I am deeply grateful to him for his support and guidance. Paula D. Matthews, Stanford Calderwood Director and Librarian, has been unwavering in her enthusiasm for this project, as was her predecessor, Richard Wendorf. Over the years, many colleagues at the Athenæum have shared my interest in the topic and helped with every stage of the process. In particular, I wish to thank Pat Boulos, Stanley Ellis Cushing, Will Evans, Carolle R. Morini, Alice Platt, Catharina Slautterback, Mary Warnement, and former colleagues Stephen Z. Nonack, Sally Pierce, and Lisa Starzyk for their expertise, kindness, and wise counsel. In addition, I benefited immeasurably from the research conducted by former members of the Athenæum's curatorial staff whose tenure had come before my own: David McKibbin, Jack Jackson, and, above all, Michael Wentworth, the former Susan Morse Hilles Curator of Paintings and Sculpture, whose scholarship and discernment continue to guide me today, a decade after his untimely death. Finally, I am grateful to the board of trustees for its unfailing support, especially Elizabeth H. Owens, chair of the Fine Arts Committee. Funding for this project was provided in part by contributions from the following trustees: Alice M. DeLana, Bayard Henry, Elizabeth H. Owens, Susan W. Paine, Sandy and Jim Righter, and Susan and Matthew Weatherbie.

I have been allowed exemplary access to the records and collections of the Museum of Fine Arts, Boston, and many staff members there have offered ready assistance and collegial encouragement. I am especially grateful to Maureen Melton, Susan Morse Hilles Director of Libraries and Archives, and Julia A. McCarthy, Manager of Collections Documentation, who generously shared not only the records under their care but also their deep knowledge of the institution's history. In the museum's library, Paul McAlpine facilitated my research with unmatched flexibility. Other members of the MFA's former and current staff also helped with different aspects of this project, among others, Marietta Cambareri, Katie Kerr, Patrick McMahon, Pamela A. Parmal, Jennifer Riley, Erin M. A. Schleigh, and Mei-An Tsu. Without their liberal assistance, this book could not have been written.

I would also like to thank the following institutions for the opportunity to conduct research, and colleagues for the invaluable assistance they offered in the forms of information, discussion, and encouragement: Shinya Araki; Department of Rare Books and Manuscripts, and Fine Arts Department, Boston Public Library; Brooklyn Museum; Rauner Special Collections Library, Dartmouth College, Hanover, New Hampshire; Craig Hanson, Librarian, Harvard Musical Association, Boston; Baker Library, Fine Arts Library, Fogg Museum, Monroe C. Gutman Library, Houghton Library, and Harvard University Archives, at Harvard University; Massachusetts Archives, Boston; MIT Institute Archives and Special Collections, Massachusetts Institute of Technology; Massachusetts Historical Society; John F. McGuigan Jr. and Mary K. McGuigan; Maryalice Perrin-Mohr, Archives and Special Collections, New England Conservatory of Music, Boston; Paul Miller, Curator, Preservation Society of Newport County, Newport, Rhode Island; Manuscripts and Archives Division, New York Public Library; Peabody Essex Museum, Salem, Massachusetts; David J. Russo; Ohrstrom Library, St. Paul's School, Concord, New Hampshire; State Library of Massachusetts, Boston; Department of Special Collections, University of California Santa Barbara; Victoria and Albert Museum, London; and Manuscripts and Archives, Yale University.

Once this book reached the manuscript stage, I gained enormously from the insightful critique of Professor Mary Crawford-Volk, Museum Studies, Harvard University, and the superb skill and unfailing good sense of Fronia W. Simpson, the redoubtable editor for this project. Pat Boulos, the Athenæum's Digital Programs Librarian, obtained images from institutions and secured permissions to reproduce them in this book. She also coordinated photography by Boston Photo Imaging of objects in the Athenæum's collections. Invaluable, too, were the thorough proofreading of Phil Freshman and the judicious indexing of Karla Knight. For the beautiful design of this book, I am indebted to Howard I. Gralla, and for distributing it, to the University Press of New England, especially Michael P. Burton, director.

Finally, I owe lasting thanks to my family and friends for their good company, infinite patience, and resolute optimism that this book would see completion. My final thanks go to my parents, who, years ago, let their only child cross the Pacific Ocean and come to Boston, where I discovered the Athenæum and much more.

HINA HIRAYAMA

"With Éclat"

THE BOSTON ATHENÆUM
AND THE ORIGIN OF
THE MUSEUM OF FINE ARTS,
BOSTON

INTRODUCTION

$\mathcal{T}$HE NEW BUILDING of the Museum of Fine Arts, Boston (MFA), was expected to open in the city's Back Bay in the summer of 1876, six years after the incorporation of the institution. Less than a year before, in the autumn of 1875, the trustees of the Boston Athenæum searched for ways to inaugurate the museum, as they put it, "with éclat."[1] A membership library founded in 1807, the Athenæum was by then known for its fine collections of books and art, its elegant edifice on Beacon Street, and its illustrious members. In October 1875 the Athenæum trustees voted, in anticipation of the MFA's opening, to spend eight thousand dollars of the institution's funds on the purchase of decorative arts objects from Italy—in bronze, wood, and textiles—and lend them indefinitely to the museum.[2] As it happened, this act of munificence was but one of many that the Athenæum offered the fledgling museum, beginning even before the museum's establishment in 1870 and continuing into the late 1880s. This desire on the part of the Athenæum to ensure success for the new museum and the collaboration that resulted from that desire are the subject of this book.

Although once vitally connected, today the Athenæum and the MFA are two distinctly separate institutions, each with its own character and well-defined collecting areas. One of the largest membership libraries in America, the Athenæum houses, in its landmark 1849 building at 10½ Beacon Street, more than 600,000 rare and circulating books as well as important collections of paintings, sculptures, prints, photographs, drawings, maps, and manuscripts, and it continues to acquire in all these areas. The Athenæum's activities are supported by a belief that knowledge and refinement come not only from books but from many other forms of culture. Accordingly, all the collections are available for enjoyment and study to the Athenæum's approximately seven thousand members in addition to researchers from across the nation and abroad. The Athenæum also offers a wide array of cultural programs, including art exhibitions, lectures, discussion groups, and concerts. The MFA, by contrast, is one of the finest art museums in the world, renowned for its encyclopedic collections of nearly

450,000 works of art from virtually all civilizations and many centuries. Since its move in 1909 to its current location on Huntington Avenue, the museum has steadily enlarged its collections and enriched its galleries. Today, it attracts more than one million visitors annually who encounter, when entering its grand edifice, original works of art as well as a vibrant selection of educational and cultural programs.

Over the years, the Athenæum has made occasional if oblique references to its past relationship with the museum. The statement that the Athenæum's "galleries of art formed the nucleus of the Boston Museum of Fine Arts" appears on one of the two brass tablets prominently displayed inside the building's entrance, but specific details of the connection have remained little known.[3] Even rarer are the museum's references to its past involvement with the Athenæum, and they are buried in the provenance of the paintings and sculptures that the museum purchased from the Athenæum in the 1970s, a full century after the Athenæum had deposited them there. Outside the two institutions, the few books that have cited the erstwhile alliance have done so, for the most part, inadequately.[4] Not surprisingly, few people—even in Boston— know that the Athenæum and the museum ever had a relation, let alone engaged in an intimate collaboration. Something has happened to fade the memory of the ardent desire that once drew the two parties inexorably close. This book attempts to retrieve that portion of the past and to find reasons for the loss of memory.

In the history of nineteenth-century American cultural institutions, the case of Boston's Museum of Fine Arts is typical. Like many other American art museums founded around the same time—New York's Metropolitan Museum of Art, also in 1870, and the Art Institute of Chicago, in 1879, for example—the museum in Boston was established by prominent local citizens who wished to correct, with education, the city's perceived indifference to art. As the thin aesthetic soil of the United States became a national concern after the Civil War, the growing wealth of certain residents of major American cities began to underwrite museums and schools of art. In those cities as in Boston, many of these institutions aimed to elevate public taste in art as well as to make art contribute to the manufacturing industry. Possessing only small collections and limited financial means, most art museums had to rely, at least in the beginning, chiefly on loans and reproductions. But toward the end of the century, many American art museums grew richer and eventually matured into confident temples of original works of art, some even comparable to their European counterparts. Not surprisingly, the coming of age of American art museums was accompanied, in most cases, by significant revisions of their original aims. The museum in Boston was no exception.

Yet circumstances specific to Boston also affected the early years of the MFA. For one thing, the museum was conceived as a successor, at least in part, to the art gallery of the Athenæum. The Athenæum, born of the bright Enlightenment belief that the world in all its departments can be understood by the systematic attainment of knowledge, has always been, on purpose, a hybrid institution. Its engagement with the fine arts began in the 1820s with the inauguration of annual art exhibitions and the formation of an art collection. In the ensuing decades, the status of the fine arts department within the Athenæum changed dramatically, and the vicissitudes experienced by the department dictated, to an extent, how the MFA came into being in 1870.

The Athenæum's internal condition before 1870, however, was only partially responsible for the MFA's creation; other factors also contributed. For one thing, Boston saw an unprecedented proliferation of cultural and educational institutions in the century's middle decades, and this development provided both a model for and momentum to the movement to organize the city's first art museum. Vital, too, was the well-timed agency of certain key figures—most critically the brothers Charles Callahan Perkins and Edward Newton Perkins—who helped unify the various groups and individuals interested in this enterprise. Furthermore, as aesthetic taste in the city shifted during the 1850s and 1860s, the relative importance of the Athenæum gallery declined, and this fact added urgency and seriousness to the effort to establish a new art institution.

At the outset, the MFA possessed no building, no collection, and few funds with which to implement its broad vision. Compared with the situation in other American cities, public assistance was scarce in Boston; the city gave the nascent institution only a tract of land on which to erect its building. The museum therefore relied almost entirely on help from private sources, and the parsimony thus forced on the fledgling museum rendered its alliances with existing institutions, especially the Athenæum, all the more crucial for its survival.

In that context, the close-knit nature of Boston's upper class was of particular importance. As wealth accumulated in Boston throughout the first half of the nineteenth century—first from maritime trade and then from the textile industry—the city's economic elite gradually coalesced, by midcentury, into a self-conscious and increasingly insular group linked through business and family. By 1870 this remarkably interconnected group funded and controlled an overwhelming majority of the city's cultural institutions and philanthropic enterprises. At its birth in 1870, the MFA was undeniably tied into this web of Boston's cultural and educational organizations through many of its trustees who also served other institutions. Among these kindred relations, the Athenæum was undeniably the closest collaborator of the new museum, and their alliance eventually developed into a complex and multifaceted partnership.

For several reasons, the MFA's protohistory—the first six years, from 1870 to 1876, when it was without a home—is especially difficult to reconstruct. These years constituted the most intense phase of the collaboration between the museum and the Athenæum, yet only a limited number of records survive from this period. For one thing, record keeping was casual and the museum published little during its formative years. For another, the extraordinary closeness between the two institutions blurred the boundaries between them.

In the twentieth century, the scholarly reassessment of Boston's nineteenth century further influenced the perception of the museum's early years. During the century when Boston grew from a peninsular town of twenty-five thousand residents in 1800 to a metropolis of more than one million in 1900, the city experienced drastic changes in its geography, population, politics, and culture, particularly after the pace of immigration into the city accelerated in the late 1840s. Just as the city's ruling economic class saw its political power gradually erode in an increasingly democratic age, the group bestowed its wealth and influence on many of the city's cultural and educational institutions. As twentieth-century scholarship gave greater attention to nineteenth-century Boston's hitherto lesser-known groups—immigrants, women, industrial workers, and others— some historians and sociologists interpreted the elite's institution-building efforts as something sinister, an attempt to monopolize culture or retain control over the city's changing population through cultural means.[5] In this context, the early museum was often maligned, along with other institutions established by the same kind of people, as harboring paternalistic and elitist intentions. The original museum of 1870 was accused of having been, variously, an exclusive mausoleum of accumulated family possessions, an ostentatious treasure house of costly chefs d'oeuvre reserved for the privileged class, or an example of a top-down initiative to impose Eurocentric taste on the American sensibility.[6] Was the original museum any of these things? Do the museum's elite origins—the fact that its founders were privileged Bostonians— necessarily mean that the institution's founding purpose was elitist? Slowly, a scholarly reassessment of the original MFA has begun, a task that this book will continue.[7]

At the popular level, too, later generations came to view the upper echelon of nineteenth-century Boston—sometimes called the Brahmins—as an antiquated, dying breed. A term with fluid definitions, Brahmins once connoted a hereditary intellectual superiority (first used in Oliver Wendell Holmes Sr.'s novel *Elsie Venner*, whose magazine installments began in 1860). The designation later acquired additional meanings—old New England roots, great wealth, high social standing, gentility, and perhaps a sense of noblesse oblige—as well as a distinct connotation of conservatism, a general opposition to change of any kind, be it the immigrant masses, the growing egalitarianism, or modern art.[8] By the time the fictive George Apley—"a true son of Boston . . . imbued with the love of his land and caste"—emerged in John Marquand's 1937 novel, *The Late George Apley*, as the mythical Boston Brahmin uncomprehending and fearful of the democratizing forces, Boston of the nineteenth century had receded far enough into the past to have acquired the sepia glaze that has since colored our impressions of the bygone century.[9] But if the later view of nineteenth-century Boston as a theater of escalating struggles between the Brahmins and the Irish has managed to unify the long and eventful one hundred years into an evocative whole, the notion has also obscured some of the specific details, nuances, and original colors of a changing city during a dynamic century.

In these ways and others, much of the MFA's early history has been veiled from our view and, with it, the Athenæum's involvement with the young museum. But some facts of the collaboration between the Athenæum and the museum have remained intact, buried among institutional records and personal papers, and can be studied afresh. By enlisting this material, this book attempts to understand the two institutions' joint travails and triumphs in their original context, as their protagonists saw them.

CHAPTER ONE

The Fine Arts at the Boston Athenæum, 1807–1870

FOR MORE than two centuries, the Boston Athenæum has been a protean sum of its changing parts. In Greek antiquity, an athenaeum was a temple dedicated to Athena, the goddess of wisdom, a public place where scholars in various fields taught their students, and orators and poets rehearsed their compositions. In their modern incarnations, athenaeums were in some cases subscription libraries and, in others, performed additional functions.[1] The Boston Athenæum began modestly in 1807 as a reading room and a library, but its founders hoped it would develop into an institution of broad learning, with collections not only of books but also of art and even scientific apparatus. Since then, different departments have emerged and evolved within the Athenæum, and to this day it has remained a hybrid institution. In 1870 the conglomerate nature of the Athenæum would play a vital role in the establishment of the Museum of Fine Arts, Boston.

The Boston Athenæum was incorporated by an act of the Massachusetts legislature on February 13, 1807. Its immediate predecessor was the Anthology Society, a group of Bostonians who in 1804 had created a literary journal, *The Monthly Anthology and Boston Review*, which contained not only materials from European magazines but also original essays, reviews, and sermons. By 1806 the society wished to set up a library of European and American periodicals and reference works as well as a reading room, where members could enjoy these materials in warm, literary fellowship. A scheme to solicit broad subscriptions for these enterprises followed. More than one hundred men subscribed to launch the Anthology Reading-room and Library, which in 1807 was renamed the Boston Athenæum.[2]

Despite such modest beginnings, the founders of the Athenæum wanted the organization to grow into an institution with a "general . . . collection in *every* branch of knowledge."[3] The prospectus issued in 1807 ambitiously proclaimed that the future Athenæum would include, in addition to the library, a "Repository of Arts" filled with works of fine art, a "Museum" of natural and antiquarian specimens, and a "Laboratory and an Apparatus" for scientific experiments and observations.[4] Intellectually, this expansive reach across diverse disciplines—literature, art, sciences—had its direct roots in the eighteenth-century Enlightenment conviction that the systematic acquisition of knowledge would allow people to understand the world in all its different manifestations. In early nineteenth-century Boston, this ideal defined the Athenæum's multifaceted composition. In the beginning, however, the Athenæum's "leading objects and chief departments" were unequivocally the reading room and the library, and additional elements—such as art—were to figure within the institution only "as far as can be done without detriment" to these two key parts.

In its organizational structure, the Boston Athenæum modeled itself most closely after the Liverpool Athenæum in England, a subscription library established in 1798.[5] The thriving port of Liverpool was a gateway to England and beyond, and the Liverpool Athenæum was known to many well-traveled Bostonians as a rising new institution. Following the example set by the English predecessor, in Boston the Athenæum's nineteen founders raised funds by the sale of shares at $300 each.[6] The 150 men who purchased the shares became the proprietors of the Athenæum, and twelve trustees were elected to direct the affairs of the institution on behalf of the proprietors.[7] At least in the early years, the trustees and proprietors executed the day-to-day operations of the reading room and the library, and the librarian was the only paid staff member. (Until 1822, even that position was filled by a founder and trustee, William Smith Shaw.) To further finance its operations, the Athenæum sold different levels of membership for its reading room and library: a subscription for life cost $100, and that for a year, $10.[8] In addition, guests and families of the trustees and proprietors were allowed to use the Athenæum, as were the leaders of Boston's religious and cultural communities. Visitors—"strangers"—with proper introduction were also admitted.[9]

Like its prototype in Liverpool, the Boston Athenæum situated itself at the nexus of the city's intellectual activity and growing mercantile prosperity. The early proprietors included ministers, lawyers, doctors, and men of letters but also a large proportion of businessmen, a necessary source of funds for an institution "humble and restricted in its first resources."[10] Genuine love of knowledge certainly prompted some to support the fledgling Athenæum, but for many prosperous Bostonians an association with the place also provided a symbolic affirmation of their cultural attainment and status. At the same time, as Boston competed against New York and Philadelphia, well-to-do Bostonians wished to make the Athenæum a tangible symbol of the city's growing affluence and culture, and supporting it constituted public display of their wealth and civic pride.

Yet, just how public an institution was the early Athenæum? At its founding, the Athenæum was envisioned as a "Publick" library, useful to "various classes of our citizens."[11] The founders firmly believed that "love of intellectual improvement and pleasure, and that propensity to reading and inquiry . . . are capable of being diffused through considerable portions of the community."[12] Even women and children, who were not admitted to the reading room until much later, were to "have more than an indirect share of the advantages of the Athenæum" through its edifying effects on men.[13] Nonetheless, the Athenæum was a subscription library, serving those who could afford to subscribe to it. It was "public" only in the early nineteenth-century sense of the word: a library was "public" or "communal" when it was not based in a home and served a constituency larger than a private household.[14] "Public" did not imply, as it does today, universal access. From the beginning, then, the Athenæum addressed not the entire population of the city but only certain segments of it. The founding prospectus conceded that "deep investigations of science and exquisite refinement of tastes . . . are necessarily confined to a few," and even the hoped-for repository of arts was meant to provide "improvement and emulation of artists, and for the correction and refinement of taste in those, who aim to be connoisseurs, and able to bestow praise and censure with discrimination."[15] At least by implication— if not by any official measures—the early Athenæum envisioned its audience to be scholars, students of letters, connoisseurs, and artists. It saw itself as a place of intellectual cultivation and fellowship for such men, not as a circulating library. True to this vision, the reading room was open for long hours, and the Athenæum's books did not begin to circulate until 1826.[16]

For years after 1807, however, the founders' ambitions far exceeded the institution's means. An economic slump followed the War of 1812, and much of the financial support for the Athenæum dried up, forcing it to abandon its building plans and even to concede, at one point, that its original vision—to encompass all areas of humanistic learning—had been too broad.[17] But toward the end of the 1810s, the city's financial climate slowly recovered, and the Athenæum's collection again began to expand by gifts and deposits.[18] The library of just over one thousand volumes at its founding had by 1822 become the third-largest library in America, housing more than twelve thousand.[19] Objects other than books also arrived at the Athenæum as gifts, and by the early 1820s the collection included an unwieldy olla podrida of objects, ranging from innumerable coins and medals to more marvelous curiosities such as fossils, air pumps, test tubes, camera obscura, and even the first fired bricks with cuneiform inscriptions to reach America.[20] A visit by a New Bedford man in 1817 attests how widely the Athenæum's collecting interest had come to be known, since the sole purpose of his call was to present to the Athenæum a "famous fish" caught recently by an "industrious mechanic" in a river in that town.[21] (He also subtly demanded remuneration for his gift.) Despite its growing collection and patronage, the Athenæum's physical presence remained modest and provisional. During the first fifteen years of its existence, the institution occupied three small temporary quarters in downtown Boston.[22]

FIG. 1 *James Perkins Estate, Pearl Street*, ca. 1822. Graphite and wash drawing on paper, 7.6 × 10.2 cm (sheet). Collection of the Boston Athenæum

FIG. 2 John and William Ridgway, "Beauties of America/Athenæum Boston." Plate with a view of the Boston Athenæum building on Pearl Street, Boston, ca. 1829. Ceramic, 15.9 cm (diam.). Collection of the Boston Athenæum, Gift of Francis J. Parker, 1870

Much needed relief came in 1822—the year in which Boston became a city—when early benefactor and trustee James Perkins (1761–1822) gave to the Athenæum his elegant mansion on Pearl Street in downtown Boston.[23] A wealthy merchant with a penchant for books, Perkins had been an Athenæum trustee since 1807 and had just retired from the post when he gave the institution its fourth—and first permanent—home. Perkins's three-story brick mansion, valued at $20,000, was one of the most opulent houses in the city, located in the residential neighborhood of Fort Hill (present-day Post Office Square), which was near enough to the wharves but also fashionable enough to suit those who had made their fortunes in maritime trade.[24] The Perkins family—headed by James Perkins and his brother Thomas Handasyd Perkins (1764–1854), who had amassed their wealth in the transatlantic and China trades—was one of the most prosperous and influential of Boston's mercantile set. James died in August 1822, only two months after the Athenæum moved into its new home. The external appearance of the Athenæum on Pearl Street is known only from a few contemporary drawings (figs. 1, 2), and no images of the interior have survived. Later verbal descriptions fondly recalled the "aristocratic dignity and repose" of the building that stood "surrounded by horse-chestnut trees full of orioles and overlooking a pasture that stretched far into the distance" in a neighborhood of stylish residences and gardens.[25] The new Athenæum soon became the "pride of Boston," and members read in rooms that were "pleasantly shaded by trees . . . [and] spacious and as silent as night" in the

cool breeze from the nearby harbor.[26] On Pearl Street, with ample space and the cachet of culture that the building and the location conferred, the Athenæum began its transformation into the multifaceted institution of learning that the founders had envisioned.

FINE ARTS EMERGE AT THE ATHENÆUM

After some alterations were made to the interior, the Athenæum moved into the erstwhile Perkins mansion in June 1822. Eleven plaster casts of antique sculptures given by trustee Augustus Thorndike soon joined the books, as did a portrait of the munificent donor James Perkins (fig. 3) by Gilbert Stuart (1755–1828), the first painting commissioned by the Athenæum.[27] These were, in retrospect, the beginnings of the Athenæum's art collection.[28] Of the eleven Thorndike casts—a standard selection of ancient sculptures from the Vatican, Borghese, and Medici collections, many of which Napoleon had taken to Paris—at least eight were in full scale, and with the collection in place, the Athenæum's reading room must have looked splendid.[29] The young Ralph Waldo Emerson (whose father had been an Athenæum founder) admired the luxurious mixture of literature and art, describing the reading room as "royally fitted up for elegance & comfort," with something of interest "to attract the eye in every corner from the tedious joys of writing & reading . . . [and] the beholder instantly feels the spirit of the connoisseur stealing over him."[30]

Within months of moving to Pearl Street, the Athenæum trustees proposed erecting a separate annex behind the Perkins mansion for "the double purpose of a Room for the delivery of Lectures, and for the Exhibition of objects of the Fine Arts." The lectures would enlighten the audience on "Natural Philosophy, Astronomy, Chemistry, Mineralogy, and in the various branches of Ancient and Modern Literature," while art exhibitions would "encourage the taste for the Fine Arts."[31] Both the lecture hall and exhibition gallery were to be open to the public for a fee and thereby produce an income. If the main building were to remain a place of solitary intellectual pursuit reserved for proprietors and subscribers, the annex would expand the Athenæum's role in Boston's cultural life. Art formed a large part of this ambitious vision, and a circular printed in 1823 characterized the proposed gallery as Boston's first "Museum of the Fine Arts."[32] This was the first concrete effort to establish a non-commercial art gallery in the city.

In 1823, however, the fund-raising campaign for the annex failed. Only in 1826 was the plan revived, when the Perkins family again came to the rescue: that year the Athenæum received two large gifts of money from Thomas Handasyd Perkins and James Perkins Jr., brother and son, respectively, of the late James Perkins. Each gave $8,000 to the building plan, amounts that were quickly matched when the Athenæum raised additional funds, and the construction of the new building began.[33] Indeed, the Perkins family's munificence was such that, in the late 1830s, when the Athenæum considered moving to a new building, the trustees seriously entertained the idea of changing the institution's name to "Perkins Athenæum."[34] When completed in November 1826, the three-story brick annex stood behind—but separately from—the Perkins mansion that housed the Athenæum's library and reading room. In the new annex, the skylit third floor formed a single large room, measuring fifty by sixty feet, "in a manner peculiarly adapted for the exhibition of paintings,"[35] and the second floor housed a spacious lecture hall that could seat as many as five hundred. Between exhibitions, the third floor was offered to local artists as studio space. The first floor was divided into several rooms, used by both the Athenæum and paying tenants such as the American Academy of Arts and Sciences.

To guide the Athenæum's new endeavors in the fine arts, a committee of trustees, called the Fine Arts Committee, was appointed in March 1827. At its founding, the committee's sole purpose was "obtaining and arranging an Exhibition of Pictures in the Exhibition Room of the New Building";[36] the formation of a permanent art col-

FIG. 4 Thomas Sully,
Thomas Handasyd Perkins, 1831–1832.
Oil on canvas, 287.1 × 195.7 cm.
Collection of the Boston
Athenæum, Purchase, 1832

lection was not yet even considered. The chairman of the Fine Arts Committee was Thomas Handasyd Perkins (fig. 4), who was at the pinnacle of his wealth and influence in the 1820s. The Athenæum was only one of Boston's innumerable educational, medical, and cultural institutions that he generously supported, but it was perhaps among those closest to his heart.[37] As the founding chairman of the Fine Arts Committee during its all-important first decade, Perkins exerted an incomparable influence over the Athenæum's early programs in art. Under him, the Fine Arts Committee comprised trustees Francis Calley Gray (who would succeed Perkins as the Athenæum president in 1832) and Franklin Dexter as well as proprietors George Watson Brimmer and Charles Russell Codman, all men known as connoisseurs of art.

The Fine Arts Committee's first task was to gather enough loans of paintings for the inaugural exhibition in the new gallery; the Athenæum possessed, at the beginning of 1827, only seven paintings. In response to the committee's call for "artists to furnish specimens of their works, and gentlemen possessing valuable pictures, to contribute to the exhibition by the loan of them,"[38] close to three hundred paintings and some twenty miniatures came out of the parlors of local residents, many of them friends and relatives of the Athenæum trustees and proprietors. To handle the practical aspects of the exhibition, the Fine Arts Committee hired a manager from the outside, a practice that would continue into the 1860s.[39] On May 10, 1827, the first annual exhibition of paintings at the Athenæum gallery opened. The display, whose official title billed it as including "specimens, by American artists, and a selection of the works of the Old Masters," in fact contained slightly more Old Master paintings, most of them copies, than works by living artists.[40] Among the "Old Master" paintings, the Dutch and Italian works of the sixteenth and seventeenth centuries popular in Boston at the time—David Teniers the Younger (1610–1690), Bartolomé Esteban Murillo (1618–1682), Domenichino (1581–1641), Aelbert Cuyp (1620–1691), Jacob van Ruysdael (ca. 1628–1682)—predominated. Most of the living artists were American and local—Gilbert Stuart, Washington Allston (1779–1843), Chester Harding (1792–1886), Francis Alexander (1800–1880), Alvan Fisher (1792–1863)—and almost half of their canvases were portraits, the rest divided among landscapes, genre pictures, and history paintings. For 25¢ (or 50¢, for a season ticket), anyone, including women who were still barred from the reading room, could visit the exhibition from eight o'clock in the morning to sunset.[41] This inaugural exhibition was extremely popular, and when it closed on July 8, 1827, brisk sale of tickets and catalogues had brought in a gratifying $4,000, of which $2,600 was profit.[42]

The Athenæum's first four exhibitions were spectacularly successful. In 1828 the second exhibition generated a profit of $2,500, and in 1829 the figure rose to almost $3,000. By 1830 the exhibitions had produced a combined revenue in excess of a remarkable $10,000. There were a number of reasons for this pleasing outcome. For one thing, the Athenæum gallery distinguished itself from Boston's other commercial and temporary installations that typically mixed natural and ethnological curiosities with paintings and sculptures.[43] In the 1820s, for example, the New England Museum on nearby Court Street exhibited "3,000 reptiles preserved in spirits" and a mechanical panorama, interspersed with portraits and sculptures including a full-length likeness of Emperor Alexander of Russia and a marble statue of Venus by Antonio Canova (1757–1822).[44] In comparison, the Athenæum gallery was—or at least appeared—decidedly more serious and high-minded: the exhibitions were housed in an elegant building, more narrowly focused on the fine arts, and intended to cultivate taste rather than commercial gain.

The Athenæum's early exhibitions also owed much to the remarkable cohesion among the trustees and their circle of friends, many of whom lent eagerly to the shows and, in turn, derived particular rewards from their participation. Created to foster the "improvement and emulation of artists" as well as "the correction and refinement of taste in those, who aim to be connoisseurs,"[45] the Athenæum gallery nevertheless functioned, from the late 1820s on, as a venue for a close-knit circle of the emerging local connoisseurs to showcase—and validate—their taste. Unlike the National Academy of Design, founded in New York in 1826 by professional artists for their own benefit, the Athenæum gallery was organized almost entirely by the trustees and their friends, who were collectors, not practicing artists. Just as men who cherished their personal libraries had earlier supported the formation of a "public" library at the Athenæum, those with art collections lent their possessions to the Athenæum gallery for public display. Even though this clubby cohesion worked in favor of the Athenæum's early exhibitions, it also rendered the gallery's purpose fundamentally ambiguous: Did it serve living artists or aspiring connoisseurs? Throughout its existence, from 1827 to 1874, the Athenæum gallery was neither completely an artists' organization nor a collectors' club but remained a sometimes uneasy combination of the two.

The monies raised by the exhibition in 1827 added a new and important responsibility to the Fine Arts Committee: the formation of a permanent art collection. But this new function emerged almost inadvertently, only after the first installation in the gallery had brought in ample cash. In fact, during the fund-raising campaign for the annex, in 1826, Thomas Handasyd Perkins was of the opinion that the income from the future lecture hall and art gallery—which he estimated would be "one thousand dollars and upwards" per year—should benefit "the increase of the periodical and other publications."[46] A permanent art collection was not mentioned. Even in early 1827, with the inaugural art exhibition already on the horizon, the trustees recommended to the proprietors, only in general terms, that the Athenæum "devote the net proceeds of such exhibition to the promotion of the fine arts."[47] What, exactly, did "promotion" mean?

At the beginning of 1827, as noted, the Athenæum's art collection consisted of only seven paintings, the eleven Thorndike casts, and one other sculpture.[48] Five of the paintings had entered the collection as gifts, and two were portraits that the Athenæum had commissioned of its important officers (James Perkins and William Smith Shaw). In contrast, between 1827 and 1839, the Athenæum acquired, chiefly by purchase and some by gift, an impressive total of almost eighty paintings and forty-six sculptures, making these years the most active period of art acquisition in the institution's history.

In 1828 alone, the committee bought *Portrait of a Man* (fig. 5) attributed to Annibale Carracci (1560–1609), *The Sortie Made by the Garrison of Gibraltar* (fig. 6) by John Trumbull (1756–1843); *Pat Lyon at His Forge* (1826–1827; MFA) by John

FIG. 5 Attributed to Annibale Carracci, *Portrait of a Man*, 1592. Oil on canvas, 52.1 × 41 cm. Collection of the Boston Athenæum, Purchase, 1828

Neagle (1796–1865); *King Lear* (fig. 7) by Benjamin West (1738–1820); and *Benjamin Franklin* (ca. 1786; Monticello, Charlottesville, VA) after the French painter Joseph-Siffred Duplessis (1725–1802).[49] These early acquisitions clearly gave the Fine Arts Committee confidence and clout, and in the 1830s the committee spent its own funds as well as monies raised by subscription on purchases of important works, some of them iconic American paintings. In 1830, for example, the Athenæum commissioned Chester Harding, the most popular portraitist in Boston after Stuart's death in 1828, to execute a full-length portrait of John Marshall, chief justice of the United States (fig. 8). The following year, the committee ran a remarkably successful subscription campaign for the purchase of *George* and *Martha Washington* (1796; jointly owned by the MFA and the National Portrait Gallery, Washington, DC)—known as the Athenæum portraits—by Gilbert Stuart. In 1834 a combination of the committee's funds and subscriptions paid for four large mid-eighteenth-century views of Rome by the Italian artist Giovanni Paolo Panini (1691–1765; fig. 9).[50] In sculpture, too, the committee acquired, either by purchase or subscription, works by the first generation of American sculptors that still distinguish the Athenæum's sculpture collection today: a marble bust of *John Quincy Adams* (fig. 10) by Horatio Greenough (1805–1852) and a series of portrait busts of illustrious men by John Frazee (1790–1852), to

FIG. 6 John Trumbull, *The Sortie Made by the Garrison of Gibraltar*, 1789. Oil on canvas, 180.3 × 271.8 cm. Purchase, Pauline V. Fullerton Bequest; Mr. and Mrs. James Walter Carter and Mr. and Mrs. Raymond J. Horowitz Gifts; Erving Wolfe Foundation and Vain and Harry Fish Foundation Inc., Gifts; Gift of Hanson K. Corning, by exchange; and Maria DeWitt Jesup and Morris K. Jessup Funds, 1976 (1976.332). The Metropolitan Museum of Art, New York. Photograph by Geoffrey Clements. Image © The Metropolitan Museum of Art. Source, Art Resource, NY

FIG. 7 Benjamin West, *King Lear*, 1788, retouched by West 1806. Oil on canvas, 271.8 × 365.6 cm. Museum of Fine Arts, Boston, Henry H. and Zoe Oliver Sherman Fund, 1979.476. Photograph © 2013 Museum of Fine Arts, Boston

name a few. Once the Athenæum became known as an art-collecting organization, gifts of works of art also increased.

Even as the committee made these important purchases, however, the proprietors had not accepted the trustees' 1827 recommendation that the proceeds of exhibitions be devoted to "the promotion of the fine arts," so that the Fine Arts Committee was required to request the board's approval piecemeal each time it contemplated a purchase.[51] As late as 1831 a sense of uncertainty lingered in the committee's report about the disposition of the income from the exhibitions: "Presuming that it is the purpose of the Trustees to apply the proceeds of the Annual Exhibition to the acquisition of valuable works of art & that the committee would be expected to give some attention to this subject they have taken some pains to ascertain what paintings of merit can now be procured."[52] Even though no objections to the committee's purchases were

FIG. 8 Chester Harding, *John Marshall*, 1830. Oil on canvas, 242.8 × 153 cm. Collection of the Boston Athenæum, Purchase, 1830

FIG. 9 Giovanni Paolo Panini, *Interior of St. Peter's, Rome*, 1756–1757. Oil on canvas, 164.1 × 235.6 cm. Collection of the Boston Athenæum, Purchase, 1834

FIG. 10 Horatio Greenough, *John Quincy Adams*, 1828–1829. Marble, 59 × 35.7 × 21.7 cm. Collection of the Boston Athenæum, Purchase, 1829

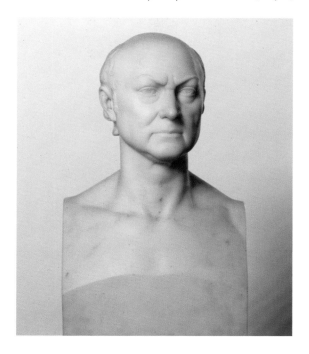

raised, no official statement was made either to indicate that the Athenæum now collected art or that the Fine Arts Committee was to carry out that task. Equipped with ample funds and the momentum created by the gallery's ascendancy, the committee made significant additions to the art collection and the committee's importance and visibility grew, but its function within the larger Athenæum was never officially defined. In the absence of an institutional vision for its permanent art collection, the acquisition process remained informal, dependent on personal recommendations by the trustees, proprietors, and other unofficial advisers connected to the Fine Arts Committee.

While its responsibilities gradually settled into exhibition and acquisition, the Fine Arts Committee also took seriously the education of living artists, one of the objectives listed in the 1807 prospectus. As early as 1816, William Tudor, one of the Athenæum founders and the creator of the magazine *North American Review*, had proposed the establishment of an art academy in Boston, an "Institution for the Fine Arts," equipped with casts of all the sculptures at the Musée du Louvre and a space suitable for art exhibitions.[53] Even though the Athenæum never became an art academy, the trustees made small attempts to assist local artists. In the original Perkins mansion, where the Thorndike casts remained until 1839, the reading room was heated three evenings a week so artists could go and draw from the sculptures there.[54] When Harding requested a more secluded setting for the casts, the trustees swiftly moved the Thorndike collection from the reading room to a north-facing hall.[55] In the new annex, the committee invited the city's best painters—Gilbert Stuart and Washington Allston, for exam-ple—to use the third floor as a studio when it was not occupied by exhibitions. As with exhibitions and acquisitions, though, the Athenæum's patronage of its favorite artists was often through personal connections, and the institution proved an astonishingly loyal patron to several important local artists. At any rate, taking charge of these three interconnected areas—exhibition, acquisition, and education of artists—the Fine Arts Committee came to wield, in less than a decade after its tentative beginning, significant influence within the institution.

Not surprisingly, as the Athenæum's commitment to the fine arts grew deeper in the 1820s and the 1830s, objects other than paintings and sculptures gradually receded into the background. For one thing, the storage and management of curiosities and scientific specimens were becoming problematic. Already in 1825 the new librarian, Seth Bass, complained of the clutter in Room 13 (in the Perkins mansion), which housed "Minerals, Shells and other articles, not arranged nor catalogued (and may be called a Museum burlesque)!!"[56] Before long, "some person, unknown" broke into the popular Room 12, where coins, medals, and engravings were kept.[57] By 1829 the trustees had little choice but to decline "stuffed skins of animals" and, a few years later, "shells and minerals."[58] Although the Athenæum's holdings continued to include some "curios" well into the 1860s, dwindling space encouraged selectivity, and the fine arts came into clearer focus.

Unfortunately, the popularity of the annual exhibitions was not long-lived. Already in the early 1830s attendance declined and profits diminished. The novelty and excitement wore off, and the Fine Arts Committee's ambitious policy never to present the same works twice—except for the objects belonging to the institution—created an inevitable difficulty. In addition, skeptical murmurs about the authenticity of many of the so-called Old Master paintings on view could not long be ignored, especially because most of them were indeed copies, many of them *roba di milord*, the kind of third-rate forgeries foisted on gullible American travelers in Europe. Despite the Fine Arts Committee's efforts—borrowing from new sources and offering cash prizes for contemporary works, for example[59]—the waning of patronage was a trend difficult to reverse. Moreover, artists in the city increasingly resented the fact that any profits realized benefited solely the Athenæum's art collection and not the exhibiting artists. Before long, the dissatisfaction led Harding and his associates to establish, in 1834, an exhibition space—Harding's Gallery—on School Street, within walking distance of the Athenæum. The Athenæum gallery's unresolved dichotomy of purpose—did it serve working artists or collectors—was exposed.

Furthermore, as the 1830s wore on, the Pearl Street neighborhood, once lined with elegant houses, grew ever more commercial and crowded with warehouses, making the area unsuitable for the sophisticated cultural center that the Athenæum had aspired to be. Finally, after years of declining attendance, the Athenæum closed the lecture hall in 1839. The space was immediately converted into a sculpture gallery, to which the Thorndike collection of plaster casts was moved from the original Perkins mansion, and where the first of the Athenæum's sculpture exhibitions opened that same year. The 1839 exhibition, for the first time featuring both paintings and sculptures, momentarily brought popularity and high profits back to the gallery, but thereafter the annual exhibitions on Pearl Street never again replicated the financial triumphs of their earlier years.

In addition, the physical management of the Athenæum's expanding art collection, as with the curiosities and scientific specimens, was proving increasingly difficult. By 1839 the Athenæum's collection, after a decade of growth, comprised more than eighty paintings (including the original seven)—several of them enormous—with twenty-one more on deposit. More than forty-five works of sculpture had entered the collection in the 1830s, and thirty more would come in the following decade. The annex was fast running out of space. Besides, at the close of each annual exhibition, the committee had to vacate the skylit third floor for artists to use by moving most of the paintings to the lower floors for storage. This yearly pilgrimage of paintings so exasperated the Fine Arts Committee that its report of 1839 indignantly declared that the committee did not "consider these pictures safe in the possession of this Institution, subject as they are to be yearly taken down from their places, to be carried up & down long and inconvenient flights of stairs with more or less care and consigned for many months to the damp rooms on the ground floor of the Fine Arts Building."[60] The idea of a permanent gallery was discussed at this time, but nothing came of it.

By 1842 William T. Andrews, the chairman of the Fine Arts Committee, was compelled to conclude that the overall "condition of the Fine Arts department [was] not encouraging."[61] The exhibition of that year had been "almost wholly unproductive,"[62] and in the 1840s the annual income from the exhibitions—in the 1820s almost $4,000 —dwindled to mere hundreds.[63] In acquisitions, too, further additions were rendered difficult in a building already too small to house the existing collection. To be sure, the decade did see some of the Athenæum's most brilliant acquisitions, such as *Orpheus and Cerberus* (fig. 11) by the American sculptor Thomas Crawford (1813–1857), in 1844. Even then, the sculpture gallery proper was deemed inadequate for the display of Crawford's statue, so his supporters raised $300 by subscription to erect a separate, small structure solely for the purpose. Furthermore, the criticism of the temporary nature of the Athenæum gallery, which was closed for long periods between exhibitions, grew increasingly clamorous from the public and artists who wished to study the valuable art collection more frequently. Eventually, the annex of 1826, once the raison d'être and pride of the Fine Arts Committee, proved an insurmountable obstacle in achieving almost all that the committee wished to accomplish.

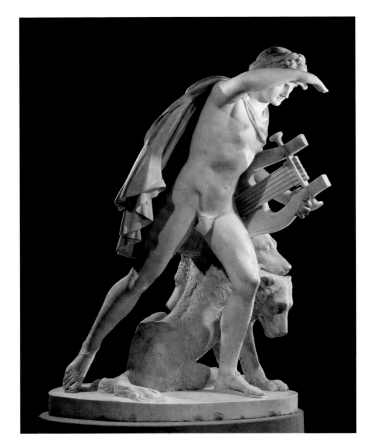

The Fine Arts Committee's woes alone, however, would likely not have led the
Athenæum's administration to conclude, as it did, that a move to a larger building in
a more central location was essential to the organization's survival. An even more
pressing problem was the desperate shortage of space for its books. As prominent as
the exhibitions and art collection had become, the library was still the heart of the
institution; in the late 1840s the books were three times more valuable than the art
collection.[64] Since 1822 the Athenæum's library had grown steadily: ten thousand
volumes in 1827, thirty thousand by 1839, and close to fifty thousand by midcentury.
In addition, the commercial bustle in the Pearl Street neighborhood increasingly
disturbed the tranquility necessary for serious study. The library of the Athenæum
was no longer the luxurious, serene setting cherished by its early patrons.

Finally, in 1843, the trustees and proprietors approved the search for a new site.
After one false start, the Athenæum secured a parcel of land in its current location on
Beacon Street, halfway between the State House and King's Chapel.[65] Among the
many opinions voiced about the future Athenæum, one distinct stipulation, made by

the proprietors in 1845, was of far-reaching significance. This was that the new edifice be built "in such a manner as will, either by lecture rooms, picture galleries, offices or shops or some combination of any or all of these yield an income at least equal to the interest on sixty thousand dollars."[66] In essence, the nonlibrary portions of the Athenæum were expected to generate income for the institution as a whole. The idea of a large lecture hall was eventually rejected as a potential financial risk, but an art gallery remained integral to the plan, assuming a major fiscal and public role in the future Athenæum. To fund the building project, the Athenæum issued new shares. After a competition, Edward Clarke Cabot (1818–1901)—not only a trustee and a grandson of Thomas Handasyd Perkins but also a nephew of Thomas Greaves Carey, the Athenæum's sitting president—was chosen in 1846 as the architect of the new build-ing, to be assisted by George M. Dexter (1802–1872), an architect with more experience. Construction began in 1847, and the façade was completed by 1848.

Disastrously, however, by 1848 the Athenæum had already spent, on the building's exterior alone, the entire sum it had raised for the whole project ($70,000). The need for more funds was obvious and acute, and the Athenæum was to struggle for years with the consequences of this financial calamity. In this predicament, the Athenæum must have found highly tempting the twice-repeated proposal from the city that the institution become, or at least serve as the foundation for, Boston's first public library. In 1848 the proprietors considered the city's offer that it pay the Athenæum $50,000 up front and thereafter $5,000 annually in exchange for the use of its library (although not the reading room), but they refused.[67] The city therefore established, that same year, the Boston Public Library. When the city asked the Athenæum, in 1852, to merge with the new public library, a violent controversy within the Athenæum ensued. A considerable number of the proprietors supported the idea, among them George Ticknor, Harvard professor and the host of an intellectual salon, while others objected to the idea, most notably Josiah Quincy, the retired Harvard president and mayor of Boston.[68] In the end, the proprietors again declined the proposed merger because it would contradict "the wishes and intentions of many of its founders and benefactors, and . . . the best interests of Literature and Science in this Community."[69] The pro-prietors were unwilling to surrender to the city the Athenæum's right to define that "community" on its own terms.

At issue was the definition of the Athenæum's constituency. The proposed public library was to be supported by the city's funds and accessible to all of Boston's inhabi-tants over sixteen years of age. When this new definition of the word "public" emerged with the promise of universal access, the earlier sense of the word "public" as "com-munal"—as the Athenæum founders had understood it—was no longer tenable. The proprietors' refusal to join with the new public library made explicit the exclusivity that the Athenæum had thus far imposed only implicitly. The two debates forced the

Athenæum to declare, irrevocably, that its library was private, belonging to a group of people who increasingly considered themselves separate from the larger population.

The first chapter of the Athenæum's history was approaching its end. In the four decades since its founding, the institution had enlarged its membership and collections as well as gained enormously in cultural stature. The Athenæum had changed internally, too: as the historian Ronald Story has demonstrated, between 1807 and 1860 seven interconnected family groups occupied a disproportionately large share of the Athenæum's administrative posts.[70] Under the leadership of this relatively small group of Bostonians, the Athenæum came to confer a status of culture and breeding on its mostly hereditary membership. In an increasingly diverse city—by one account, fully one-quarter of its residents in 1850 were Irish by birth[71]—the Athenæum came to function, at least in part, as a self-conscious marker of the emerging class lines, standing firm as a bastion of old, rather than new, Boston.

The Athenæum on Beacon Street

On July 27, 1849, at ten o'clock in the morning, the Athenæum proprietors gathered on the second floor of the new Athenæum on Beacon Street and proclaimed the place open. Situated in the center of the city, the three-story building was the Athenæum's fifth home and the first that had been built expressly for it (fig. 12).

Behind the imposing façade of rosy-hued sandstone, however, much of the interior space lay unfinished. Only the second floor, the location of the library, had been completed, while parts of the first and third floors, intended to house sculpture and paintings galleries, respectively, remained under construction. The books had been moved to the new building, whereas the majority of the paintings and sculptures stayed behind on Pearl Street, and some canvases were being repaired elsewhere. (As an exception, Crawford's *Orpheus and Cerberus*—the largest marble in the collection—had traveled to Beacon Street in early 1849, when "snow favored its transport."[72]) Nearly two more years would pass before all of the Athenæum's art collection moved into the new building. Finally, the picture (or paintings) gallery on the third floor opened in 1850, and the statuary (or sculpture) gallery on the first in 1851.

When the Athenæum's new quarters were completed, the building became something of an architectural jewel in Boston, "the most beautiful and imposing specimen of architecture in the city . . . an honor to our city."[73] While no one could deny its impressive grandeur, some disapproved of the new Athenæum as "a building of extraordinary pretensions," a manifestation of "the mania for showy edifices."[74] The structure's stately presence and obvious ostentation clearly irked some who, like Charles Fairbanks, the Athenæum's assistant librarian from 1847 to 1853, missed the personal scale and understated charm of the Athenæum on Pearl Street. The swagger,

FIG. 12 *The Boston Athenæum*, 1852. Salted paper print, 33.3 × 27.9 cm (mount). Collection of the Boston Athenæum

though, was almost the very point; the palatial new quarters announced the institution's growing stature with an unmistakable self-consciousness.

In the new building, books occupied the second-floor library (fig. 13)—praised by Nathaniel Hawthorne as a "noble hall . . . [which] looked splendidly with its vista of alcoves"[75]—as well as the western one-third of the first floor, where the reading room was located. Much of the rest of the building served purposes unrelated to

FIG. 13 Merrill G. Wheelock,
*Interior of the Athenæum
Library*, 1849. Pen and ink,
wash drawing on paper, 9.2 ×
9.8 cm (image). Collection of
the Boston Athenæum

books: the majestic vestibule and staircase showcased large paintings and sculptures
(fig. 14); the third floor, atop the grand but exhausting staircase, housed the four
rooms of the picture gallery; and, on the first floor, the eastern two-thirds was the
statuary gallery (fig. 15). (At the northeast corner of the second floor was a room
called the "museum," which contained an assortment of curios and natural history
specimens that remained in the Athenæum's collection.) As on Pearl Street, the
library and reading room were open only to members and qualified visitors, while the
picture and statuary galleries were available to the public for a fee during exhibitions.

The first exhibition of paintings in the new building opened in May 1850, and
that of sculpture in September 1851. The new picture and statuary galleries boasted
ample space as well as splendid accommodations. The third-floor picture gallery was
lit with skylights and made even brighter by gaslights.[76] Heat from a hot-water fur-
nace in the basement—a marvel of modern technology—warmed the galleries,
inducing the visitor, some imagined, "to believe that he feels the influence of Italy
while he gazes upon the artistic treasures from her classic shores."[77] Worried initially
about the "bareness and drabness of the rooms,"[78] the Fine Arts Committee expended
considerable attention and funds on furnishing the rooms with carpets and covering
the walls with drapery to make the new picture gallery even more attractive than its
elegant predecessor on Pearl Street. By the mid-1850s the gallery was deemed, with
understandable Boston exaggeration, "among the best in the world (fig. 16)."[79] On the

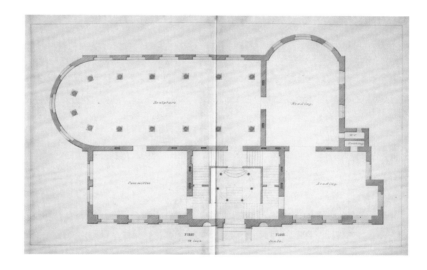

first floor, the statuary gallery provided an eighty-foot-long perspective in which to view what some considered the "richest collection of . . . statuary in the country."[80] At the rounded end of the room, a cast of Michelangelo's *Night and Day* sat prominently on a specially designed pedestal, surrounded by the Athenæum's sizable collection of sculptures in marble and plaster (fig. 17).[81] The grand vista of the new statuary gallery, under the high ceiling and framed with arches, pleased the Fine Arts Committee immensely, and once the sculptures were in place, the committee even declared that the room had "proved better adapted for its purpose than was ever anticipated."[82]

FIG. 16 Attributed to
Henry Bricher, after
Asa Coolidge Warren,
"Gallery of Paintings at
the Athenæum." From
*Ballou's Pictorial Drawing
Room Companion* 8
(March 31, 1855): 201

In the attractive new space, the Athenæum's exhibitions were popular. They ran for a longer time than before, usually from late spring to early winter. The statuary gallery was open even longer, for almost nine months of the year, a boon for artists and students. The exhibitions grew in both size and variety, containing by the end of the 1850s more than three hundred paintings and one hundred sculptures. Some famous works of American paintings—by Thomas Cole (1801–1848) and Frederic Edwin Church (1826–1900), for example—made appearances at the Athenæum gallery during the 1850s, as did some contemporary French works, including the avant-garde pictures by such Barbizon painters as Jean-François Millet (1814–1875), making their American debut. The gallery was also host to several well-publicized traveling exhibitions, which brought to it contemporary European paintings in scales larger than ever before. For example, in 1852 the Düsseldorf Gallery, a touring exhibition, brought more than one hundred paintings by contemporary German artists; in 1858 an exhibition of British art comprised close to two hundred paintings and watercolors by the British Pre-Raphaelites.

Apart from these noteworthy pieces that appeared occasionally in the gallery, the Athenæum's exhibitions continued to feature, for the most part, the same mixture of the institution's holdings, local artists' submissions, and loans. The assortment was essentially arbitrary; the Athenæum's programs in art still lacked a well-defined purpose. In the 1840s the existence of the art gallery in the future Athenæum had been justified chiefly as a means of producing income, but few since then had discussed what role the fine arts would play. On Beacon Street, the purpose of the gallery remained as vague as it had been in 1827, even though the paintings and sculpture galleries occupied fully half the space in the building and functioned as the decidedly public portion of the institution. Even while Boston's artistic climate began to change

FIG. 17 Attributed to Henry Bricher, after Asa Coolidge Warren, "Statuary Room of the Athenæum." From *Ballou's Pictorial Drawing Room Companion* 8 (March 31, 1855): 201

dramatically after midcentury, the Athenæum's Fine Arts Committee developed no clearly articulated criteria of selection, artistic or otherwise, for its exhibitions. Instead, in the genteel words of Edward Newton Perkins, the chairman of the committee, the purpose of the Athenæum gallery was simply to "delight and instruct."[83] As before, a majority of the loans to the exhibitions came from the trustees-cum-collectors, proprietors, their families, and friends.

Moreover, in the 1850s, the Athenæum's exhibitions, which were popular but also more costly because of their larger scale, brought in smaller profits than the trustees had anticipated; the highest, in 1850, netted $2,683.12. In 1852, when the proprietors requested that the galleries stay open between exhibitions so that the institution's own art collection could be more available to the public, the Fine Arts Committee happily agreed to the proposal, but the full board of trustees categorically rejected the idea because "any attempt to make the exhibition permanent would be unprofitable."[84] Increasingly, the gallery was discussed solely in terms of money.

Perhaps a partial explanation lies in the fact that, just as it settled into its stately new home, the Athenæum found itself on the brink of the worst financial crisis in its history. The architect's original estimate of $59,000 had more than tripled to an astounding $190,000 by 1849,[85] and the institution was in debt, uncertain of its ability to afford the new building. In the spring of 1850 the Athenæum's financial outlook was so bleak that the proprietors hoped not for "development or growth" but only "mere preservation" of its book and art collections.[86] At that year's annual meeting, the entire board resigned, with comical gravity, as a gesture of contrition, although all the trustees were reelected on the spot.[87] Various fund-raising and economizing efforts followed—selling the Pearl Street property, issuing new shares (bringing their total number up to the current 1,049), and soliciting funds from the trustees and proprietors—and these eventually restored the institution's coffers. Still, the near-fiscal collapse was not easily forgotten, and in 1855 the proprietors issued a stern warning to the trustees to "confine, for the future, the annual expenses of the Institution within its actual annual receipts."[88]

In this extraordinary financial predicament of the 1850s, the dynamics between the Athenæum's two major parts—library and the fine arts—began to shift. Most significant for our story was the establishment, in 1852, of the Library Committee. This new committee of trustees provided crucial institutional backing to the library, an area that had hitherto been managed solely by the librarian and his assistants with only occasional, informal help from the trustees. Initially, the committee's only duty was to compile a new catalogue of the Athenæum's books. (The last comprehensive catalogue had been issued in 1827.) But soon the committee asked for a clarification of its duties, and its responsibilities were expanded to include the general direction of the library and the reading room. The committee was also put in charge of purchases of books and periodicals, with full control of the two large funds recently given by two proprietors—John Bromfield, in 1846, and Samuel Appleton, in 1853—that were devoted exclusively to book acquisition.[89] In contrast, the Fine Arts Committee, though much older, had at its disposal only the relatively small Fine Arts Fund, the accumulated revenue from the annual exhibitions. Moreover, the Library Committee had a staff in place even before its formation, whereas the Fine Arts Committee had no in-house staff under its influence. Most critically, the Library Committee asked for and received a clear definition of its role within the Athenæum, something that had eluded the Fine Arts Committee since its beginning in 1827. In apparent ascendancy by the mid-1850s, the Library Committee confidently predicted "the probability of [the library's] more rapid growth hereafter than ever before."[90]

In fact, in the new building on Beacon Street, the library had entered the period of its most dramatic growth, and the increasing funds and enthusiasm of the newly formed Library Committee only accelerated the expansion. The library of 50,000 volumes in 1849 grew to one of 70,000 by 1858, and doubled in size by 1867.[91] Circulation, too, was vigorous: in 1859, for example, members took out almost 12,000 books.[92] Inevitably, the expanding book collection demanded ever more space in the building. When William Frederick Poole, assistant librarian since 1851, became the Athenæum's fourth librarian in 1856, his professional enthusiasm combined with his exacting nature to exacerbate the already serious competition for space. Furthermore, Poole's system of identifying each book by its fixed location on a shelf—a standard practice before the introduction of subject-based call numbers—meant that, as the library grew and books were shifted, the librarian constantly had to remark each book with its new location. The task must have driven Poole to more than occasional despair, and with each passing year his diatribe against the shortage of space for books grew ever shriller.

Poole's campaign proved effective: as early as 1859 the board ordered the Fine Arts Committee to remove paintings from the "pamphlet room" on the third floor, next to the picture gallery, so that books could move in.

Perhaps because of this escalating territorial rivalry, and possibly also from fiscal caution, in 1854 the board sought to determine "a proper proportionate contribution from the proceeds of the Annual Exhibitions towards the general expenses of the Athenæum."[93] A temporary committee was appointed to investigate the institution's records to discover the original terms of the Fine Arts Fund, the budget of the Fine Arts Committee. The findings were soon reported: the only official stipulation adopted so far on the matter had been the proprietors' vote of 1829, which allowed the net proceeds of the annual exhibitions to be devoted to "the promotion of the fine arts." Unfortunately for the Fine Arts Committee, these extremely unspecific terms adopted in 1829 came back to haunt it in 1854, since they allowed too wide a margin for interpretation. The startling recommendation was made that $4,000 from the more than $5,000 that had accumulated in the Fine Arts Fund be transferred to the Athenæum's general funds. The reason behind this demand was simple and incontestable: it would help defray "the large expenditure made in the erection of the Athenæum building for the accommodation of the collections of paintings & sculpture, and for the Annual Exhibitions."[94] As if that were not enough, the temporary committee also proposed that $250 from the proceeds of annual exhibitions be paid—not only in the present and the future but also from the previous two years—to the general operating account "as a fair proportionate contribution from the Fine Arts Department."[95] A year later the board approved the committee's recommendations, and the Fine Arts Committee lost control of a considerable portion of its monies.[96] With diminished funds, the Fine Arts Committee purchased only sporadically in the 1850s and 1860s, with none of the focused zeal of the 1830s. As a consequence, from then on the growth of the Athenæum's art collection depended largely on gifts.

In 1854, the catastrophic year for the Fine Arts Committee, Thomas Handasyd Perkins died at ninety. The death of the committee's first chairman in that year was no more than a coincidence, but it nevertheless epitomized the disappearance of the Athenæum's founding generation. By the early 1850s Josiah Quincy, president of the Athenæum from 1820 to 1829, had taken to identifying himself—with a mixture of pride and wistfulness—as "the Sole Survivor of the first Five Subscribers to the Athenæum," and members of the next generation had already begun to occupy positions of power at the Athenæum.[97] When the move to Beacon Street and the ensuing fiscal debacle had encouraged the induction of new members into the ranks of the trustees and proprietors, many of the faces were naturally those of the grandsons of the Athenæum's early officers and benefactors.

Born in the 1820s, these younger men were connected closely to the Athenæum by both ancestry and exposure. Many of them had witnessed the Pearl Street Athenæum flourish and eventually decline, and had come into Athenæum proprietorship in the 1840s (usually after graduation from Harvard). Some of them became Athenæum trustees in the years surrounding 1850, and a considerable number of these trustees would play a central role, two decades later, in the birth of the Museum of Fine Arts.

On the Fine Arts Committee, too, younger faces began to predominate. After frequent changes during the 1850s, the committee's membership gradually settled in the early 1860s into a group of five trustees who would stay on the committee for the next two decades.[98] In particular, Edward Newton Perkins (1820–1899), the committee's chairman from 1862 into the 1890s, would play an important role in the Athenæum's collaboration with the Museum of Fine Arts in the 1870s and 1880s. His brother Charles Callahan Perkins (1823–1886), an Athenæum proprietor since 1845, would become the de facto founding director of the MFA in 1870, and thereafter the brothers would collaborate closely with each other. Not incidentally, Edward and Charles Perkins were grandsons of James Perkins, who donated his Pearl Street mansion to the Athenæum in 1822.

THE 1860S: A DECADE OF TRANSFORMATION

In the 1860s the competition for space within the Athenæum escalated to the extent that it became acrimonious. Already in 1862 a member of the Library Committee suggested with unmasked hostility that a room in the Allston Hall, a public space on nearby Tremont Street, "might be hired for $1,000 per annum for the Department of Fine Arts," presumably for exhibitions, so that books could take over the picture gallery.[99] Even the attic did not escape the searching eyes of the librarian, to whom the trustees gave $150 for "preparing a portion of the attic for the use of the library."[100] At the annual meeting of 1863, a proprietor questioned with unusual bluntness if "the Fine Arts department did not have devoted to it too large a portion of the building, interfering with the convenient arrangement of the books."[101] That same year, a trustee ominously suggested that the fine arts department be "by and by given up and the space thus saved be diverted to the books."[102]

Just when the Fine Arts Committee was having increasing trouble defending its physical and budgetary independence within the Athenæum, the committee faced another difficulty that came from without: the Civil War. As the nation descended into war, attitudes emerged like the one expressed by a writer criticizing the Athenæum's exhibition of 1861: "This is the first time in our experience when anything in public affairs has made it seem of doubtful propriety to bestow especial attention upon topics belonging exclusively to the fine arts. . . . it seems almost like treason to think of aught that does not directly concern our national danger."[103] Shipping paintings from distant cities was made difficult by the war, and the Athenæum had to rely even more heavily than before on its own collection and local loans. The Fine Arts Committee made several attempts to counter sagging attendance, and some of them bore fruit: distributing free admission tickets to all the proprietors brought in a gratifying twelve thousand visitors in 1863,[104] and in the winter of 1863–1864 the collaboration with the Sanitary Commission raised $1,200 for the agency. Ultimately, though, the fine arts simply could not compete with the gravity of the conflict.

Although the war ended in 1865, internal pressure on the Fine Arts Committee only intensified. To the great annoyance of the committee, the annual exhibition of 1864 was forced to close early by order of the board so that the gallery could be used for an outside exhibition.[105] The profit from an annual art exhibition exceeded $2,000 for the last time in 1865, but for some reason $2,000 of it was paid to the treasurer and only $42.25 was credited to the Fine Arts Fund. In 1866 the trustees voted that "hereafter one half of the net proceeds of the exhibitions of the Fine Arts Department, not exceeding $1,000 per annum, be paid to the Treasurer for the general purpose of the Athenæum."[106] Although the vote was rescinded within months, the trend was unmistakable.[107]

The predicament of the Fine Arts Committee was fundamental. In the fewer than twenty years since the move to Beacon Street, the art collection had grown only slowly. Further acquisition of art was hampered by the lack of adequate space and funds, and the annual exhibitions had become stagnant. Most alarming, however, was the looming prospect of the fine arts' losing their physical territory to the growing library. Edward Newton Perkins, the embattled chairman of the Fine Arts Committee, admitted plaintively in 1864 that "the Library increases so rapidly that it will not be many years before the Fine Arts must find other quarters."[108] He conceded two years later that "the great need of the Fine Arts Department is a new and permanent home."[109] Forced to recognize its secondary place within the institution, the Fine Arts Committee had begun by the mid-1860s to save the diminished but still accruing balance of the Fine Arts Fund for a future gallery.[110] In his good moments, Perkins hoped that "many friends of the Athenæum would give freely both of money for the building, and of works of art to adorn it" if ever such an art gallery were to be erected.[111]

Finally, in 1866, the Fine Arts Committee's fate was decided by an official declaration: in March, the Standing Committee concluded unequivocally that the art collection should be removed, since the building had become too small to house both it and the library. To support this position, the committee listed the "purposes which the Fine Arts department [had] especially served to promote":

1st To form & gratify a refined taste in the community by the exhibition of objects of great & historic beauty, and by furnishing to Students in Art models of those works which have won the admiration of the world.

2d To add something to the annual income of the Institution, by the net proceeds of the annual exhibitions.

3d To adorn & dignify its halls, & render them more attractive to the stranger, and more interesting and dear to the daily visitor.

After decades of ambiguity, this was the clearest statement yet of the Fine Arts Committee's function within the institution, issued—ironically—at the exact moment when the Athenæum decided, essentially, to eliminate the committee. Although the Standing Committee condescendingly praised the fine arts department for having "added interest & dignity to the Library . . . and contributed to draw public favor towards the Institution generally," the report concluded that the "connection" between the two departments was not "absolutely necessary." Astoundingly, the report did not even mention the sizable collection that the Fine Arts Committee had formed in the four decades of its existence. In the final opinion of the Standing Committee, the only remedy was "a separate building, perhaps a separate Institution, for the Fine Arts."[112]

Given the Standing Committee's conclusion, the Fine Arts Committee had no choice but to contemplate a "new and permanent home," a separate building "adapted in all respects to the Fine Arts."[113] But the Fine Arts Committee's means—the $11,376.50 in the Fine Arts Fund—fell far short of the likely cost of securing a suitable space elsewhere in the city.[114] When the Library Committee declared, with brimming confidence, that "the time is not very far distant when our books will occupy all our rooms,"[115] the imminent prospect of the Fine Arts Committee becoming homeless compelled Perkins to call the situation, in 1867, a "crisis."[116]

One possibility was to build an art gallery on a lot next to the Athenæum on Tremont Street that the institution had purchased in 1864 as an investment. At least one drawing was made for a gallery to be erected on this site, by Edward Clarke Cabot, who had designed the Athenæum's Beacon Street building. In its function, the proposed gallery was to inherit and continue the responsibilities that the Fine Arts Committee had come to assume: the annual exhibitions, the art collection, and the education of the artist and the public. But the Fine Arts Committee struggled with the question of how the new space was to be connected, physically and philo-sophically, to the library of the Athenæum. In Cabot's drawing of about 1866 (fig. 18), the proposed gallery was adjacent to the Athenæum's existing building but featured a separate entrance on Beacon Street and was not internally accessible from the rest of the Athenæum.[117] At least physically, the new space was to be a distinct institu-tion. How the new entity would have related to the Athenæum otherwise can never

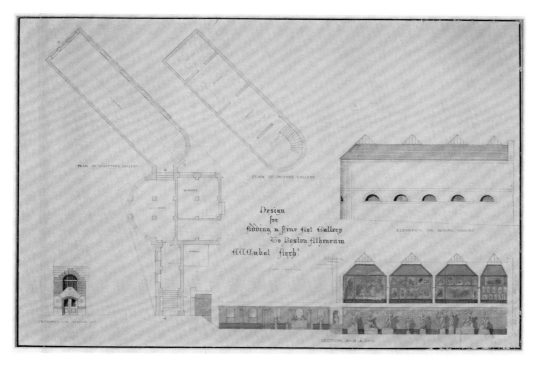

FIG. 18 Edward Clarke Cabot, "Design for Adding a Fine Art Gallery to Boston Athenæum," ca. 1866. Pen and ink, wash drawing with graphite on paper, 47 × 67.6 cm (sheet). Collection of the Boston Athenæum

be known, because the Fine Arts Committee abandoned the plan, deeming the site too small for the purpose.

Following the Standing Committee's momentous decision of March 1866, trustees and proprietors busily contemplated, in a series of lively meetings and detailed reports, "the means of preserving and extending the Department of Fine Arts."[118] At issue, most pressingly, was the statuary gallery that occupied two-thirds of the first floor (fig. 19). By early 1867 the Library Committee had made the ingenious claim that "the room used as a statuary gallery was originally designed for the use of the Library."[119] A statuary gallery had been allowed to move in, the Library Committee contended, only because the Athenæum had "the space unoccupied and could so appropriate it with entire convenience" at the time of the institution's move to Beacon Street.[120] The final report on the matter, issued by the joint committee of trustees and proprietors in March 1867, accepted the Library Committee's argument. The joint committee further claimed that the Pearl Street Athenæum had had two distinctly separate buildings, one for the library and the other for the art gallery, and argued that the same arrangements should be adopted on Beacon Street.[121] The report was accepted and printed in the *Boston Daily Evening Transcript*.[122]

FIG. 19 Stephen Fellows Adams, *Statuary Gallery, Boston Athenæum*, ca. 1865. One-half of a stereograph. Collection of the Boston Athenæum

Finally, in May 1868, the trustees authorized the Standing Committee to make "all proper arrangements" to convert the first-floor statuary gallery into a library.[123] With his characteristic meticulousness, the librarian, William Frederick Poole, had already calculated that, by adding a mezzanine level, the conversion would provide enough shelf space to hold exactly 18,216 additional volumes.[124] (In late 1868, however, Poole abruptly resigned, at the very moment the library triumphed over the fine arts.[125]) The Athenæum began its vast physical transformation. Every space within the building was surveyed, and every object inspected. As a result, many remnants of the highly variegated collections welcomed by the early Athenæum left the institution about this time, most of them placed on deposit at other cultural institutions. More than 130 ethnological objects, for example, were transferred to the Peabody Museum of American Archaeology and Ethnology, established at Harvard in 1866, as were several natural history specimens to the Museum of Natural History, erected in the Back Bay by the Boston Society of Natural History in 1862.[126] In the early 1870s an unspecified number of architectural casts were deposited at the recently established architecture department of the Massachusetts Institute of Technology.[127] The Fine Arts Committee dreamed of a wholly new institution with rooms for "occasional exhibition by artists, or artists' clubs, and perhaps for advanced schools of design,"[128] but no specific site for such an entity was within view. Meanwhile, when the annual exhibition of 1868 opened without any sculpture, the Fine Arts Committee was faced with the disheartening task of dispersing the displaced sculpture throughout the Athenæum building.

The 1860s was a period of fundamental transformation for the Athenæum. At decade's end, the Athenæum emerged with a profoundly altered institutional identity: it was now to be primarily a library. With this revision, the Fine Arts Committee essentially lost its status as an equal half of the institutional body. Still, the committee could not peremptorily abandon either the art collection or its own original mission—the encouragement of the fine arts in Boston. Provisions for their continuation on some level, however greatly diminished, had to be made. The committee was left with this difficult task while its independence and power—and its true institutional affiliation and support system—grew more ambiguous than before. This uncertain position, however, proved in the end to be an asset, since it gave the Athenæum's Fine Arts Committee both particular urgency and exceptional flexibility in its later collaborative relationship with the MFA. Threatened by the possibility of extinction, the committee was desperate, yet, half divorced from the larger Athenæum, it was no longer constrained by its original institutional parameters.

THE LAWRENCE BEQUEST

Whatever its plans, the Fine Arts Committee saw no immediate prospects of monies for the new art institution it hoped to bring into existence. At the end of 1867, the Fine Arts Fund stood at a modest $14,000, and with the revenues from the annual exhibitions continuing to dwindle, the committee could do little but appeal to the proprietors and the public alike for monetary help for the proposed museum.[129] A bequest of $10,000 received in 1867 from a Henry Harris, to be used for art acquisition, was a welcome bit of bright news, but lack of space prevented the committee from making immediate purchases.[130]

Then, in the spring of 1869, the Athenæum received the bequest of a large collection of arms and armor from Colonel Timothy Bigelow Lawrence (1826–1869; fig. 20), an Athenæum proprietor since 1846. Lawrence was a son of Abbott Lawrence who, with his brother Amos, had ushered in the glory days of textile manufacture in New England and who served as a congressman as well as ambassador to Great Britain between his many philanthropic projects. After Harvard, the younger Lawrence filled various diplomatic posts abroad, following in the footsteps of his powerful father, and was consul general to Italy when he died unexpectedly in 1869, on a business trip to Washington, DC.[131]

By a contemporary account, the Lawrence collection was "as perfect for its size as any now known, either in England or upon the continent," comprising a wide variety of weapons from both the East and the West.[132] Like some of his wealthy contemporaries, Lawrence had gathered examples of arms and armor with wild abandon on his many European sojourns and formed, it would seem, an encyclopedic assortment of

weapons from various cultures and dates. Elizabeth Chapman Lawrence (1829–1905) vividly described a week's worth of rapid-fire purchases her husband made in London in 1855:

> a headsman's sword which has been used many times & is very old; the sword of a Malay Pirate adorned with bunches of human hair!; an exquisite silver gilt Damoscene [*sic*] sword; a Russian Bayonet picked up at the Battle of the Alma; & a powder flask taken from the dead body of a Cossack. A gun mounted in silver such as are only carried by the chiefs in Indian battles, axes, cross-bows, guns, daggers & swords innumerable & the most awful *savage*-looking weapons from the East strew the house in every direction.[133]

Instead of remaining at the Lawrences' villa in Florence, Italy, where the couple had lived, the collection came to the Athenæum following the childless collector's death.[134] Unfortunately, lack of adequate space at the Athenæum forced the vast assemblage to be stored temporarily in a warehouse in downtown Boston.

The Lawrence bequest had fortuitously come with an express condition that it be exhibited to the public in an appropriate space. To discuss this stipulation further, the Fine Arts Committee was in communication with Lawrence's widow almost immediately after her husband's death in March, and by November she had offered an additional $25,000 toward "establishing in this City a gallery" that would house and exhibit, "on a scale larger than is now possible," her husband's collection as well as "paintings, statuary and other objects of virtu and art."[135] Twenty-five thousand dollars was a substantial sum for an individual donation—the Lawrence collection itself was valued at $15,000[136]—but creating a new art museum clearly required even more money, and Mrs. Lawrence's offer had come with the condition that matching funds be raised from other sources. Originally from Pennsylvania, Mrs. Lawrence had developed, through her marriage, strong ties to Boston and many of its prominent citizens. After her husband's death, she lived primarily in Pennsylvania and Washington, DC, but her interest in the proposed gallery remained strong. As it happened, her timely offer in November 1869, clearly worked out in partnership with the Fine Arts Committee, added crucial financial backing and momentum to what had so far been a dream. Soon, others joined the proposed enterprise and money was raised, and in February 1870 Boston's Museum of Fine Arts was established. In this new institution, the Lawrence collection of arms and armor was to occupy, appropriately, a place of pride as one of its centerpieces.

CHAPTER TWO

Toward 1870: The Perkins Brothers, the Athenæum Gallery, and Changing Taste in Boston

B Y 1870 Boston was a metropolis far different from the small town it had been at the beginning of the century. The city's population grew tenfold in the intervening seventy years, from 25,000 in 1800 to 250,000 in 1870, and the relative homogeneity that had existed earlier among its residents disappeared with the influx of immigrants, especially from Ireland, that increased dramatically in the late 1840s. Economically, Boston's prosperity toward midcentury came increasingly from the textile industry rather than from the sea, and the city remained a commercial center for the region even as it gradually lost its competitive edge to rival New York. Boston's affluence made possible, for one thing, the extraordinary feat of filling the Charles River basin, from 1857 to the century's end, which eventually created the fashionable neighborhood known as the Back Bay. For Boston, the second half of the century was a period of enormous physical and social change.

In the middle decades of the century, Boston's accumulated wealth also helped foster the proliferation of cultural and educational institutions. Some were learned societies, meant to promote particular areas of knowledge: the Massachusetts Horticultural Society was founded in 1829, the Boston Society of Natural History in 1830, and the New England Historic Genealogical Society in 1845. Others sought to make knowledge or the arts available to a wider audience: the Lowell Institute began in 1836 as a body (with no physical location) to administer a public lecture program, the Boston Public Library was established in 1848, and the Boston Music Hall opened its doors in 1852. In higher education, several new entities were instituted to accommodate the growing emphasis placed on the practical application of knowledge, especially the sciences: Harvard University founded the Lawrence Scientific School in 1846, and the same practical spirit of the age led to the creation, in 1861, of the Massachusetts Institute of Technology (MIT). The westward migration of institutions away from the cramped downtown had already begun before the creation of the Back Bay; the Athenæum's move to Beacon Street in 1849 was itself part of this development. When the newly filled land to the west of the old city became available, civic pride and economic interests combined to call for the presence of religious and cultural institutions in the freshly created neighborhood. Both new and existing organizations chose to locate themselves in the Back Bay; the Museum of Fine Arts, whose building would open there in 1876, was one among many to follow this trend.

Museums of several different varieties, too, were established during this period. Many of them focused on the sciences: at Harvard University the Museum of Comparative Zoology was created in 1859, and the Peabody Museum of American Archaeology and Ethnology followed in 1866.[1] In 1862 the Boston Society of Natural History opened the Boston Museum of Natural History in the Back Bay, on the same block to which MIT would move four years later. Museums of wider scope—some even including the fine arts—were also proposed, but none of them materialized as originally envisioned. An ambitious Conservatory of Art, Science, and Historical Relics, slated in 1859 to be erected in the newly created Boston Public Garden, for example, was to house wide-ranging displays of specimens in natural history, agriculture, manufacture, ethnology, and history, as well as the fine arts.[2] A museum was also a part of the original plan for MIT, but instead of the fine arts of painting and sculpture, the proposed museum's focus was to be chiefly on architecture and engineering. Although many lamented the absence of a permanent gallery of art in a city that prided itself on its culture, none was established until the MFA was incorporated in 1870. However, ideas and hopes about museums that developed in the middle decades of the century would contribute—directly or indirectly—to the museum's founding, and many who had earlier participated in the city's institution-building efforts would be among its earliest supporters.

Not surprisingly, most of Boston's cultural and educational institutions of midcentury origin were organized and funded by Boston's upper class. By that time, Boston's economic elite had cohered as a self-conscious and interconnected group, wielding extraordinary power over the financial, political, and cultural life of the city. By the 1860s, as the historian Ronald Story demonstrated, Boston's upper class—the Brahmins—had developed a "mature institutional constellation," a network of cultural, educational, and medical institutions linked closely by the family, business, and financial connections of their predominantly Brahmin officers and benefactors.[3] The "institutional constellation" placed the city's cultural organizations so effectively in the private control of the elite—beyond popular or governmental intervention—that the link between culture and class was reinforced. A number of historians have argued that by midcentury cultural philanthropy had also come to play a role in preserving the existing social order. Some scholars have interpreted the motives of this constellation's institution-building urge negatively, as an attempt to control the masses through culture precisely when the elite's political power began to be challenged by the city's increasingly diverse population.[4] In both views, however, the Brahmins are credited with a central role in building Boston's culture, even though their motives can be interpreted differently.

Indeed, many of the protagonists of our story—the founders and early supporters of the MFA—came disproportionately from this group of elite Bostonians, many of them scions of fortunes established in the early part of the century. The familial, professional, financial, educational, and institutional ties that bound them undoubtedly facilitated their joint endeavor, and their shared experiences of institution building clearly made smoother the complex process that eventually led to the museum's establishment. But, as we will see, the Brahmin "institutional constellation" was not always a monolithic body. In fact, in the crucial winter of 1869–1870, divisions and tensions existed among the parties that converged to negotiate the idea of an art museum. At the moment of this convergence, one vital figure joined the fray: a Bostonian named Charles Callahan Perkins.

Charles Callahan Perkins, an Inspired Advocate

In the summer of 1869, just as the Athenæum's Fine Arts Committee was working out the terms of the Lawrence bequest and gift, Charles Callahan Perkins (fig. 21) returned to Boston after years of residence in Europe. Once back in Boston, he threw himself into the work of establishing an art museum in his native city.

Charles Callahan Perkins was born on March 1, 1823, on Pearl Street, within a year of the death of his paternal grandfather, James Perkins, whose mansion had become the Athenæum's fourth home in 1822.[5] Charles was the fourth of five children born to a prosperous couple, James Perkins Jr. and Eliza Greene Callahan, niece of the spectacularly rich Gardiner Greene.[6] The Perkins children's home was next door to the Athenæum, and their great-uncle Thomas Handasyd Perkins lived nearby and doted on the younger generations of his remarkably close-knit extended family.[7] In this posh Perkins enclave in downtown Boston, where "all the appointments were luxurious and all the people kind," the Perkins children's lives began with all the privilege and comfort that their family's background assured.[8]

In 1828 their father died suddenly, and only a year later their mother remarried and soon moved to New Jersey with her new husband, leaving the children in Boston.[9] Perhaps because of these circumstances, Charles and his siblings, of whom only Sarah and Edward lived to see old age, remained extraordinarily close.[10] The Perkins children were endowed from birth not only with wealth but also with a vast social web of well-placed siblings, uncles, aunts, cousins, and family friends. Many of Charles's connections would be benefactors of Boston's cultural and educational institutions, including the Athenæum and the museum: among his cousins were, for example,

James Elliot Cabot (Athenæum and museum trustee), Edward Clarke Cabot
(Athenæum trustee and architect of its Beacon Street building), Thomas Greaves
Cary (Athenæum trustee and president), Samuel Eliot (Athenæum and museum
trustee, and, later, Athenæum president), and John Hubbard Sturgis (one of the two
architects of the museum's first building), to name but a few. Even before going to
Harvard, Charles knew several of Boston's future intellectual and cultural leaders
through his sister Sarah and her husband, Henry Russell Cleveland, a promising but
short-lived writer. A young Harvard professor named Henry Wadsworth Longfellow
was one of Cleveland's closest friends, as was an ambitious lawyer named Charles
Sumner, long before he became an influential United States senator.[11] Although her
gender denied her many of the privileges that her brothers took for granted, Sarah
eventually developed a cultural presence of her own among accomplished Bostonians
and was an intimate friend of Catherine and Grace Norton (mother and sister,
respectively, of the Harvard art historian Charles Eliot Norton), the British actress
Fanny Kemble, and Louisa Crawford, wife of the sculptor Thomas Crawford, among
others.[12]

For Charles, who had always loved music and art, Harvard's academic rigor provided more challenge than pleasure. When he sailed to Europe in 1843, the year of his
college graduation, the continent's sights and sounds therefore brought him almost
constant rapture. Charles's grand tour—with his siblings, along the traditional routes—

not only furnished him with a requisite familiarity with Europe but also changed his life: the experience awoke in him a lasting desire to succeed as an artist in his own right, and he began a period of intense study in both the visual and musical arts. After his siblings sailed home in 1845, Charles stayed in Europe until 1849. This first sojourn in Europe was followed by two more, from 1851 to 1854 and from 1857 to 1869. In total, of the twenty-six years between Charles's Harvard graduation and his final return to Boston in 1869, about two decades were spent in Europe.

In Rome, where he first went in 1844, Charles plunged into an intensive course of study in art and music. Like his great-uncle Thomas Handasyd, Charles was capable of remarkable industry. He visited galleries, churches, and concert halls, sketched (figs. 22, 23), painted, read, composed, and wrote, all the while keeping up a full and active social life. In 1844 Crawford praised Perkins's singular industry in a letter to his friend and patron Charles Sumner in Boston:

> I may say that I have never met with so young [a] person in whom I could find united the many qualifications Mr. Perkins possesses to make existence the highly intellectual state it should be. Mr. P has really been a hard worker this winter, not merely in sight-seeing, which forms a part and portion of life in Rome, but also in music, drawing, painting, and—oh, patience inimitable!—the German language. What think you? Masters in each, and half a dozen lessons a day.[13]

FIG. 22 Charles Callahan Perkins, "Lady Louisa," April 23, 1844, from a sketchbook. Graphite drawing on paper, 26 × 22.4 cm (sheet). Collection of the Boston Athenæum, Purchase, 2006

FIG. 23 Charles Callahan Perkins, "Villa Borghese," April 27, 1844, from a sketchbook. Graphite drawing on paper, 26 × 22.4 cm (sheet). Collection of the Boston Athenæum, Purchase, 2006

FIG. 24 Thomas Crawford, *Hebe and Ganymede*, ca. 1851, modeled 1842. Marble, 175.3 × 81.3 × 52.1 cm. Museum of Fine Arts, Boston, Gift of Charles Callahan Perkins, 76.702. Photograph © 2013 Museum of Fine Arts, Boston

Perkins's diligence as well as "gentlemanly deportment and truly amiable character"[14] immediately charmed the sculptor, himself on the verge of success. That same year, 1844, Crawford's *Orpheus and Cerberus* was unveiled at the Athenæum to great acclaim, and his marriage to Luisa Ward, daughter of New York's leading banker Samuel Ward and sister of Julia Ward Howe, solidified his position among Boston's cultural elite. The two Americans became fast friends in Rome, the "city of cities."[15]

A serious aspiring artist himself, Charles Perkins was also patron to many of his artist friends. From Crawford, for example, Perkins commissioned, in 1843, *Hebe and Ganymede* in marble (ca. 1851, modeled 1842; fig. 24) and, in 1853, a bronze statue of the German composer Ludwig van Beethoven, making Perkins the sculptor's second-most important patron after Sumner.[16] (Charles's sister Sarah Cleveland also purchased from Crawford, by 1850, a marble statuette, *Christian Pilgrim*, now in the Athenæum's collection.[17]) Perkins also offered opportunities for artistic cultivation and camaraderie to his friends, many of them ambitious expatriate American artists, at the many gatherings—private concerts, drawing sessions, and parties—he held at his home in Rome. Perkins's frequent guests included Crawford, the sculptor

William Wetmore Story (1819–1895), the painters Christopher Pearse Cranch (1813–1892), James Edward Freeman (1808–1884), Thomas Hicks (1823–1890), and Luther Terry (1813–1869).[18] Story, a fellow Bostonian, recollected with admiration a splendid musical gathering at Perkins's house:

> In the evening I heard some truly noble music at Charles Perkins; the grand septuor by Beethoven, which is enough to move the heart of a rock, so deep and exquisite and yearning. And a very beautiful trio by [Johann Nepomuk] Hummel, solid and various and noble. To recline on a sofa and look at the frescoes by which I was surrounded, and, with a cigar breathing about its aromatic smoke, to listen to the divine outpourings of the grandest music is a paradise of sensuous and spiritual delight.[19]

Perkins's Roman abode also functioned sometimes as a kind of artistic salon, as recalled by his friend Cranch:

> We have had many friends here this winter. . . . The only music I hear (except occasional inflictions of [Giuseppe] Verdi's operas) is at C. C. Perkins', who has soirees now and then. This excellent and accomplished young man turns his wealth to good account—goes to his studio every day, composes, has an academy at his house, where 5 of us Americans draw from the nude, gives his private concerts, where the best music is performed, and buys pictures and gives orders.[20]

The luxurious mixture of art, music, camaraderie, and comfort was one of Perkins's lifelong ideals, a dream he resurrected countless times in his private life as well as in institutional settings. Charles Perkins was, in the words of Henry James, "a master of all the amenities . . . one of the most appealing of our ghosts."[21]

As the French capital began to lure American artists-in-training away from Italy, Perkins spent a year in Paris, from 1846 to 1847. There, his chief occupation was painting, and his chosen teacher was the Dutch-born academic painter Ary Scheffer (1795–1858). Scheffer specialized in romantic pictures of literary and religious themes—taken from Dante, Byron, and Goethe—which were popular chiefly for the pious sentiments they aroused, and the painter's official success was assured by the imprimatur of his major patron, the French king Louis-Philippe, at least until he lost the throne in 1848.[22] Although Vincent van Gogh would later admire Scheffer's colors, Scheffer's technical shortcomings were undeniable, and the French critic Charles Baudelaire dismissed his pictures as "so wretched, so dismal, so blurred and so muddy . . . more like pictures by M. [Paul] Delaroche that had been left out in a heavy rainstorm."[23] For Perkins, a year's training in Paris did little to improve his draftsmanship, and there is no evidence that he ever showed his paintings anywhere.[24] But he certainly took in all that Paris offered, and a year in the city kindled in him, above all, a passionate wish to establish in Boston "musical meetings and an Academy of Design."[25]

Back in Rome, in 1847, Perkins turned to music in earnest. By early 1849 he was "deeply wrapped up in [his] symphony" and thought of "soon giving up painting altogether for music."[26] Stopping in Paris on his way home that summer, Perkins showed off the musical fruits of his Roman labor at a public concert at Salle Herz, a popular music hall. An orchestra played Perkins's symphony, and a violinist and singers performed more of his compositions, to an audience consisting of "all the best critics . . . artists . . . and all the people of distinction in Paris," including Hector Berlioz.[27] The response to the "compositeur du Nouveau-Monde" was generally positive,[28] and the elated Perkins declared, "Oh how delicious it is to hear one's own music well performed by a good orchestra—one no longer knows myself." Wishing for still more worldly success, though, he admonished himself even on the night of his triumph to "run my course with diligence & zeal—study—study—study." By the following day, Perkins was planning to compose a symphony to a poem that he would ask his friend Longfellow to write in the vein of *Evangeline*, the poet's phenomenal popular success of 1847. "An American poet & composer & subject, novelty—novelty—novelty—novelty which runs away with all the world—Success here—success in America & England certain—if I have sufficient capacity to compose the music. It strikes me as a famous idea," Perkins dreamed on feverishly.[29]

In the fall of 1849 Charles Perkins returned to Boston with a pair of musical compositions, hoping to establish himself as a composer. During his homeward voyage, he devised for himself a regimen of five hours of musical study per day—orchestration, composition, reading, and so forth—amounting to 1,825 hours a year, which he intended to follow in Boston with "stern resolution." "Courage et patience," he exhorted himself, confident that with such rigorous study, "there is no reason why I should not be a great musician some day or other."[30] When Perkins returned to America, he was only twenty-six years old.

At midcentury, those returning to the United States from Europe commonly felt a fear of cultural starvation. But Perkins suffered little of that condition during his two-year residence in Boston, from 1849 to 1851, because his wealth, social position, and gregarious nature almost immediately caused him to be active in the city's cultural life. For example, no sooner had he arrived than he began lending works of art to the Athenæum gallery. (In fact, he wrote a feisty letter to the Fine Arts Committee, reprimanding it for not having applied to him sooner for loans of works of art.[31]) In the realm of music, he frequently gave concerts and parties at his home as well as organized public recitals, many of which featured his own compositions conducted by himself.[32] Within a year of his return, Perkins had become the president and conductor of the Handel and Haydn Society (the last person to fill both capacities at once). When the society launched an ambitious campaign to raise $100,000 for its new home, the Boston Music Hall, he worked on behalf of the fund-raising committee of the Harvard Musical Association (a social organization of musical connoisseurs established in 1837) and donated a sizable sum.[33] The Boston Music Hall opened its doors in downtown Boston in November 1852.[34]

By then, however, Perkins had returned to Europe.[35] During his second sojourn in Europe, from 1851 to 1854, Perkins divided his time between Paris and Leipzig (where he studied under the piano virtuoso Ignaz Moscheles) to further his musical education, and he even published several of his scores in both cities.[36]

While in Europe, Perkins gave his friend Crawford his second major commission, in 1853, to create a statue of Beethoven for the Music Hall in Boston. Cast in bronze in Munich, the monumental work was the grand centerpiece of a royal fête given by King Maximilian in the Bavarian capital on March 26, 1855, on the anniversary of Beethoven's death.[37] By May the statue had crossed the Atlantic and was on temporary display at the Athenæum before it was carted down the street to the Music Hall.[38] On March 1, 1856, Crawford's sculpture was officially unveiled to enthusiastic applause at the Grand Beethoven Festival at the Music Hall, which featured a poem recited by William Wetmore Story, an orchestra and chorus performing the German composer's music, and a piano performance by Perkins. Towering on the stage of the Music Hall, and after 1863 in front of the colossal German-made pipe organ, the statue became a familiar symbol of Boston's musical passion (fig. 25).[39]

FIG. 25 J. H. Bufford and Company, after a photograph by Frederic L. Lay, *Great Organ, Music Hall, Boston*, ca. 1865. Tinted lithograph, 34.3 × 26.4 cm (sheet). Collection of the Boston Athenæum

In the sonorous din of the Music Hall, Perkins's dream of establishing a musical academy in Boston eventually came true, for the hall would spawn more musical institutions in the city. It was at the hall that the New England Conservatory of Music was founded, in 1867, and the Boston Symphony Orchestra, in 1881. Although these institutions would ultimately abandon the Music Hall—the conservatory moved to the South End in 1870 and the orchestra to its new Symphony Hall in 1900—Boston's first dedicated concert hall had indeed launched the kind of musical camaraderie that Perkins hoped to foster in his native city.[40]

In the 1850s, however, Boston's cultural landscape was beginning to change. For one thing, the city's increasingly diverse population demanded and supported an ever wider range of cultural entertainment. In the summer of 1855, for example, the Music Hall was host to P. T. Barnum's traveling baby show, which featured babies selected from a pool of applicants in various categories meant to be entertaining, such as the finest, the fattest, the ugliest, and the like.[41] Vulgar and cheaply produced, the show nevertheless proved irresistible to a large audience. Perkins publicly objected to the use of the Music Hall—"a place consecrated to the endeavor to elevate the taste of the community"[42]—for so tasteless and commercial an enterprise and threatened to rescind his gift of the Beethoven statue.[43] But the baby show ran for two weeks with high profits, and Perkins never took the statue back. Commercial entertainment was nothing new to Boston, but as such spectacles as the baby show became ever more popular among the city's changing population, the established cultural hierarchy that people like Perkins had taken for granted began to loosen.

Perkins's return to Boston in 1854 was most likely related to his marriage, the following June, to Frances Davenport Bruen. Daughter of a prominent New York family who summered in Newport, Rhode Island, Frances had met Perkins in Rome, about 1847, probably through Crawford, whom the Bruen family had long patronized.[44] Through his marriage, Charles Perkins's ties to Newport grew strong. There, spending summers at the villa originally built by his mother-in-law, he befriended many of the artists and writers as well as the rich, who would transform the once idyllic community into a mecca of conspicuous consumption by the end of the century.[45]

Perkins's third and longest European residence began two years after his marriage, in 1857, this time with his growing family: his wife, daughter (two sons would be born in Florence), mother-in-law, and sister-in-law. In Europe, Perkins's studies in art and music continued. In Paris, he was one of the earliest American students in etching of Félix Bracquemond (1833–1914) and Maxime Lalanne (1827–1886), two of the most forward-looking printmakers of the era.[46] In Florence, he and his family settled in Villa Capponi, a handsome Baroque villa perched on a hill to the south of the city.[47] Happy in marriage and ensconced on a beautiful Tuscan hillside, he was within reach of all that Florence—and, indeed, the rest of Italy—offered. Still, he must have felt a degree of disappointment in not having become an established practitioner of either music or painting. At this crucial moment, a friend in Florence, Alexis-François Rio (1797–1874), gave Perkins an opportune piece of advice: become an art historian.[48] A French historian of Christian art, Rio judged art primarily by the sincerity of religious sentiments expressed in it rather than by the realistic effect produced by the use of perspective, classical proportions, and naturalistic coloring that had been practiced since the Renaissance.[49] Perkins shared Rio's art historical views to an extent—as did John Ruskin—but Rio's greatest gift to the Bostonian was the suggestion of a career in art history, and Perkins acknowledged his gratitude by dedicating his first book to the Frenchman.

Art history was a fitting field for Perkins. For years he had looked, sketched, and researched art of many centuries and in diverse media and accumulated a vast amount of art historical knowledge. Perkins, an exceptionally facile writer and lecturer, was a skilled disseminator of that body of knowledge. He had already delivered, in 1857, a lecture entitled "Rise and Progress of Painting to the Beginning of the Sixteenth Century" at Trinity College in Hartford, Connecticut, one of the first lectures on art history given at an American college.[50] His logical next step was to publish.

The history of Italian sculpture from the Middle Ages to the sixteenth century was to be the subject of Perkins's first book. Although abundant in Italy, the great works of Italian sculpture, unlike paintings, were "not to be found in splendid and commodious galleries, but in scattered churches and palaces," making a survey of them difficult for "any but careful observers."[51] Few books had discussed the subject, especially for the general reader. Jacob Burckhardt's *Der Cicerone*—a handbook of architecture, sculpture, and painting in Italy—had come out in 1855, in German, but its English translation of 1873 would cover only the portion devoted to paintings. Moreover, postmedieval Italian sculpture had been judged—usually negatively—against the standards of the antique, a standard that was not applied to the pictorial art because few examples of antique paintings had survived. Perkins wished to correct this bias by publishing what he had learned during his years of peregrinations throughout the Italian Peninsula. His first book, *Tuscan Sculptors: Their Lives, Works, and Times; With Illustrations from Original Drawings and Photographs*, published in two volumes in London in 1864 (in French translation in 1869), addressed sculpture of Tuscany only. In 1868, in *Italian Sculptors: Being a History of Sculpture in Northern, Southern, and Eastern Italy*, also published in London, he expanded his treatment beyond this region. Like Rio and Ruskin, Perkins located the high point of Italian sculpture in the 1400s and considered Michelangelo the last of the masters before the decadence of the later Renaissance set in. In both publications, however, he was more factual than moralistic, his writing more descriptive than interpretive. His text was remarkably neutral in tone and embellished by copious engravings made after his own sketches (fig. 26).

FIG. 26 An assemblage of several sculptures by Michelangelo. After Charles Callahan Perkins, from *Tuscan Sculptors* (London, 1864), 2: frontispiece

Perkins's tomes were a popular and critical success. Although not the most original in conception or execution, his books nevertheless filled a perceived gap in the existing art historical literature by presenting a body of material hitherto unavailable to a wide audience. In official recognition of his contribution, Perkins was created a *chevalier* of France's *Légion d'honneur* on July 15, 1867, and was made, on April 24, 1869, the first American corresponding member of the Académie des Beaux-Arts of the French Institute.[52] He had become one of the earliest American practitioners of art history, a field not yet established as a scholarly discipline.

Edward Newton Perkins (fig. 27), Charles's older brother by three years, is also central to our story.[53] Born on Pearl Street on April 18, 1820, and graduated from Harvard in 1841, Edward promptly took his own grand tour of Europe from 1841 to 1842 with his cousin Samuel Eliot, followed by a second sojourn there with his siblings, including Charles, from 1843 to 1845. Edward clearly relished the cultivated pleasures of Europe; in a portrait painted in 1845 by the Italian artist Bernardino Riccardi (1814–1854), Edward is a polished and well-heeled connoisseur, surrounded by the customary

FIG. 27 *Edward Newton Perkins*, n.d. From Mark Antony DeWolfe Howe, *Later Years of the Saturday Club, 1870–1920* (Boston, 1927), n.p.

FIG. 28 Bernardino Riccardi, *Edward Newton Perkins* (detail), 1845. Watercolor on paper, 33 × 26 cm (sight). Collection of the Boston Athenæum, Gift of the estate of Miss Eliza Callahan Cleveland, 1914

accoutrements of taste (1845; fig. 28). Unlike Charles, however, Edward wished neither to become an artist nor to organize institutions of art and music. After his marriage, in 1846, to Mary Spring of Watertown, Massachusetts, he settled into the tranquil life of a country squire at Pinebank, the family's summer residence, in Jamaica Plain, where the childless couple was active in the affairs of the Episcopal Church.[54] Although the couple would take frequent trips abroad, Edward's life centered primarily on Boston.

Philanthropy—almost a requisite of Edward's family name and wealth—suited his private and altruistic nature particularly well. Beginning in the mid-1840s Edward was benefactor to innumerable institutions, including Harvard University, St. Paul's School in Concord, New Hampshire (both his alma maters), the Perkins Institution for the Blind, and the Boston Episcopal Charitable Society, among others. He divided "his time between Church & Charity," as his sister Sarah observed with affectionate bemusement, often falling into his "old ways of helping every human creature in his own delightful way."[55] Of the many causes Edward supported, the Athenæum— familiar to him since his childhood by both lineage and physical proximity—was perhaps of greatest interest to him. During the many decades he served as an Athenæum trustee (from 1851 to 1898, with a hiatus from 1852 to 1856 while he was in Europe) and the chairman of the Fine Arts Committee (from 1862 to 1898), the mundane work of meetings, record keeping, and correspondence on behalf of the institution filled Edward's days, and he worked diligently without ever seeking the spotlight for himself.

Notable events for Edward Perkins tended to be those in his private life. Henry Wadsworth Longfellow gave a vivid description, for example, of Perkins's elegant wedding at Pinebank:

> a superb *fête champêtre*. . . . The evening, the blue lake, the boat with its white sail; the music, the dance on the greensward; the broad-spreading tent, "like a morning-glory inverted"; the crowd, well-dressed, and fair to see; the gleam of lamps through the gathering twilight, the procession to supper—the young bride led on by the white-haired Mr. Otis—all made a picture in my mind of great beauty. Then followed fireworks; and as we drove away the broad moon rose over the trees.[56]

Far more private than his gregarious brother, Edward led a quiet, privileged life of unobtrusive distinction.

Art, for Edward Perkins, was neither passion nor a profession but an expected part of life, like a fine house. For his 1848 renovation of the first Pinebank, the summer residence built by his grandfather James Perkins, Edward hired (after finding his cousin Edward Clarke Cabot's plans unsatisfactory[57]) the Paris-trained Jean Lemoulnier (dates unknown; in Boston 1846–1851), who crowned Pinebank II with fashionable French mansard roofs.[58] Ultimately, though, Edward's interest in art was superficial and his taste conventional. His loans to the Athenæum's exhibitions were mostly run-of-the-mill copies of Old Master paintings and picturesque Italian views, and he rarely commented on art in private or in public, even in his capacity as the chairman of the Athenæum's Fine Arts Committee. Instead, Edward deferred to his brother Charles on all matters of art.

The Athenæum Gallery vis-à-vis Boston's Changing Taste

The evolution of Boston's taste in art after midcentury is a familiar story that has been covered elsewhere by a number of art historians.[59] Before 1850 the city's exposure to paintings had been limited primarily to those by the Old Masters (or, more often, copies after them), American artists, and the slightly older generation of academic French painters such as Horace Vernet (1789–1863), Ary Scheffer, and Paul Delaroche (1797–1856). In the 1850s a greater number and variety of recent European paintings came to the city, causing taste in Boston to grow more diverse.

One significant event in this development was the city's swift embrace, in the 1850s, of contemporary French paintings, especially those of the Barbizon School. A key figure in this shift was the American painter William Morris Hunt (1824–1879), who returned from Paris to Boston in 1855. A scion of a prosperous Vermont family and educated at Harvard, Hunt had been in Europe since 1843 and went to Paris in 1847 (the same year as Charles Perkins). There, his first teacher was Thomas Couture (1815–1879), from 1847 to 1852, and the second, Jean-François Millet in Barbizon, from about 1853 to 1855, two artists who increasingly defied the ideals of the official French academy. When he returned to Boston, Hunt introduced the latest French aesthetics to the city. His own paintings incorporated the lessons he had learned from his French masters—fresh application of paint, less finish, and contemporary subject matter—and they were a regular presence at the Athenæum gallery throughout the 1850s and 1860s. As a teacher, he influenced a generation of American artists in Newport and Boston.[60] A charismatic arbiter of taste, Hunt also introduced to Boston paintings by Millet and other Barbizon artists, and several collectors in the city began to purchase such pictures with Hunt's counsel. Prominent Bostonians eagerly sat to him for portraits, too, especially after his marriage in 1855 to Louisa Dumaresq Perkins, granddaughter of Thomas Handasyd Perkins (and therefore Charles and Edward Perkins's second cousin), which confirmed the artist's already considerable social standing in Boston. In 1869 Hunt was the first artist to be elected a member of the Saturday Club, whose distinguished membership consisted of Boston's most illustrious men of letters and other intellectuals. Even after Hunt's death, in 1879, Boston's penchant for French, especially Barbizon, paintings persisted. By 1880 more than half of the pictures owned by the city's collectors were French.[61] Twenty years later, nearly 150 works by Millet had entered Boston collections.[62]

For much of the 1850s, the Athenæum gallery mirrored at least something of the growing diversity of artistic taste. Younger collectors, many of them new Athenæum proprietors or trustees, lent fresh works to the exhibitions in the gallery. In 1853 the first Barbizon canvas to be seen in Boston, *Study from Nature, Sketch at Fontainebleau* (1852; MFA) by Eugène Cicéri (1813–1890), was on view at the Athenæum, lent by Hunt's friend and fellow artist Edward Wheelwright (1824–1900). The following year, the Athenæum's exhibition featured the first painting by Millet to be shown in America, *Harvesters Resting* (1850–1853; fig. 29), from the collection of Martin Brimmer (1829–1896).[63] Brimmer, the son of the Boston mayor by the same name, had become in that year a trustee of the Athenæum at the age of twenty-five. He had met Hunt in Paris in the early 1850s and through him, Millet, and become the French artist's first major patron and one of the earliest American collectors of Barbizon paintings. Brimmer's eclectic holdings eventually included more than two dozen paintings and pastels by Millet, which entered—some of them in 1876, and others after his death in

FIG. 29 Jean-François Millet, *Harvesters Resting (Ruth and Boaz)*, 1850–1853. Oil on canvas, 67.3 × 119.7 cm. Museum of Fine Arts, Boston, Bequest of Mrs. Martin Brimmer, 06.2421. Photograph © 2013 Museum of Fine Arts, Boston

1895—the collection of the MFA. Thomas Gold Appleton, son of the millionaire Nathan Appleton and brother-in-law of Henry Wadsworth Longfellow, was another important Boston collector. A close friend of both Charles Perkins and Hunt and one of the first Bostonians—along with Perkins—to patronize contemporary French artists, Appleton collected widely, and his collection eventually included many works by such Barbizon painters as Constant Troyon (1810–1865; with whom the collector had informally studied in Barbizon), Narcisse Diaz de la Peña (1807–1876), and Théodore Rousseau (1812–1867), as well as those by the American artists influenced by the contemporary French aesthetics.[64] Appleton regularly exhibited works from his collection at the Athenæum gallery in the 1850s and 1860s.

During the 1850s, the Athenæum gallery also allotted space to a variety of paintings that had little to do with the French style. The city's newest and largest art gallery naturally attracted some high-profile loans, including those from other cities. In 1852, for example, the gallery was host to a selection of more than one hundred paintings from the Düsseldorf Gallery, an exhibition of contemporary works by German artists associated with the Rhineland city of Düsseldorf, which had been on view in New York City since 1849.[65] The paintings that came to Boston—many of them landscapes and history paintings—showed rigorous figure drawing, high finish, and strong narrative content, all characteristics of the Düsseldorf School, to a city that had seen few such works.[66] During that decade, the Athenæum gallery also welcomed works by several Hudson River School painters. Landscapes by Asher B. Durand (1796–1886) and Jasper F. Cropsey (1823–1900) regularly graced the gallery walls. From 1854 to 1857 five large canvases of the historical landscape series *The Course of Empire* (1833–1836; The New-York Historical Society) by Thomas Cole made much-touted appearances at the Athenæum gallery. Another celebrated artist of the Hudson River School, Frederic Edwin Church, displayed in 1855 his grand equatorial landscape *Andes of Ecuador* (1855; Reynolda House Museum of American Art, Winston-Salem, NC) to much acclaim.

When, in 1858, another traveling exhibition came to the Athenæum gallery, it brought the influence of the English critic John Ruskin (1819–1900). He believed that art mirrored the moral condition of the society that created it, and his early writings had provided an intellectual framework for questioning the supremacy of the classical and the naturalistic ideals in art that had been accepted since the Renaissance.[67] In the practice of painting, he prized "truth to nature," a faithful depiction of the factual appearance of God's creations. His teachings inspired a group of British artists—the Pre-Raphaelites—to reform painting by rejecting the classically inspired, ideal compositional formulas practiced by European masters since Raphael.

In this country, Ruskin's disciples were more numerous and active in New York than in Boston. In New York, his tenets gave particular encouragement to the artists of the Hudson River School, who endeavored to depict nature, especially *American* nature, with utmost fidelity and truthfulness.[68] Boston was home, though, to Charles Eliot Norton, Ruskin's closest American friend and literary executor. Having met Ruskin in 1850, Norton, who would become Harvard's first art history professor in 1874, preserved the English critic's teachings in a city whose artists and collectors increasingly turned away from them.[69] Norton was an Athenæum trustee in 1858, when a traveling exhibition brought to the gallery almost two hundred contemporary British paintings and watercolors, including those by the Pre-Raphaelite artists Ford Madox Brown (1821–1893) and William Holman Hunt (1827–1910) as well as a quintessentially Ruskinian sketch of a rock by the critic himself (fig. 30).[70] The Pre-Raphaelites' style—with its strong delineation, meticulous details, and high finish—certainly brought a shock of the new to Boston.

FIG. 30 John Ruskin, *Fragment of the Alps*, ca. 1854–1856. Watercolor and gouache over graphite on cream wove paper, 33.5 × 49.3 cm. Harvard University Art Museums/Fogg Museum, Gift of Samuel Sachs, 1919.506. Photo: Katya Kallsen © President and Fellows of Harvard College

The momentary surge of excitement that the Athenæum gallery had experienced in the early 1850s, however, did not last. As the Fine Arts Committee's relative position within the Athenæum grew weaker during the institution's financial crisis of the 1850s, the committee continued to operate without a clear vision or a mechanism to steer its exhibitions. At the same time, outside the Athenæum, a number of new art organizations and venues emerged in the city, and some of their exhibitions deprived the Athenæum gallery of the more progressive works and a responsive audience that would have enlivened its exhibitions. The short-lived Massachusetts Academy of Fine Arts, founded in 1852, soon became the Boston Art Club, part artists' guild and part social club.[71] After its first exhibition at the Athenæum gallery, in 1855, the club began to hold its exhibitions in its own space, with a much clearer focus than the Athenæum on contemporary American works.[72] The Allston Club, an artists' group founded in

FIG. 31 Ary Scheffer, *Dante and Beatrice*, 1851. Oil on canvas, 180 × 99 cm. Museum of Fine Arts, Boston, Seth K. Sweetser Fund, 21.1283. Photograph © 2013 Museum of Fine Arts, Boston

FIG. 32 Peltro William Tomkins, after Correggio, *Madonna of the Basket*, ca. 1806–1820. Watercolor on paper, 25.2 × 17.8 cm. Collection of the Boston Athenæum, Bequest of Thomas Dowse, 1858

FIG. 33 William Marshall Craig, after Rembrandt van Rijn, *The Mill*, ca. 1806–1820. Watercolor on paper, 27.2 × 32.4 cm. Collection of the Boston Athenæum, Bequest of Thomas Dowse, 1858

1866 by William Morris Hunt, specifically chose to display French and French-inspired American works, a direction that more closely matched the prevailing preference among Boston's forward-looking artists and collectors.[73] Commercial art galleries and European dealers eagerly catered to these and other collectors, too, and a growing number of Bostonians traveled and purchased works of art abroad.[74] While thousands of French pictures came to Boston in the second half of the century, the Athenæum gallery exhibited, in its entire existence, fewer than one hundred French paintings.[75]

By the 1860s the relative importance of the Athenæum gallery in the city was clearly on the wane. A large part of the loans represented older taste; many came from Charles Perkins, most of them Old Master copies, American works by his friends, and European paintings of a generation earlier. Among others Perkins showed, from 1856 to 1869, Scheffer's saccharine canvas *Dante and Beatrice* (1851, a replica of the original of 1846; fig. 31). The picture must have appeared more irrelevant with each passing year in a city where, by the late 1860s, the pre-Barbizon works of the 1830s and 1840s looked decidedly *retardataire*.[76] Commenting on the Athenæum's 1869 exhibition, a reviewer concluded that "the exhibitions have scarcely been worth the toil up the stairs and the twenty-five cents admission fee."[77] The gallery that had debuted as a splendid new presence on Beacon Street in 1850 had become, less than two decades later, an exhausted and stagnant venue, no longer vital to the city's artistic life.

The Fine Arts Committee's difficulties also extended to the area of acquisition. In fact, after 1850, additions to the Athenæum's art collection were few, and most of them came as gifts rather than by purchase.[78] The largest single addition during this period was a set of fifty-two nineteenth-century English watercolor copies of Old Master paintings (figs. 32, 33), given in 1858 by the estate of the late Bostonian Thomas

Dowse.[79] Although technically fine copies, the watercolors added to the collection little that was new when they made annual appearances in the Athenæum gallery. In 1869 a reviewer called the Athenæum's holdings mostly "fossils," and in 1870 another critic dismissed them as a "feeble collection of antique casts, copies, and modern pictures."[80] The Athenæum's golden age of collecting—the 1830s—had long since passed, and its art collection had lost the vitality and importance it had once had. One reason, to be sure, was the committee's reduced budget since the institution's financial crisis of the 1850s. More fundamentally, the committee lacked a comprehensive collecting program as well as support from the rest of the institution. During the 1850s and 1860s, the committee occasionally attempted subscription campaigns for art acquisitions, but the process depended on informal, personal negotiations among the institution's trustees rather than on a well-defined vision.

A case in point was the Fine Arts Committee's response, in 1859–1861, to the proposal of James Jackson Jarves (1818–1888) to sell his collection to the Athenæum. The peripatetic art critic from Boston had lived in Paris and Florence for much of the 1850s and in 1859 proposed to sell to the Athenæum about 120 paintings by the Italian "primitives." Ranging in date from the thirteenth to the seventeenth centuries, Jarves's pictures included some very important early Italian works: for example, two fragments from an altarpiece of about 1435 by Sano di Pietro (1406–1481), depicting episodes from the life of Saint Anthony Abbot (fig. 34), and *Portrait of a Lady with a Rabbit* (ca. 1505; Yale University Art Gallery) by Ridolfo Ghirlandaio (1483–1561).

Jarves first proposed the sale to the Athenæum in October 1859 through his friend the Athenæum trustee Charles Eliot Norton, but the Athenæum's subscription campaign to raise $20,000 for the purchase of the collection failed. The following summer, Jarves, still hopeful for the Athenæum's patronage, accompanied his pictures to Boston. The Athenæum remained unmoved, and the collection, sequestered in a warehouse, was never seen in Boston. When, in the winter of 1860–1861, the paintings puzzled and amused the viewers in New York but failed to find a buyer, Jarves made one last overture to the Athenæum, only to be disappointed, in April 1861, by a final refusal.[81]

Officially, the Athenæum gave no reason for its decision. To be sure, $20,000 was a sizable sum, especially for a collection whose merit was assured chiefly by the Ruskinian camp. The visual language of these and other early masters had begun to be taken seriously only in the first half of the nineteenth century; in the 1850s these "primitive" paintings were still far from being universally accepted. In addition, the financial panic of 1857–1858 undoubtedly cast a lingering pall, and other subscription schemes being advanced concurrently in the city competed for its limited resources.[82] Furthermore, Jarves's name may have aroused particular caution at the Athenæum, since one of the two paintings he had tried to sell to the institution in 1855, *Danäe*,

FIG. 34 Sano di Pietro, *Saint Anthony Abbot Tormented by Demons*, ca. 1435. Tempera and gold on panel, 47.5 × 34.3 cm. University purchase from James Jackson Jarves, 1871.58. Yale University Art Gallery, New Haven, Connecticut. Photo, Yale University Art Gallery/Art Resource, NY

FIG. 35 Bernardo Daddi, center panel: *Christ on the Cross between the Virgin and Saints Mary Magdalene and John the Evangelist*; left panel: *The Agony in the Garden and Saints Peter and Paul*; right panel: *Saints Catherine of Alexandria and Margaret of Antioch, Saints James Major and Benedict*, 1334. Tempera and gold leaf on panel with engaged frame, 62.3 × 54.2 cm (overall). Harvard University Art Museums/ Fogg Museum, Friends of the Fogg Art Museum Fund and William M. Prichard Fund, 1918.33. Photo: Imaging Department © President and Fellows of Harvard College

purportedly by Titian, was publicly denounced as a forgery during its exhibition at the Athenæum gallery.[83] That Jarves lacked an influential family name or a Harvard degree (he had dropped out of the school for health reasons) also denied him due respect in Boston, even after the publication, in 1855, of his *Art Hints: Architecture, Sculpture, and Painting*, arguably the second important American book on art.[84]

Beneath the surface, the Athenæum's refusal had much to do with the personal opinions of the trustees and their allies, especially the Perkins brothers. In late 1859, shortly after Jarves's initial offer, Edward, on a visit to Florence, counseled Norton against the collection.[85] Perkins assured Norton that his brother Charles agreed with him on the matter, and Edward also wrote to fellow Athenæum trustee Samuel Eliot to the same effect.[86] Particularly puzzling is Charles's disapproval of the Jarves collection, for he clearly admired the Italian masters of the thirteenth and fourteenth centuries and even owned a rare triptych from 1334 by the Florentine painter Bernardo Daddi (active ca. 1320–1348), a pupil of Giotto (fig. 35).[87] In retrospect, the fact that Jarves collected beyond his means at the visible expense of his family probably cast him as a kind of fanatic and likely offended genteel Bostonian sensibility. Also, Jarves's combative style—in person as well as in writing—did little to endear him to the more elegant crowd in the city. Norton himself never lost faith in the merit of Jarves's pictures, but the Perkins brothers were close family friends, and Norton thereafter did little to persuade the Athenæum to purchase the collection. The fruits of Jarves's labor, now widely regarded as one of the finest collections of the Italian "primitives," slipped away from Boston forever. In 1871 Yale University purchased his pictures.[88]

It becomes clear that Charles Perkins—as artist, connoisseur, and art historian—occupies an ambiguous position in the mid-nineteenth-century history of taste. Like Ruskin, he believed in the reforming power of art: art should not only be beautiful but also improve people's lives by offering comfort and moral uplift. Perkins admired, on the one hand, ancient Greek art for its skilled realization of a pure ideal and, on the other hand, medieval art for conveying faith and religious truth. Compared with these two ideals, "modern art," by which he meant contemporary art, "does not aim to be the exponent of a religious ideal. Its aims are practical, like those of the century."[89] As late as 1870 Perkins declared that, apart from Hippolyte Flandrin (1809–1864), Scheffer, and Delaroche, "no modern French painter has ever succeeded in infusing the slightest religious feeling into his pictures."[90] In remaining true to such feelings, Perkins was not able to appreciate the art of his own time. Ultimately, he was at once a social reformer and a connoisseur, and his allegiance remained divided between the moral and the aesthetic. Unable to commit fully to either, Perkins grew increasingly interested in the use of art in education: the cultivation of the sense of the beautiful in all people, for the betterment of the whole society.

Despite his sympathy for Ruskin, however, Charles Perkins was by nature not doctrinaire enough to qualify as a Ruskin acolyte, like Charles Eliot Norton. Perkins's view of art history was more empirical than theoretical, and therefore less judgmental than that of some of his more impassioned contemporaries. In other ways, too, he differed from Ruskin and his followers. Ruskin distrusted the masses, whereas Perkins genuinely liked people. William Morris, one of Ruskin's heirs, hated his century; Perkins thrived in it even while he bemoaned some of its artistic productions. In retrospect, however, this comfortable adjustment to his milieu probably made Perkins a less provocative arbiter of taste than Ruskin, Hunt, or Jarves. "Sugary . . . full of sweetness and light . . . especially sweetness": so Henry James described Perkins with a hint of sarcasm. Perkins's "sweetness" clearly earned him friends and admiration in his own time, but James nevertheless pronounced him "careful and sound, but without the divine afflatus."[91]

In the late 1860s, as his scholarship received international recognition, Charles Perkins finally enjoyed a measure of professional satisfaction that had long eluded him. At this fulgent moment, however, when opportunities in Europe opened to him,

Perkins and his wife decided to return to Boston.[92] Their three children were thirteen, eleven, and nine, respectively, and the parents wished them "brought up and educated in America."[93] In the summer of 1869 Perkins and his family left Europe after twelve years of residence there and settled, by the early fall, in their new house at 2 Walnut Street on Beacon Hill.

THE FALL OF 1869: A CONVERGENCE

When he returned to Boston, Charles Perkins threw himself into a schedule full of social and organizational engagements. There must have been days when he shuttled from one meeting to another and then to a dinner party or a concert, all the while generating a steady stream of business and personal correspondence as well as manuscripts for publications and lectures, at a pace that would have exhausted anyone less energetic. In 1871 he revived the dormant Boston Art Club and served as its president until 1881. As a member of Boston's School Committee from 1872 to 1884, Perkins influenced how art was taught in the city's public schools. Eager to elevate public taste in art, he also published and lectured widely on art and art education.[94]

Above all, Perkins's chief passion—the best venue for his vision—was the founding of an art museum in Boston. His return to the city in the crucial summer of 1869, just when his brother's Fine Arts Committee at the Athenæum was negotiating with Mrs. Lawrence the possible erection of a museum to house her late husband's bequest, added decisive momentum to that effort. Perhaps more significant, Charles also provided an important corrective to the Athenæum's earlier vision of an art museum. Instead of being merely a larger version of the Athenæum gallery, the new institution would be, in his view, a didactic museum dedicated to education. By 1869 he was an ardent disciple of the relatively new educational ideals espoused by the South Kensington (today's Victoria and Albert) Museum in London, whose purpose was to improve both public taste and industrial design through displays of the best examples of art and design.[95] To advance this vision, in the fall of 1869, Charles Perkins found a perfect vehicle in an organization called the American Social Science Association.

Organized in Boston in 1865, the American Social Science Association was a loosely defined group of professionals, social reformers, and businessmen with an extraordinarily broad mission: "to collect all facts, diffuse all knowledge, and stimulate all inquiry, which have a bearing on social welfare."[96] The members discussed diverse topics in the emerging field of the social sciences in the hope of improving human and societal conditions, and education was one of their main areas of focus.[97] The organization's scope was so all-encompassing, however, that it would lose its purpose by the early twentieth century; its Education Department met its demise even earlier, in the late 1870s.[98] For a time in the 1860s, however, the association was a relevant arena where people with different interests met to deliberate on a roster of social ills and possible remedies for them. Not surprisingly, some of its influential members were trustees and benefactors of Boston's many cultural institutions, including the Athenæum. Among others, William Barton Rogers, the founding president of MIT, was the association's first president, from 1865 to 1868; Samuel Eliot, an Athenæum trustee since 1866, followed Rogers as president from 1868 to 1872; and Edward Clarke Cabot, an Athenæum trustee from 1857 to 1875, was also an active member.

In the late summer of 1869, just when he returned from Europe, Charles Perkins joined the association and by October had become the chairman of its Committee on Art in Education, a subcommittee within the Education Department. The other committee members were James M. Barnard, a well-to-do Boston merchant, philanthropist, and a passionate advocate for art education, who had preceded Perkins as chairman; William Robert Ware, the founding professor of the architecture department at MIT; Edward Clarke Cabot; and, briefly, John Quincy Adams Ward (1830–1910), the New York sculptor who was concurrently involved in the founding of the Metropolitan Museum of Art in that city.[99] Even before Perkins's arrival, the committee had planned to install in Boston's public schools galleries of representative plaster casts and consulted European "experts" on their selection. Such galleries were to develop "a taste for the beautiful" among students.[100] To this project, which was already in progress, Perkins's knowledge, both of art history and of the latest European practice in art education, was an immense asset.

It proved difficult, however, to find in existing public schools space that was suitable for the envisioned galleries of casts. Instead, during the fall of 1869, the Committee on Art in Education began to discuss the possibility of constructing a new building devoted solely to the display of plaster casts. By November 22 Charles Perkins tested the committee on the "feasibility of establishing a regular Museum of Art at a moderate expense."[101] Evidently, he had been exploring this possibility for some time, and at the same meeting

> it was stated that it appears that there are two other parties in the field proposing to do something in the way of art in Boston, one a new body & the other a committee of the Boston Athenæum.[102] Members of each of these two movements have been seen by the members of this committee, & an attempt is to be made to unite or harmonize the 3 movements. It being understood that the committee of the Athenæum have invited this committee to meet them next Wednesday it was voted that our Chairman be ready to present our plans at the art meeting & to advocate an independent & entirely new movement.[103]

Two days later, the committee met with the Fine Arts Committee at the Athenæum, where Perkins proposed the idea and Cabot presented his architectural drawings (now unlocated) of the projected museum.[104] On behalf of the association, Barnard also recommended that the proposed organization draw its trustees, while remaining an independent body, from "among the Trustees or active members of the Athenæum, Harvard University, Institute of Technology, Social Science Association, &c."[105] All these proposals must have been music to the ears of the Athenæum's Fine Arts Committee members, who were desperate to find a suitable alternative to its cramped quarters. At this meeting, however, the Fine Arts Committee was powerless to "join any other plan or society for the same purpose," and "nothing definite was arrived at."[106]

Nonetheless, Charles Perkins and his associates persevered. They invited more men to join their plan, and Perkins was to prepare a newspaper article to rally public support.[107] Within days, a new committee was formed to frame "a suitable organization to harmonize the various interests and to govern the Museum when established,"[108] and eighteen men met on December 3, under Perkins's leadership, at the office of the American Social Science Association at 13 Pemberton Square, across the street from the Athenæum. All prominent Bostonians, many of the attendees occupied important positions at the cultural institutions involved with the project: the Athenæum, Harvard, MIT, the Boston Public Library, and the American Social Science Association.[109] Somewhat surprisingly, the Athenæum at first declined the invitation to join forces with other institutions for this project. It was thought that the Athenæum "had already some money means & some objects of Art to commence their works with,"[110] and, as the Athenæum's president, John Amory Lowell, smugly declared, "the Athenæum could not join any other association or body of men in the establishment of an Art Museum, and that it would be [for] others to join" the Athenæum in its plan.[111] Eventually, however, the parties came to an agreement, and the Athenæum promised to deposit its art collection at the future museum. Others followed suit: Harvard offered to lend the collection of engravings bequeathed to it by Francis Calley Gray in 1857; and MIT, its collection of architectural casts (amassed chiefly by William Robert Ware) for which it lacked adequate space. More meetings followed, and a basic outline of the proposed museum gradually emerged. During this process, the American Social Science Association—and especially Charles Perkins, its chief spokesperson in this project—played a crucial role by serving as the all-important mediator for the disparate parties and their respective interests.

Finally, on December 21, 1869, yet another committee of fourteen men was created specifically to apply to the state legislature for an act of incorporation to establish "a Museum of Art" in Boston.[112] By then, several more men of financial, political, or social influence had been added to the earlier lineup, clearly so that their practical expertise would benefit the future museum.[113] For example, the name of Martin Brimmer, who would soon become the museum's founding president, appeared for the first time when he joined this committee. Not surprisingly, the new additions replaced some of the committee members of the American Social Science Association whose chief contribution had been their vision and passion rather than their wealth and influence. Barnard, for instance, an active member of the association who worked tirelessly to further educational charity while adopting a "modest scale of living" for himself, quietly receded into the background after December 1869.[114]

When the committee duly filed an application to the state legislature, at last the establishment of an art museum in Boston became a concrete possibility. On February 4, 1870, the Massachusetts legislature passed an act of incorporation for the Museum of Fine Arts, and Boston's first art museum was born. But would it survive its infancy? A positive answer was anything but certain in the early spring of 1870.

CHAPTER THREE

The Founding Vision for the Museum, 1870

O N MARCH 10, 1870, one month after the state legislature passed the act of incorporation for the Museum of Fine Arts, Boston, the new institution's founding trustees gathered "for the purpose of considering whether they [would] accept the Act of incorporation granted to them by the General Court."[1] They eagerly accepted.

So was born Boston's first art museum, but at the beginning it possessed no building, no collection, and few financial resources. Immediately, practical questions pressed for answers: Where would the museum be? How would it be organized? How would it be funded? At the same time, the institution's philosophical direction also demanded definition: What would be its purpose? Whom should it serve? What should it collect and exhibit? Only one of these questions found a quick answer when, in May 1870, the city gave the museum a grant of land for its future building. Others, however, required time for deliberation, and some—such as that of funds—remained unresolved for years.

The original board of the MFA consisted of twenty-six men, appointed by three different methods. The first twelve were the incorporators. It was they who had applied in December 1869 to the state legislature to establish the museum; in February 1870 they were in turn named the museum's incorporators. The nine men in the second group were institutional representatives: according to the terms of incorporation, each of the three institutions that had helped found the museum—the Athenæum, Harvard University, and MIT—was required to appoint three persons annually to the board. The last five men were ex officio appointments, all but one from the city government and its educational agencies: the mayor of Boston, the president of the Boston Public Library, the superintendent of the Boston public schools, the secretary of the city's Board of Education, and the director of the Lowell Institute.[2] The customs of the day dictated that no women be considered for trusteeship, not even Mrs. Lawrence, who had contributed the single largest amount of money toward the museum's establishment.[3]

By design, the twelve incorporators were those who could give practical help to the young institution. In December 1869 they were chosen deliberately from a variety of fields: men of influence in the areas of finance, local politics, real estate, and manufacture were added to balance those "on the Fine Arts side."[4] The incorporators were a variegated bunch: although all prominent and civic-minded men of native stock, they ranged in age from thirty-three to seventy-three, and only seven of the twelve had gone to Harvard. Five were members, either by birth or marriage, of unquestionably well-established, illustrious Boston families (Martin Brimmer, Charles William Eliot, Samuel Eliot, Charles Callahan Perkins, and Benjamin Smith Rotch), who lent their names, wealth, and influence to innumerable cultural institutions and philanthropic enterprises. Three others hailed from outside Boston, all sons of professional fathers, and had achieved prominence through their intellectual and professional prowess (George Barrell Emerson, Francis Edward Parker, and William Barton Rogers). The remaining four were successful men of business who had turned their talents to the city's political, cultural, and financial institutions (John Tisdale Bradlee, William Endicott Jr., Henry Purkitt Kidder, and Otis Norcross) (see Appendix).

The remaining members of the board—the required institutional and ex officio appointments—were obviously expected to strengthen the museum's connection to the city's existing political, cultural, and educational structures. The young institution's overwhelming need for practical assistance was probably the reason why the American Social Science Association, despite its significant contribution to the museum's creation, had no formal representation on the board; the association, possessed of no funds, real estate, or collections, could offer little tangible help.

The greatest strength of the founding board lay in the cohesion that already existed among many of its members. Not only did they share familial and business ties, but they also had worked with one another through their overlapping institutional affiliations. The specific histories, needs, and interests of the institutions that could help the MFA were common knowledge to the majority of these men, making communication smooth. As if to symbolize the group's pedigree, the board held its meetings in the building of the Massachusetts Hospital Life Insurance Company, a trust and investment firm that handled a large proportion of the money belonging to wealthy Bostonians and the institutions they patronized.[5] From February 1870 into the 1880s—well past the museum's opening in 1876—board meetings continued to take place at the insurance company's office in downtown Boston. Once the museum was established, the institutional boundaries that had occasionally divided the negotiations of the winter of 1869 swiftly disappeared. For example, John Amory Lowell, who as the Athenæum's president had flatly declined to join the American Social Science Association in establishing the museum ("the Athenæum could not join any other association or body of men") became, by the spring of 1870, one of the MFA's

FIG. 36 Hayman Selig Mendelssohn Studio, London, *Martin Brimmer*, ca. 1880. Albumen photograph, 29.8 × 23.2 cm (mount). Collection of the Boston Athenæum, Gift of Charles H. Parker, 1938

most active trustees (representing the Lowell Institute) and spearheaded the effort to organize the new institution's administrative structure.[6]

By the end of March, the bylaws and the officers of the new museum were in place: Martin Brimmer (fig. 36) as president, Henry P. Kidder as treasurer, and James Elliot Cabot (representing the Athenæum) as secretary. Of the three, Brimmer would leave a particularly strong mark on the museum: during his long tenure as president, from 1870 to his death in 1896, he was directly responsible for raising funds and, as chairman of the Building Committee, for erecting the institution's first structure. He also generously gave and bequeathed a number of important paintings to the museum. Following the election of these officers, multiple committees came into being in rapid succession: the Committee on Organization was to devise an organizational structure; the Finance Committee, to seek some form of financial foundation; and another committee was to petition the city council for a grant of land. Once the museum received from the city, in May, a parcel of land abutting what would later be named Copley Square, the Building Committee began to plan the structure. Yet another committee was to negotiate the contracts by which other institutions would deposit their collections at the future museum.

The members of the board also endeavored to define the museum's purpose and contents. What the trustees accomplished in 1870 undoubtedly exceeded what has survived in the museum's scant early records. The several handwritten drafts of official documents—bylaws and mission statement, for example—are heavily marked with corrections by multiple hands, unquestionably a result of many unrecorded discussions.[7] In February the act of incorporation had declared the MFA's three goals only in the broadest of terms: erection of a museum building for the exhibition of art, formation of a permanent collection, and instruction in the fine arts. A more specific plan—for the institution's purpose, audience, and contents—needed to be developed without delay. On March 17 the trustees announced the "Plan and Objects of the Museum." It listed the institution's tripartite aims: first, to make available "to the public and to students, such art-collections already existing in the neighborhood"; second, to nurture such collections so that they would grow into "a representative Museum of Fine Arts, in all their branches, and in all their technical applications"; and third, to provide instruction in studio arts through "lectures, practical schools, and a special library."[8] As for the contents of the future galleries, several organizations—the Athenæum, Harvard University, and the Boston Public Library[9]—had already promised to lend (deposit) parts of their collections, and loans from private sources were also anticipated. Notably, the trustees also listed as a major component of the museum's display "a commencement . . . of what is intended ultimately to become a comprehensive gallery of reproductions."[10]

Among the committees established in the spring of 1870, the one responsible for collecting and exhibiting works of art—two of the museum's most essential tasks—was the Committee on the Museum, with Charles Callahan Perkins as chairman. Even though the museum's building did not open until 1876, this curatorial committee began work in 1870 on the institution's exhibitions and acquisitions. The committee carried out a remarkable number of tasks that in today's museums are performed by a variety of highly trained specialists: curator, registrar, exhibitions director, collections manager, editor, facilities manager, fund-raiser, and communications officer. The committee's central importance was confirmed in 1873, when its report was printed for distribution as the institution's first annual report. (No other reports were published until 1876.) As chairman of this important committee, Perkins exerted a singular influence on the museum's early curatorial direction.

This committee was a loosely defined entity, and a few devoted men discharged its responsibilities in informal capacities, donating their time and knowledge. In part because of the scarcity of the early museum's records, the committee's early accomplishments have been underdocumented. Despite overseeing the museum's entire curatorial operations from 1870 on, Perkins had no official title until 1876, when he was made the ambiguous "Honorary Director," the word "honorary" denoting only the

absence of salary, not an auxiliary status. Perhaps because of this, Perkins has generally been less well known than Brimmer, the museum's first president, and Charles Greely Loring (1828–1902; fig. 37), who was given the title of "Curator" in 1876.[11] In reality, however, Perkins's curatorial responsibilities were greater than those of either of the other two figures. To be sure, Brimmer worked tirelessly as the museum's public face and steered the construction of its first building, but he apparently had little to do with its day-to-day curatorial activities, signing far fewer documents for loans, purchases, and gifts than Perkins did. And while Perkins assumed full curatorial duties almost from the moment of the museum's incorporation, Loring was not officially involved with the institution until 1872, when Perkins invited him—a friend and an amateur Egyptologist—to help with one section of the museum's exhibition. Moreover, in 1876, when Loring received the title of curator, the board stipulated that the honorary director was to direct the overall curatorial activities of collecting and exhibiting, while the curator was to handle the more mundane aspects of curatorial duties, which are today performed by building manager, registrar, and custodian.

Perkins played a major role in shaping the trustees' March 1870 statement. Less than a month before the Plan and Objects were announced, on March 17, he had delivered a lecture, on February 22, in which he called for the establishment of both "educational museums of art" and schools of design, which together would provide the "means of forming a standard of taste through knowledge of the masterpieces of the past."[12] According to Perkins, it was a matter of course that a museum should consider education its foremost aim, and if educational museums could acquire masterpieces for their collections to serve that end, as some galleries had done in Europe, that was all well and good. But in the United States, he advised, where there was no governmental support for museums and little art had accumulated from the past, museums by necessity must strive for a different goal. With single-minded pragmatism, Perkins stated that an art museum in the United States of 1870 was to aim at "collecting material for the education of a nation in art, not . . . making collections of objects of art."[13]

In 1870 the fundamental justification for the MFA's existence lay in its educational role. Even before the museum was incorporated, education had been cited as its chief purpose: the proposed museum was to be "a means of popular education and enjoyment."[14] In March 1870 the trustees themselves pledged that they would run the museum with "the sole view to [its] greatest public usefulness."[15] The didactic character was confirmed nowhere more clearly than at the ceremony for the opening of its building, in 1876, when Boston mayor Samuel Crocker Cobb proclaimed the museum "the crown of our educational system,"[16] and Samuel Eliot, a museum trustee, affirmed that "every museum is not only an institution of fine art, but it is a school."[17]

THE SOUTH KENSINGTON MUSEUM: ART IN THE SERVICE OF INDUSTRY

Much evidence confirms that the most salient model for Boston's new museum was the South Kensington Museum in London, founded in 1852 (originally as the Museum of Manufactures).[18] As early as January 1870, Brimmer referred to the proposed museum in Boston as the "project of a South Kensington Museum to be established here on a scale proportioned to the modest capacities of the place."[19] In February 1870 Perkins characterized the MFA as "an educational institution, like the South Kensington Museum."[20]

The London museum was founded in the aftermath of the Great Exhibition held in that city in 1851, where British products had performed poorly. One of the museum's original aims, therefore, was to improve the nation's manufacturing industry. Art was to be applied to manufactured goods—hence the nineteenth-century sense of the term "applied arts"—and science utilized in industrial processes, in order to make British products more competitive in the international market. At the same time, the museum was part of Britain's educational-reform movement that sought to expand vocational training and public schooling. Teaching of necessary skills to future workmen—especially drawing—was deemed particularly important, and a number of publicly funded schools of design had been established throughout the country, including the Government School of Design in London in 1837.[21] At midcentury, this reform movement and the mandate to improve British design joined hands, forming a new national system of art education. In 1852 the study collection of the Government School of Design—books, prints, paintings, plaster casts, skeletons, stuffed birds, and specimens of manufacture such as "silks, bronzes, porcelains, inlaid and carved woods"[22] —was transferred to the newly founded Museum of Manufactures (called the South Kensington Museum after 1857) and joined the objects purchased from the Great Exhibition, together forming the nucleus of the new institution's collection (fig. 38). The school itself was renamed the South Kensington School of Design (now the Royal College of Art) and trained drawing teachers for the nation's schools. Following in the footsteps of the London museum, the new institution in Boston considered it one of its primary goals to contribute to the manufacturing industry. The trustees' March 1870 statement specifically promised instruction in various branches of art "with their industrial applications." A draft for the statement had even included the word "manufacture": the museum was to offer "instruction in Drawing, Painting, Modelling, and designing for Architecture, Manufactures, and Decoration" by establishing a free school of design.[23]

The South Kensington Museum implemented many practices that were relatively new to public museums. Its display focused chiefly on decorative arts, although fine arts were also present: examples of decorative arts showed designs and skills that had

FIG. 38 John C. L. Sparkes, *Marlborough House: Fourth Room*, 1856. Watercolor on paper, 31.7 × 30.7 cm. Victoria and Albert Museum, London. Photo © Victoria and Albert Museum, London

been applied to man-made objects in diverse cultures during different historical periods, while paintings and sculptures demonstrated accepted artistic taste and standards. The museum was also decidedly didactic in its display and programs, using a variety of pedagogical devices such as labels, catalogues, and lectures that were meant to instruct the audience in no uncertain terms on the correct principles of ornament and design. (The famous "Chamber of Horrors" filled with "Examples of False Principles of Decoration" left little room for ambiguity.) Finally, the museum, clearly "designed to afford instruction . . . to the masses, as well as to the *élite* of society,"[24] instituted measures that made it available to a wider audience than had London's other public museums, the British Museum and the National Gallery. The South Kensington Museum was open for longer hours on more days than the other two, making it easier for working people to visit. Its open atmosphere and innovative amenities, including the world's first museum restaurant, which opened in 1857, welcomed the visitor. Significantly, in Boston, the museum would endeavor to adopt many of these policies implemented at the South Kensington Museum.

From the beginning, however, the South Kensington Museum's purpose entailed an inherent dichotomy: the vocational training of people in manufacturing was one goal, while documenting the history of taste for the education of the public was another.[25] Mindful of this fact, Henry Cole, the museum's influential first director from 1852 to 1873, addressed not only the producer of manufactured goods—the designer and the artisan—but also the broader public, the consumer of industrial products:

> Our first and strongest point of faith is . . . to elevate the Art-Education of the whole people, and not merely to teach artisans. . . . Our first object, therefore, has been to . . . promote all the several interests involved in the improvement of public taste. The interest of the public, as consumer and judge—the interest of the manufacturer, as the capitalist and producer—and the interests of the artisan, as the actual workman.[26]

By the 1860s the emphasis of his educational enterprise had undeniably shifted from design education to public display. In the 1870s the South Kensington Museum was criticized for exhibiting showy and expensive treasures, more for the entertainment of the general public than for any serious instruction in design, and, after Cole retired, the museum's reputation in its own country began to falter. Nonetheless, the museum continued to attract accolades overseas, and new museums emulating the South Kensington model multiplied in Europe as well as in North America. Boston's Museum of Fine Arts was one prominent example.

To interested Americans in 1870, the South Kensington Museum was a highly successful educational innovation. In the fewer than twenty years since its establishment, the museum and its affiliated School of Design had become an acknowledged "centre of education in the arts of design for teachers and pupils throughout the whole kingdom,"[27] and they claimed a large share of the credit for the improved performance of British manufactured goods at the world fairs of the 1860s. Britain's visible success had induced the governments of France, Germany, and Austria to found institutions with similar aims and programs. By contrast, in the United States, even though the nation was newly concerned with the weak performances of its manufactured goods at international fairs, the British model inspired a number of private—not governmental—efforts to emulate it. The South Kensington idea found its way into the plans for many of the art institutions that emerged in major American cities during the 1870s and 1880s. New York's Metropolitan Museum of Art, incorporated only two months after its Boston counterpart, initially espoused a set of objectives bearing all the hallmarks of the South Kensington model: "encouraging and developing the study of the fine arts, and the application of the arts to manufacture, of advancing the general knowledge of kindred subjects, and, to that end, of furnishing popular instruction and recreation."[28] In 1876 the Pennsylvania Museum and School of Industrial Art (today, the museum is the Philadelphia Museum of Art and the school, the University of the Arts) was chartered for the purpose of establishing "a Museum of Art, in all its branches and technical application, and with a spherical view to the development of the art and textile industries of the state."[29] In Boston, too, the museum at its founding clearly embraced the London museum's mandate to make art contribute to industry.

In Boston, the impact of the educational ideals of the South Kensington Museum and its affiliated school was not limited to the MFA. The British model just as strongly influenced the city's ongoing effort to promote industrial art education, which culminated in May 1870, only three months after the museum's incorporation, in "An Act Relating to Free Instruction in Drawing." Commonly known as the Massachusetts Drawing Act, the law, written in two sections, made Massachusetts the first state to mandate drawing an essential component of the free universal education of all people. The first section required that drawing be taught in public elementary schools as a compulsory subject, just like reading and writing;[30] the second, that every Massachusetts community with a population of more than ten thousand provide "free instruction in industrial or mechanical drawing" to students aged fifteen and older.[31] In 1870 twenty-three cities and towns in the Commonwealth were populous enough to be required by the law to offer free drawing classes to their residents.[32]

Even before this, Massachusetts had led the nation in the standardization and professionalization of public schools. Schools had long existed in America, but under Horace Mann, the secretary of the newly created Board of Education (the first such position in the United States) from 1837 to 1848, schools in Massachusetts were made nonsectarian and attendance was made compulsory. Toward midcentury, schools in

Massachusetts began to offer graded classes and standardized curricula, both innovations in public education. School systems, which had hitherto consisted of only teachers and pupils, began to employ professional administrators, whose job was to manage the teachers, and Boston's first superintendent of schools was appointed in 1851. Teachers' training became professionalized, too, and Boston founded in 1852 its first Normal School—"normal" because it established teaching standards, or norms— to prepare high school graduates for the teaching profession. By the 1870s all the rudiments of a modern school system were in place, and many of the state's educational innovations would become the standard American way of schooling.

At the same time, Boston's extraordinary transformations in the century's middle decades—from an agrarian to an industrial economy, from a homogeneous to a diverse population—pointed out the necessity of teaching practical skills in public schools. The ability to draw legible images with clear outlines (fig. 39) was considered necessary for future workmen in a state where, by 1870, fully half of its working population was employed in the manufacturing industry.[33] Successful European attempts to institute universal drawing instruction, first in Prussia and more recently in Britain, had prompted several American cities—Baltimore, Philadelphia, Cleveland, Cincinnati, New Haven, and Hartford, among others—to experiment with similar programs. By the end of the 1860s Massachusetts industries, faced with mounting competition from Europe and the American South and West, had come to favor legislation that would make drawing an essential part of public education.

In June 1869 twelve men and two businesses filed the petition for what would become, almost a year later, the Massachusetts Drawing Act. The petition had a manifestly commercial motive: to ensure "great proficiency in mechanical drawing and in other arts of design" on the part of "the skilled workmen."[34] Not surprisingly, the petition cited the British system—the South Kensington Museum and its school— as its direct model.

As it turned out, many of the founding trustees of the museum were active supporters of the Massachusetts Drawing Act. Two, John Amory Lowell and William Gray, had signed the petition for the act in June 1869. After the law's enactment, three other trustees were directly responsible for its implementation: John D. Philbrick, the superintendent of Boston's public schools; his successor, Samuel Eliot; and Alexander H. Rice, the state's educationally minded governor. In addition, Joseph White, a museum trustee in his capacity as secretary of the Massachusetts Board of Education, would in 1875 petition (unsuccessfully) to amend the 1870 law to make it even more beneficial to industry. Then there was Charles Perkins, who in 1870 began informally advising a subcommittee on drawing within Boston's School Committee. In that role, Perkins was responsible for the hiring of Walter Smith, a graduate of the South Kensington School of Design, for two positions charged with administering the new

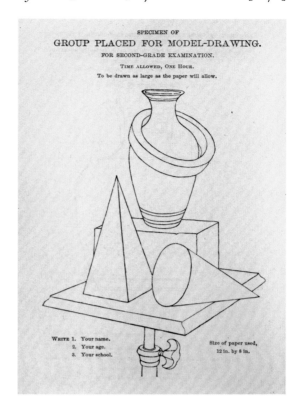

law: the Director of Art Education for Massachusetts and the Director of Drawing
for the Boston public schools.[35] After Smith arrived in Boston, in October 1871, he
and Perkins, who would be elected to the Boston School Committee the following
year, dominated the state's effort to promote art education for the rest of the decade.
In May 1872, when an exhibition showcasing the results of the free industrial drawing
classes was held, the organizing committee for it consisted of three museum trustees—
Philbrick, Perkins, and Robert W. Ware (who would become a museum trustee in
1875)—and Smith.[36] Largely through the efforts of Perkins and Smith, in 1873 the
state established the Massachusetts State Normal Art School (now the Massachusetts
College of Art), the nation's first publicly funded school for the training of art teachers,
with Smith as its first director.

In 1870 the nascent museum clearly aligned itself with the Massachusetts Drawing
Act, considering itself part of a coordinated plan to institute in Boston a system of
industrial art education after the British model. While public schools taught drawing as a compulsory subject, the museum's contribution was to exhibit examples of
decorative and fine arts. In March 1873, when Smith, Perkins, and Philbrick petitioned the state to allocate $15,000 for the establishment of the State Normal Art

School, the MFA's full board quickly approved the proposal, officially pronouncing it "most worthy of a favorable hearing, inasmuch as it aims to attain an object of the utmost importance to the industrial and artistic interests of Massachusetts."[37] Perhaps it was an overstatement, but Smith referred to the MFA as "a Boston museum of fine and industrial art."[38]

Within a few years, however, the support for universal drawing instruction declined in Massachusetts. Especially after the financial panic of 1873, the public resented having to pay for a program that served only a narrow segment of the population—namely, the artisans-in-training and the industrial capitalists who would benefit materially from a well-trained workforce. Differences of opinion within the Boston School Committee also contributed to the program's demise, as did the personal unpopularity of Walter Smith, a dogmatic and arrogant taskmaster.[39] Boston's art community roundly disliked him, too. On the one hand, William Morris Hunt despised Smith's methodical, rigid drawing curriculum; on the other, Harvard professor Charles Herbert Moore, a Ruskinian and a Hunt critic, publicly condemned his "amazingly stupid and mechanical teaching now furnished under the auspices of the State."[40] Smith's influence waned as precipitously as it had waxed, and by 1882 he had been dismissed from all three of his positions.[41] He returned to England the following year, and Perkins lost his seat on the School Committee in 1884. By the mid-1880s the art-in-the-service-of-industry model that was so passionately embraced in 1870 by the city and the state—and by many of the museum's founding trustees—had lost much of its force.

Art History Rationally Displayed for the Public

As important as the South Kensington model was for the museum in 1870, another type of institution was also available for emulation: the encyclopedic public museum of nineteenth-century Europe, dedicated to a systematic display of the history of art for the edification of the general public. Even while upholding the improvement of industrial design as a major goal, the trustees also wished their institution to grow, eventually, into a "representative Museum of Fine Arts."

Beginning in the Renaissance, the display of princely collections had long been accessible only to the noble, the powerful, the rich, or the learned. Only after the revolutions of the late eighteenth and early nineteenth centuries did parts of the vast aristocratic accumulations of art move from private to public ownership, and some of them became available to the general populace for the first time. Sponsored either by the state or by enlightened monarchs, the new public art museums aimed to illustrate, with their comprehensive art collections, "the rise and progress of the arts and their gradual decadence" in displays arranged rationally and chronologically.[42] This new brand of museum was concerned not so much with the improvement of industrial design, as was the South Kensington Museum, but with the dissemination of art historical knowledge to the broader public.

As the new type of public art museum offered art to an expanding audience, the function of displays of art also shifted. In the words of the art historian Carol Duncan, the earlier, aristocratic art galleries had

> addressed the visitor as a gentleman and reinforced this identity by enabling him to engage in and re-enact the kind of discerning judgments that gentlemanly culture called "good taste." By asking him to recognize—without the help of labels—the identities and distinctive artistic qualities of canonized masters . . . the visitor-cum-connoisseur could experience himself as possessing a culture that was both exclusive and international, a culture that marked its possessor as a member of the elite.[43]

In contrast, this new art museum considered its visitor "a bourgeois citizen who enters the museum in search of enlightenment and rationally understood pleasures."[44] In these art historical exhibitions, schools of art and their principal masters punctuated the long progress of art through time, and objects were presented in logical order in well-lit (and, in some cases, fireproofed and heated) galleries, accompanied by didactic labels aimed at members of the general public who were neither connoisseurs nor scholars.

It was this new kind of encyclopedic public art museum, such as the Musée du Louvre in Paris and the Königliches Museum in Berlin (built between 1823 and 1830 and renamed the Altes Museum in 1845), that many of the MFA's founding trustees— and other American museum builders of the period—had seen and admired in Europe. Earlier, when the Athenæum gallery had opened in 1827, the venue still retained some residual character of the older form: entering the space and knowing how to appreciate the works on view confirmed the visitor's membership in the elite circle of connoisseurs. By 1870 the ideal had clearly shifted in favor of the newer, didactic displays, systematically laid out to communicate art historical instruction. James Jackson Jarves astutely described the contrast in 1870: the older galleries had featured "capricious gatherings of royal and aristocratic patrons . . . [displayed for] princely ostentation" with "no historical sequence, nor . . . adequate means to study the development of art at any fixed period," whereas the new public art museums were "organized on a popular basis to instruct the public at large, [and were] chronologically and scientifically arranged."[45]

As for the school attached to the museum—clearly one of the aims outlined in the Plan and Objects in March 1870—it began operation as the School of Drawing and Painting in the museum's basement on January 2, 1877, six months after the museum's opening.[46] For years, however, the school's purpose, audience, and connection to the museum remained ambiguous. In 1870 the school had been envisioned as something closer to the South Kensington School of Design than an art academy for the fine artist. Yet by 1876, when museum trustees contemplated the opening of a school, their ambition had shifted to the establishment of "a public Drawing School, of the higher class, which may ultimately develop into an Academy of Painting."[47] At first, though, the students were predominantly women, most of them amateurs, and the new school settled for the somewhat limited role of creating an appreciative audience for art: "To give to amateurs the training they require is accordingly one of [the school's] first duties. . . . If he can learn to see things as the artist sees them he will better understand the artist's purpose and will have a more just appreciation of the artist's work."[48] In the late 1870s the museum's basement also housed several schools of practical arts—plaster carving, pottery painting, needlework—which were established by outside organizations. These schools, however, failed to attract enough pupils and closed within a few years.[49]

At the same time, the school's connection to the museum remained surprisingly unclear. Even though many museum trustees welcomed the school—one trustee declared that "without the Drawing School, the Museum was like a body without a soul; with it, it is alive"[50]—the school did not officially belong to the museum until 1901. In the intervening years, the school's administrative and fiduciary responsibilities rested with the Permanent Committee, consisting of several museum trustees as well as artists, architects, and connoisseurs.[51] The three trustees who sat on this committee from 1876 on (Brimmer, Loring, and Perkins) worked closely with the school, inspecting the students' work every Saturday, and their deep involvement at first created a warm, familial relationship between the two bodies. In point of fact, however, the museum had no formal jurisdiction over the committee or the school, and, as the years wore on, the absolute and lifelong—oligarchic—nature of the Permanent Committee grew increasingly untenable. In 1901 both the School of Drawing and Painting and the Permanent Committee ceased to exist, and the former was renamed the School of the Museum of Fine Arts. Only then was the school officially entrusted with "the responsibility of doing a part in [the museum's] educational work."[52]

"Attainable Objects": Decorative Arts and Reproductions

In order to achieve, with inadequate funds, all the ambitious goals set by the founding trustees, the fledgling museum had little choice but to collect and exhibit "attainable objects."[53] One category of such objects was the promised loans, and another was specimens of what was called art industry, that is, examples of decorative arts. Although bearing the name of a museum of fine arts, the museum aimed initially to collect and exhibit not only paintings and sculpture but also textile, ceramic, metalwork, glass, carved wood, jewelry, furniture, and more. Decorative arts were to form a major component of the displays, equal in status, not secondary, to examples of the fine arts.

Another group of "attainable objects" was reproductions. The amount of money, the argument went, that in Europe would be expended on a single original picture or statue could erect in America "a fire-proof building and fill it with reproductions of antique and mediaeval works in metal, ivory, etc., etc., obtained by electro-type, galvano plastic, various processes of casting, elastic moulding, and photography, all of which are quite as efficacious for educational purposes as the originals which are out of our reach."[54] A vocal proponent of this vision, Charles Perkins confidently asserted that "your libraries are . . . not filled with original manuscripts, neither need your museums be filled with original marbles."[55] Accordingly, in March 1870 the founding trustees clearly stated their wish to create "a commencement . . . of what is intended ultimately to become a comprehensive gallery of reproductions."[56]

Among different kinds of reproductions, plaster casts were deemed the most useful. Although foreign to our modern notion of what an art museum ought to collect and exhibit, until the twentieth century plaster casts had played a role almost equal to that of originals in the study of the visual arts.[57] Long a requisite component of European aristocratic collections, plaster casts acquired a new importance in the nineteenth-century art museums as a tool for didactic illustration, for which the casts' ability to fill the "missing links"[58] in art history—to achieve chronological thoroughness—was particularly valuable. In the second half of the century, commercial producers supplied an ever greater number of casts of sculptures and architectural details to homes, schools, and museums. Museums in Europe systematically collected hundreds of plaster casts,

FIG. 40 J. Davis Burton, *South Kensington Museum, North Court, Showing Casts*, late 19th century. One-half of a stereograph. Victoria and Albert Museum, London. Photo © Victoria and Albert Museum, London

FIG. 41 T. E. Marr, *Museum of Fine Arts Boston, Copley Square Location.* Sculpture Gallery, 1902–1903. Museum of Fine Arts, Boston. Photograph © 2013 Museum of Fine Arts, Boston

and some employed *formatori* (ornamental plaster makers) to produce casts for sale from the objects in their own collections or from monuments abroad.[59] At the South Kensington Museum, the acquisition of casts accelerated throughout the 1860s and culminated in the opening, in 1873, of the gargantuan cast courts (fig. 40).

This international vogue for amassing plaster casts undoubtedly reassured the museum trustees in Boston. The medium's increasing availability and relatively low cost made casts all the more irresistible to the trustees, who genuinely believed that "as a rule, original work is beyond our means."[60] In addition, plaster casts matched the museum's multiple educational aims: to show examples of high skill to workmen, to illustrate a comprehensive history of sculpture, and to show standards of beauty for the elevation of public taste. For much of the nineteenth century, the fundamental purpose of a museum display was to instruct and enlighten, not necessarily to induce the aesthetic delight that modern sensibilities have come to believe only originals inspire. Originals and plaster casts were sometimes considered interchangeable, serving the same didactic function. In fact, in the 1870s some praised plaster casts on aesthetic grounds: cleaner and more uniform in surface, "reproductions are better than most original antiques."[61] In Boston, one museum trustee even considered plaster casts a defense against potential mistakes in acquisition: by building a cast collection, the museum would be "prevented from squandering [its] funds upon the private fancies of would-be connoisseurs."[62] For all these reasons, the MFA zealously purchased hundreds of plaster casts from European sources in the late nineteenth century. In 1874 the trustees unhesitatingly

sold a large portion of the late Senator Charles Sumner's bequest to the museum—ninety-four paintings and more than hundred engravings, most of them European—for $3,856 in order to purchase more casts with the money.[63] Moreover, the importance attached to plaster casts was such that the opening of the new museum building, initially scheduled for May 1, 1876, was postponed until July 3 to accommodate a delay in the arrival of fifty cases of casts ordered from London.[64] At its height in the early 1890s, the MFA's cast collection contained more than nine hundred examples (figs. 41, 42).

A PROVISIONAL MUSEUM OF 1870

During the year 1870, multiple aspirations gradually coalesced into a coherent vision for the museum. Wishing at once to contribute to industry, to educate the public in art history, and to train artists, the museum sought to build a collection comprising fine and decorative arts, original works if available, and the rest in reproductions. Even while adhering to the South Kensington model, the museum trustees recognized that, without the British Museum and the National Gallery, which in London complemented the South Kensington's holdings, "what London . . . [is] obliged to do partially, *we in America must do wholly.*"[65] The museum would deliver the panacea of art to "the benefit of all classes of the community."[66] It was an ambitious plan indeed.

As if to signal the maturing of the museum's sense of self, the trustees took up the matter of the official seal in February 1871. The Committee on the Museum was assigned the task of designing the seal, and in May the committee gave a verbal proposal for the seal's basic components: "three interlaced rings, inscribed with the words 'Art' in the upper ring—'Education' in that to the right, & 'Industry' in that to the left."[67] The board immediately approved the plan, and soon a seal exactly matching this description was produced (fig. 43).[68] The seal appeared on the title page of the museum's annual report as late as 1954, long after the institution's founding vision had been drastically modified.

The vision of 1870 was a provisional one, subject to change almost from the moment of its announcement. Most critically, lack of funds constricted the museum in 1870 and beyond, and the museum's "long wearisome struggle against poverty" continued well into the 1890s.[69] Unlike the situation in Europe, where the state had emerged as the guardian of museums in the first half of the nineteenth century, in the United States the government's involvement in art had been limited, and even in the rush of museum building that began in the 1870s, most new museums had to rely primarily on private citizens for both funds and works of art.[70] In 1870 the wealth that would in the next generation bring a vast amount of art to America was in the making, but the MFA's founding trustees nevertheless, and rightly, considered their institution disproportionately poor for its oversize ambition. Although they certainly dreamed of a glorious future when the museum would possess ample funds and even original works of art, *festina lente*—make haste slowly—was the operative mode in the museum's early days.[71]

By the end of 1870 the founding trustees had secured a parcel of land for the museum's building, defined the museum's expansive vision, and registered the museum's existence in the public consciousness. Nonetheless, the MFA still existed in name only, almost entirely as an idea yet to be realized. Surely it was with keen anticipation, not irony, that Sarah Perkins Cleveland, sister of Charles Perkins, wrote in September 1870, more than six months after the museum's incorporation: "There is good hope for a Museum of Fine Arts in Boston."[72] Her comment underscores the highly precarious state in which the ambitious enterprise found itself in the year of its launch. When the museum received its very first gift, in November 1870, Washington Allston's *Elijah in the Desert* (1818; MFA), a special committee was appointed "to consider the best means of exhibiting this picture" at some appropriate location, but the committee found no immediate solution.[73] Even the following spring, a welcome gift of a Gobelins tapestry had to be placed "in the rooms of the [Boston] Art Club for safe-keeping."[74] It is clear that much practical work lay ahead.

In the beginning, the MFA considered education its foremost goal. In retrospect, this didactic focus removed the young institution from taking part in the clash of diverse visual tastes that had come to characterize Boston's artistic community in the 1860s. By attempting to form, at least for the moment, a collection of reproductions and applied arts—along with original works of fine art that happened to be available—in order to fulfill its didactic mission, the early museum aspired not so much to endorse accepted taste of the day (as the Athenæum gallery had done in 1827) or to promote specific artistic opinions, styles, or groups (as art clubs and commercial galleries had done since midcentury) but, instead, to instruct a broad segment of the population—the working people, the artisan, the public, the artist—with as comprehensive a display of art and design history as it could afford. As the museum endeavored to do this, the fledgling institution's desperate financial needs required that it accept any assistance that was offered, rather than to quibble about the source and content of the aid on aesthetic or intellectual grounds. Willingly, eagerly, and gratefully, the young museum received help in all areas: money, loans and gifts of objects, gallery space, advice, and goodwill.

In retrospect, the nascent museum's detachment from contemporary artistic developments, as well as its extraordinarily broad purpose, put the Athenæum in a particularly advantageous position to assist the younger institution. Indeed, if the museum had had the will or the means in 1870 to align itself more definitely with one artistic camp or another, the Athenæum, which had lost much of its aesthetic vision by the end of the 1860s, would have had little to offer. In time, the MFA's finances improved, its artistic aims grew clearer, and it ceased to require assistance from the Athenæum. But during the museum's earliest years, particularly between 1870 and 1876, the Athenæum provided vital support, without which the whole enterprise might well have foundered in its infancy.

FIG. 43 Original seal of the Museum of
Fine Arts, Boston, designed 1871

CHAPTER FOUR

The Athenæum and the Museum, 1870–1876

O N JANUARY 17, 1870, more than two weeks before the Museum of Fine Arts was incorporated, the Athenæum trustees formally offered the use of its third-floor gallery for "an art loan exhibition . . . to forward the movement in favor of the proposed Museum of the Fine Arts."[1] The Athenæum's eager proposal proved premature, and no exhibition took place on behalf of the museum that spring. Nevertheless, the gesture was a fitting preamble to the extraordinary collaboration that would develop between the two institutions.

Between 1870 and 1876, the two curatorial committees of the Athenæum and the museum—the Fine Arts Committee and the Committee on the Museum, respectively—worked particularly closely with each other. Sharing the goal of launching the museum, the two committees were also intimately connected by their overlapping members. Of the five members of the Athenæum's Fine Arts Committee, all but one were museum trustees; all five members of the Committee on the Museum were either Athenæum trustees or proprietors, three of them members of the Fine Arts Committee.[2] The chairmen of the two committees were, respectively, Charles Callahan Perkins, at the MFA, and his brother Edward Newton Perkins at the Athenæum. It was hardly surprising, then, that between 1870 and 1876, while the MFA's building was under construction, the Committee on the Museum held its biweekly meetings at the Athenæum.

At the Athenæum, the 1870s had begun with a palpable sense of relief on the part of the Fine Arts Committee, for finally a future home had been found for the art collection. The competition for space between books and art had ended, and the arrival in 1868 of the genial Charles Ammi Cutter as the Athenæum's fifth librarian fostered a more harmonious relationship between the Library and Fine Arts Committees. But peace brought a kind of doldrums: the exhibition of 1870 scarcely differed from those of the 1860s, featuring the Athenæum's holdings combined with loans from a similar lineup of owners. Among the familiar mixture of portraits and Old Master copies, only a smattering of contemporary French works could be found, including *The Quarry* (*La Curée*) (1857; MFA) by Gustave Courbet, shown by the Allston Club, and none was by the Barbizon painters.[3] In fact, the 1870 exhibition contained "no new works from abroad," and the Fine Arts Committee wearily predicted that the next year's exhibition would "have to depend for its attractions upon the pictures which may be in this city."[4]

In the spring of 1871, the Athenæum's special installation "Exhibition of Paintings for the Benefit of the French" brought an unexpected change. Since the outbreak of the Franco-Prussian War in July 1870, Bostonians had eagerly devoured news from France. The destruction of the French capital during the siege of Paris in the winter of 1870–1871 particularly affected the many well-to-do Bostonians who had enjoyed the City of Light in all its Second Empire gaiety in the preceding decades—the boulevards, the gaslights, the cafés. In the spring of 1871, Boston was host to a legion of lectures, concerts, and fairs organized to raise funds for beleaguered France, and in late February the Athenæum decided to join the effort with a special exhibition.[5] Running from April 15 to May 6, it coincided with the French Fair, a large charity bazaar held at the nearby Boston Theater from April 11 to 22, which raised $85,000 in twelve days.[6]

At the Athenæum gallery, the French installation, which raised money for France but included many non-French works, was a modest affair, even smaller than the institution's regular exhibitions.[7] The show's topical nature apparently attracted fresh works from new sources. (Loans constituted about one-third of the works on view.) Gone were the perennial champions of older taste, such as Charles and Edward Perkins and Henry Joseph Gardner. The new lenders presented more recent European works, including a few Barbizon landscapes by Constant Troyon and Émile Charles Lambinet (1813–1877) as well as academic paintings by Isidore Pils (1813–1875) and Charles Baugniet (1814–1886).[8] Americans were well represented, too, with nine Copleys, nine Allstons, and four Stuarts.

Although the fact is little known, it was in the Athenæum's special 1871 show that the MFA's small holdings made their first public appearance. At that time, the one-year-old museum owned only three paintings, one sculpture, and one tapestry: *Elijah in the Desert* by Washington Allston; two magnificent paintings by François Boucher (1703–1770), *Halt at the Spring* (1765) and *Return from Market* (1767; both, MFA); *Hebe and Ganymede* by Thomas Crawford; and a Flemish tapestry.[9] Allston's painting and the marble sculpture had been the only two gifts that the museum received in 1870. The paintings by Boucher and the tapestry had been among the furnishings of the Deacon House, a French-style mansion in downtown Boston, and had been presented to the museum in March 1871.[10] In April these objects—the MFA's entire collection—quietly joined other loans in the Athenæum's special exhibition.

In retrospect, the Athenæum's 1871 installation for the French marked the last time an Athenæum exhibition offered something substantially new. Thereafter, the gallery contained, for the most part, the predictable fare of portraits and Old Master copies. Some thirty Copleys appeared in the 1871 regular exhibition, for example, as did growing numbers of Stuarts and Allstons in subsequent shows, making the Athenæum gallery a veritable mausoleum of old-stock Boston clans. In 1873 fifty-one chromolithographic reproductions of Old Master paintings published by the Arundel Society, to which the Athenæum subscribed annually, joined the exhibition, but they hardly introduced artistic styles or subject matter hitherto unknown to the viewer.[11] Shrinking in size each year, the Athenæum's exhibitions were effectively moribund. In a few short years, the museum's founding in 1870 had redefined the function of the Athenæum's Fine Arts Committee to be almost solely that of supporting the new institution.

The first two exhibitions to be held in the name of the Museum of Fine Arts took place one year later, in the spring of 1872. The first was a highly anomalous show mounted in a room at the jewelry store of Bigelow, Kennard, and Company in downtown Boston (fig. 44), and the second was installed in one of the four rooms of the Athenæum gallery.[12] The first of the two exhibitions had particularly narrow content and purpose: the entire display consisted of more than five hundred archaeological specimens from Cyprus, and the whole purpose was to raise monies so the museum could purchase the objects.

The Cypriot objects had come from the Italian-born Brigadier General Luigi Palma di Cesnola (1832–1904), an amateur archaeologist who later became the first director of the Metropolitan Museum of Art in New York.[13] After success as a cavalry officer in the Austrian and Crimean wars, Cesnola came to the United States,

FIG. 44 John Andrew and Son, *George Lyon and Company*, wood engraving on paper. The building in downtown Boston where Bigelow, Kennard, and Company was located. Advertised in the *Boston Directory* (1871–1875)

earned military honors in the Civil War, and in 1865 secured the illustrious appointment as the first United States consul to Cyprus. While there, the enterprising Cesnola excavated many of the island's archaeological treasures, clearly with a view to profiting from his discoveries. Situated to the south of Turkey and to the west of present-day Syria and Lebanon, Cyprus sat, since ancient times, at the crossroads of many civilizations, whose influences it absorbed through bustling trade and innumerable wars. Excavated chiefly in the nineteenth century, Cypriot antiquities were thought to provide the missing link between the ancient Egyptian, biblical, and classical worlds, a notion that Cesnola fully exploited in his pursuit of fame and fortune.[14] He was certainly not alone: many European consuls, officials, and traders were digging on the island and along the shores of the Mediterranean, hoping to profit from the sale of their finds. And profit they did, for Cypriot antiquities were popular: the Musée du Louvre acquired dozens of them in 1863, and other museums and collectors were eager to follow suit. Cesnola's collection, which by 1870 contained well over thirteen thousand objects, was the largest assemblage of Cypriot antiquities to date, comprising bronzes, terra-cotta and limestone sculptures, inscriptions on stone, vases, glass, and gold ornaments that were believed, at the time, to range in date from 1000 to 100 B.C. (figs. 45, 46).[15] In 1870 Cesnola left Cyprus (only to return in 1873) and successfully auctioned some of his finds in Paris, and major European museums were showing an active interest in acquiring more from him.

Cesnola's most famous excavations were made in March 1870, in Golgoi (sometimes called Golgos in the nineteenth century). There, in the tombs of the temple of Aphrodite, Cesnola unearthed stone sculptures that bore strong Greek influence and were thought to represent the crucial link between the Cypriot and Greek civilizations. When he heard this news, Charles Perkins apparently sent a congratulatory telegraph to Cesnola, which began a correspondence between the two. As early as June 1870—four months after the museum was incorporated—Perkins recommended to its board that it purchase the Cesnola collection, the first acquisition proposed for the new institution.[16] Cesnola initially offered the entire collection, but the price of "$80,000 in gold" was prohibitive.[17]

As it turned out, Boston was only one of Cesnola's many prospective clients. To secure the highest price and maximum prestige, Cesnola hoped to sell his collection en bloc, even while retailing portions of it piecemeal. In July 1870 he almost found a purchaser in the antiquities-loving French emperor Napoleon III, but the deal fell through within weeks when the emperor lost his throne in the war against Prussia. Cesonla's negotiations with the Russian Imperial Hermitage Museum also failed, because the Russians were unwilling to buy the entire collection. Something of Cesnola's flamboyant dealings must have been known to Perkins in Boston, for he sought advice from Carl Friederichs, a friend and distinguished archaeologist at the

FIG. 45 Stephen Thompson, photograph of objects discovered by Cesnola in Cyprus. Left: Male statue, probably 5th century B.C. Limestone. Right: Male figure, probably 6th century B.C. Limestone. Bottom right: Relief of a lion, bull, and two figures, n.d. Limestone. From *The Antiquities of Cyprus Discovered (Principally on the Sites of the Ancient Golgoi and Idalium) by General Luigi Palma di Cesnola* (London, 1873), pl. 4. The relief is in the collection of the Metropolitan Museum of Art, New York, acc. no. 74.51.2878.

FIG. 46 Stephen Thompson, photograph of objects discovered by Cesnola in Cyprus. Left: Jug, probably 1600–1450 B.C. Terra-cotta. Right: Two-handled bottle, n.d. Terra-cotta. From *The Antiquities of Cyprus Discovered (Principally on the Sites of the Ancient Golgoi and Idalium) by General Luigi Palma di Cesnola* (London, 1873), pl. 17

Berlin Museum. Friederichs, who had had an unfriendly encounter with Cesnola in Cyprus in 1868, advised Perkins to acquire only a small portion of the Italian's collection, because Boston "could get all that . . . would be desirable . . . for a small sum of money."[18] Perkins accordingly requested from Cesnola a selection worth $2,000 and asked the consul to send it to London for inspection by a friend. To Perkins's annoyance, however, the hard-driving Cesnola sent boxes of Boston-bound objects directly to a warehouse in New York. Apparently, Cesnola was in a desperate rush to get his collection out of Cyprus before the Turkish government's export ban on Cypriot antiquities took effect in late 1871. By early 1872 Cesnola managed to transport to London "the most and best" part of his collection, while sending to Boston, in his own words, "mere trash," an assortment that the consul boasted he had formed "without spoiling [his own] collection."[19] In London, Cesnola's hope to sell more than five thousand pieces to the British Museum languished and eventually died, but by the end of 1872 the collection was snatched up by New York's Metropolitan Museum of Art.

Trash or not, the boxes bound for the MFA, containing about five hundred objects, were shipped from New York to Boston in mid-February 1872.[20] Perkins quickly arranged for the items to be displayed at Bigelow and Kennard's, and the exhibition was open to the public by early March. Although he had by then come to find Cesnola mildly annoying, Perkins approved of the Cypriot specimens that finally arrived in Boston, for they illustrated the transmission of diverse artistic influences in the ancient world. The museum's first exhibition was a success and closed around April 25, when the trustees formally expressed gratitude for "the practical good will" that Bigelow, Kennard, and Company had shown to the museum in giving "the use of an excellent room for the exhibition of the Cyprus Collection, free of expense, during the previous two months."[21] With the subscriptions raised during the exhibition, the Cesnola collection became the MFA's first major purchase in May 1872. These specimens represented a fortunate and welcome exception for the young museum, which had largely resigned itself, because of its modest funds, to buying reproductions.[22] It was expecting to receive more Cypriot objects from Cesnola, and on May 3 the balance of the museum's purchase—forty-one boxes and eighteen baskets—left Cyprus for Boston. Sadly, though, on leaving Beirut, where the ship had stopped en route to collect wool and olive oil, the bark caught fire and the entire cargo sank to the bottom of the sea.[23]

Boston's purchase preceded by six months the much larger acquisition by the Metropolitan Museum of Art—for $50,000, to be paid in three installments—of the remaining, main bulk of the Cesnola collection. The objects arrived at the Metropolitan in early 1873, with Cesnola himself as part of the package. The museum soon hired Cesnola to arrange his vast collection, commissioned him to return to Cyprus to undertake more excavations (1873–1876), and appointed him its first director in 1879.[24]

A dilettante archaeologist and shameless self-promoter, Cesnola came under criticism, even during his lifetime, for his lax documentation, exaggerations, and even lies. The much-publicized discovery of the "Kourion treasure" during his second sojourn on Cyprus, for example, was soon exposed as an invention, for the "treasure" consisted of objects of dates and styles too diverse to have come from a single source, as Cesnola had claimed. Sued in 1884 for "deceptive alterations and unintelligent restorations,"[25] he was exonerated at the time, but today his transgressions are a matter of historical fact. The vast number of Cypriot objects that Cesnola (and others) unearthed without scruple eventually helped to bring about the advance of archaeological knowledge that called some of his claims into question.

As soon as the Cypriot exhibition closed, the Committee on the Museum asked for the use of the Athenæum gallery "for the safe keeping and exhibition of works of art belonging to the Museum."[26] The Athenæum instantly obliged, by offering one of the four rooms of its third-floor picture gallery. Preparations proceeded apace, as the two committees from the two institutions—the Committee on the Museum and the Fine Arts Committee—began attending to myriad practical details. The MFA's committee ordered display cases and placed an inscribed tablet over the doorway to announce it as the museum's room,[27] while the Athenæum's counterpart painted and decorated at its own expense the space allocated to the Museum of Fine Arts. After some discussion, the museum trustees agreed to bend their original wish—to offer their exhibitions free of charge—to comply with the Athenæum's long-standing practice of charging an admission fee (25¢ in 1872, as it had been since 1827), because the museum's room was accessible only through those occupied by the Athenæum.[28] Finally, the museum's holdings, which had hitherto been integrated in the Athenæum's exhibitions, were brought into the one gallery devoted to the museum, to join the newly acquired Cesnola collection and several loans. The preface to the catalogue of the MFA's first exhibition in the Athenæum gallery, written by Charles Perkins, was dated June 16, 1872.

This 1872 exhibition introduced a refreshingly new look to the Athenæum gallery that had housed only paintings for two decades, for it consisted predominantly of archaeological specimens and decorative arts. Astonishingly, of the 539 objects listed in the catalogue, only three were paintings (the same three that had been included in the Athenæum's exhibitions in 1871). Because the Athenæum's sculpture gallery had closed in 1868, statues and busts from both the museum and the Athenæum were scattered throughout the Athenæum building, not in the gallery.[29]

Numerically, the Cesnola collection of more than five hundred Cypriot objects (grouped into 349 lots in the catalogue) dominated the museum's 1872 exhibition. Case after case of archaeological artifacts was a common sight in countless late nineteenth-century museums. In Boston, too, the collection was deemed worthy of the MFA's educational goal of creating a physical illustration of art history. In June 1872, during the run of that year's exhibition, the museum's archaeological collection grew more than tenfold thanks to the gift of the Way collection of Egyptian antiquities: figures, ornaments, and utensils in bronze, marble, stone, terra-cotta, glass, and wood, as well as several mummies, totaling almost five thousand objects.[30] To accommodate this large collection, the Athenæum immediately offered to the museum a second room on its third floor, an act that the latter gratefully characterized as "a renewed proof of [the Athenæum's] identification with the interests of the Museum."[31] After Charles G. Loring spent a full year cataloguing and arranging it, the large Egyptian collection debuted in the museum's exhibition in 1873, becoming, in addition to the Cesnola collection, one of the chief attractions of the MFA's exhibitions.

In 1872 the rest of the museum's exhibition comprised items in glass, ceramics, bronze, plaster casts, and medals, most of which were lent by a relatively small circle of museum and Athenaeum trustees, supporters, and their relatives. Mrs. Lawrence showed her maiolica and furniture (as well as a fragment purported to be from Dante's coffin) next to the twenty-eight pieces of non-Western weapons from her late husband's collection bequeathed to the Athenæum in 1869. Charles Perkins displayed more than forty assorted decorative arts objects—plaster casts of architectural elements, Della Robbia ware, illuminated manuscripts, carved ivory, and "pieces of stucco from the Alhambra,"[32] among others—and his mother-in-law, four. George Washington Wales, a trustee of both the Athenæum and the museum, contributed an assortment of Greek pottery, maiolica, and Asian porcelain, totaling almost forty objects, while Thomas Gold Appleton exhibited some forty Greco-Italian vases. These examples of decorative arts underscored the MFA's allegiance to the South Kensington model and created, albeit on a modest scale, "an artistic microcosm, well calculated to teach the visitor something of the character and quality of the art-industry of many nations during a long period of the world's history."[33]

To its credit, the Committee on the Museum, which organized that institution's exhibitions at the Athenæum, readily acknowledged that the objects on view were small in number and far from comprehensive. As Perkins repeated in his preface to several of the exhibition catalogues in the early 1870s, the committee hoped that the few objects shown on the Athenæum's third floor would induce "the wealthy and generous" to "be moved to give us the means of increasing them."[34] The museum's early exhibitions at the Athenæum were provisional in character and clearly different from the displays in its own building after 1876. For one thing, the MFA, in the middle of a difficult fund-raising campaign for its building project in the early 1870s, could spend little money on exhibitions. For the 1872 exhibition, the trustees had resolved to spend no more than $350, but the expenses climbed to $430.[35] By June 1872 the museum was unable to offer insurance to lenders: "all objects of art loaned to the Museum should be at the risk of the owner."[36] Under these circumstances, the continued availability of the Athenæum gallery, free of charge, constituted welcome financial assistance. In a very real sense, the museum's exhibitions at the Athenæum were "the means of keeping alive an interest in the Museum of Fine Arts which might otherwise have died out."[37] At the close of the MFA's first exhibition at the Athenæum, in 1872, the Committee on the Museum gratefully acknowledged the Athenæum's liberal support.[38]

While the museum's displays grew in size and variety between 1872 and 1874, the Athenæum's Fine Arts Committee, whose own exhibitions shrank year by year, never betrayed a sense of competition. On the contrary, in true fraternal fashion, the Athenæum's Edward Perkins not only recognized the MFA's ascendancy but also celebrated it: in his report for 1873, he praised the museum's display as "the most interesting part of the [combined] Exhibition," while conceding that the year had gone on "in the even tenor of its way . . . with no event of much interest to record" for his Fine Arts Committee.[39]

THE BUILDING PROJECT FOR THE MUSEUM

While the Committee on the Museum mounted—with effort—exhibitions and kept the young museum in public view, the Building Committee struggled with the fund-raising for, and the construction of, the institution's first building. On May 26, 1870, less than four months after its incorporation, the museum received a gift of land from the city of Boston. The gift came with the condition that a building costing "no less than one hundred thousand dollars" be erected on the site "within three years from May 1, 1870," and that the future museum be open free of charge at least four days each month.[40] Within ten days, the Building Committee was formed with Martin Brimmer, president, as chairman. All of the committee members were museum trustees as well as either a trustee or a proprietor of the Athenæum: James Elliot Cabot was an Athenæum trustee, and William W. Greenough, Otis Norcross, and Charles C. Perkins were all Athenæum proprietors. Through these and other men who were connected to both institutions, the Athenæum and the museum cooperated—informally but closely—on the younger organization's building project.

The museum's site was at the corner of Dartmouth Street and St. James Avenue on the newly created land in the section of the city known as the Back Bay. The filling of the tidal flat to the west of the original Boston peninsula had begun in the late 1850s, but in 1870 the new land that included the museum's lot was still a windswept expanse of dirt, only one block away from the west-facing shoreline. The portion of the landfill that would include the museum, owned since 1856 by the Boston Water Power Company, was conveyed to the city in 1870 "to be used for an Institute of Fine Arts or for an open square."[41] Cultural institutions and parks were understood to raise the value of properties nearby, and the MFA was one of the centerpieces of this financially motivated scheme. The museum opened in 1876, followed by Trinity Church in 1877, both facing the open space that the city would purchase and rename Copley Square in 1883; the Boston Public Library would join them in 1895.[42]

On the very day in May 1870 when the city deeded the 91,000-square-foot site (a little more than two acres) to the MFA, the museum issued a circular soliciting funds for "the first Art Museum in this country."[43] By early 1871 "a few public-spirited citizens" had added to the original $25,000 from Mrs. Lawrence to make the total available $130,000.[44] Clearly much more was needed.

To raise funds, a well-attended public meeting took place on February 3, 1871, at the Boston Music Hall. Martin Brimmer presided, and illustrious speakers urged support for the enterprise, including Boston mayor William Gaston, author and Unitarian minister Edward Everett Hale, and Ralph Waldo Emerson.[45] Many of the speeches, echoing the museum's founding vision of March 1870, touted the moral and practical benefit that art education would bring to industry and to the public of all classes. The most evocative of the orations was by Emerson, who recalled the Athenæum on Pearl Street almost half a century earlier, where the Thorndike casts—the first sizable collection of plaster casts in the city—"fed the eyes of young men like nectar."[46]

The goal was to raise $300,000 by June. To achieve this ambitious task, a group called the Committee of Fifty was organized under the chairmanship of the museum trustee William Gray. Reporting to this committee were numerous subcommittees, each representing a business or an industry and charged with the task of canvassing "their respective classes, professions, and trades" for pledges of monetary contribution.[47] The subcommittees were as varied as commercial Boston itself: "printers," "line engravers," "city officers," even "door, sash, and blind makers."[48] Each subcommittee kept a subscription book, and the tallies of accumulating funds and donors were published weekly in the newspapers. Perhaps because of this broad outreach, a remarkably democratic spirit permeated this citywide effort to contribute to the projected museum: "everyone has an interest in [the MFA's] success," a newspaper article exhorted, and "its usefulness will not be exclusive, confined to a narrow circle."[49] It is "a people's movement, in which [even] the poorest should feel an interest," wrote Albert J. Wright, the chairman of the subcommittee of printers.[50] The circle of supporters extended to artists, and the sculptor Richard Saltonstall Greenough (1819–1904) exhibited his latest statue, *Grief*, for the benefit of the museum, personally bearing all shipping costs and donating the entire proceeds.[51]

The Committee of Fifty also looked beyond Boston. It sent printed circulars about the planned museum to members of the United States Congress, American government officials abroad, and potential friends in Europe, soliciting their cooperation in securing funds, objects, or information useful to the new institution.[52] Throughout the spring of 1871, pledges of donations both large and small arrived from diverse sources. The trustees reciprocated this demonstrated goodwill by presenting anyone who contributed more than one dollar with a certificate—bearing an image of the museum's newly minted seal—that designated the donor, officially, a "founder."[53] The list of contributors published in 1876 began with Mrs. Lawrence, whose promise of $25,000 in 1869 had launched the whole enterprise, and it ended, after more than one thousand names, with Lewis Albrett, who had given 50¢. By the summer of 1871, a remarkable $260,000 had been pledged toward the museum's first building.[54]

Immediately following the gift of land, serious discussions about the architecture of the museum building itself also got under way.[55] On June 15 the Building Committee issued *Proposals for Designs for Museum of Fine Arts*, a circular calling for an architectural competition and setting November 1, 1870, as the deadline for submissions.[56] For the cash-strapped museum, cost was the single most important concern. Even though the competition called for designs of the whole building, the circular included the caveat that the museum intended to erect, at first, "only so much of the building as shall not exceed in cost the sum of one hundred and twenty-five thousand dollars."[57] Despite the erroneous impression shared by some that "there will be no lack of funds" for the project,[58] the trustees categorically sought "economy of space rather than architectural display" and aimed for a functional building well suited to the MFA's modest means and educational mission.[59] Warning against the folly of spending "all our money in erecting a huge building whose empty walls will do but little," Charles Perkins, the chairman of the Committee on the Museum, advised "building only for the purpose of placing collections already bought or given" and postponing until later the "erection of such a building as will be an honor and an embellishment to any city."[60] The museum's board apparently concurred with this view, and Perkins reiterated this belief at the opening ceremony in 1876: "it is not the building which makes the Museum, but the works of art that you place in it."[61]

Fourteen submissions were tendered to the Building Committee. The architects came from both within and outside Boston and ranged from the well established to the beginner, but when six finalist designs were chosen for the second round of consideration, all were by Boston firms.[62] During the winter, the Building Committee studied and compared the six designs in terms of "space, light, convenience, economy and architectural effect,"[63] tallying up square footage devoted to every purpose in each plan and working with architects to modify their initial submissions. By early February 1871, the firm of Sturgis and Brigham had won the coveted prize of designing Boston's first art museum.[64]

At the time, the architectural office of John Hubbard Sturgis (1834–1888) and Charles Brigham (1841–1925) operated in both England and America. Typically, Sturgis in London expressed the architectural vision for the firm's designs, and his partner Brigham attended to the practical details in Boston, dealing with contractors and keeping clients happy. Born in China to Russell Sturgis, a wealthy Boston merchant and later a partner in Barings Bank in London, John Sturgis was extremely well connected in Brahmin Boston, an asset that undoubtedly bolstered his architectural career. The younger Sturgis spent much of the 1850s in England, studying art and architecture and absorbing the influence of Ruskin. Returning to Boston in 1861, he joined the firm of Gridley J. F. Bryant and Arthur D. Gilman, the city's largest architectural office, and met Charles Brigham from Watertown, Massachusetts, a competent young architect with the business acumen to accommodate Sturgis's artistic vision. In partnership since 1866 (when Sturgis returned to England), the two architects designed a number of public buildings in Boston as well as private residences in the Back Bay

and Newport, Rhode Island, for wealthy citizens, with many of whom Sturgis had family connections (on both his parents' sides as well as through his wife, Frances Anne Codman).[65]

The building proposed by Sturgis and Brigham was to extend 210 feet along St. James Avenue and 300 feet along Dartmouth Street, although, as we will see, only a portion of the original plan was executed.[66] In the architects' original plan, the museum's front elevation, with the main entrance, faced west on Dartmouth Street, which was then expected to become a major thoroughfare (fig. 47). The three-story building (plus a basement) enclosed north and south courtyards, designed to bring maximum light into the galleries (fig. 48). The exterior was to feature terra-cotta ornaments and red brick, in what became one of the earliest major terra-cotta installations on exterior walls in the United States (fig. 49). Terra-cotta, made from fine-grained clay with such a high vitreous content that it bakes to a hard surface, is virtually indestructible as a building material. In England, the use of terra-cotta on building exteriors had become particularly popular after midcentury. The South Kensington Museum's 1860s addition had incorporated terra-cotta embellishments and mosaic panels against red bricks on the façade, creating the fashionable polychrome effect. This successful use of terra-cotta at the London museum undoubtedly reassured the museum trustees in Boston, giving the material a South Kensington stamp of approval. The plan by Sturgis and Brigham was chosen, according to the Building Committee, for a design that was "simple, convenient & easily adapted to any purpose of a Museum."[67]

In addition to the architectural merit of the plan, Sturgis and Brigham possessed a definite advantage of having known many of the museum trustees. Sturgis in particular—a quintessential Brahmin—counted many cousins and close friends among them. Martin Brimmer, a friend, for example, wrote to the architect as early as January 1870

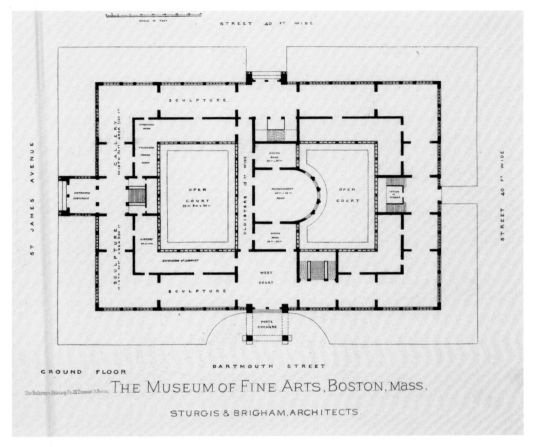

FIG. 48 Floor plan of the Museum of Fine Arts, Boston, as originally proposed. From *American Architect and Building News* 8 (October 30, 1880): n.p.

FIG. 49 John H. Sturgis, Terra-cotta ornaments. From "Details of the MFA, Boston," *American Architect and Building News* 3 (April 13, 1878): n.p.

about the proposed institution even before it was incorporated. In reply, Sturgis, an ardent admirer of the South Kensington Museum in London, wrote to Brimmer:

> For some years past I have had an Earnest hope that some such thing might be started at home. . . . Being intimately acquainted with the S.K.M. & knowing the vast amt. of good it has done in Eng'd toward the Art training of the many & its more intimate appreciation by the few. I have had many conversations & discussions with the officials of the Museum . . . relative to the feasibility of planting a germ in American soil. . . . It is, I trust, needless for me to state how cordially I would co-operate with or aid you in anyway in my power—either by giving you information as to the size, & progress & practical working of the Parent Museum in this country or in choosing or buying casts, Electrotypes, Photos, or any other objects wh. it may be thought well to obtain.[68]

As early as February 1870 Sturgis had learned through intensive research the exact amount of money that the South Kensington Museum had saved by using terra-cotta, compared with the cost of building the British Museum, which used carved stone.[69] His intellectual devotion to the South Kensington ideal precisely matched the Boston museum's original vision, and terra-cotta's apparent economy further recommended the material to the trustees. In the spring of 1870, Edward Perkins, a second cousin, specifically referred, in his correspondence with Sturgis, to "terracotta design" for the future museum building.[70] Charles Perkins also advocated for "employing Terra Cotta for the ornamental portion of the [museum's] building, brick for the walls & stone for the substructure."[71] By the time Sturgis and Brigham won the competition, Sturgis had been in communication about the museum with his friends in Boston for more than a year. It is no wonder that Brimmer, the Building Committee chairman, commended the architects, after their selection, as having "the ability & taste requisite for so important a work."[72]

Sturgis had a particularly close connection to Edward Perkins, the chairman of the Athenæum's Fine Arts Committee and an MFA trustee, for whom Sturgis had been doing architectural work since 1868. Perkins's cherished second Pinebank (1848, by Lemoulnier) had burned down in February 1868. That October, Perkins—on a European tour to recover from the ordeal—had asked Sturgis to design a new house to be erected on the remaining foundation.[73] After months of frequent correspondence between Sturgis in London and Perkins in the various European cities he visited, Perkins settled on the use of ornamental bricks and terra-cotta for the house's exterior. The latest English fashion was comparatively economical, attractive, and new to America; in fact, it was so novel that the architect H. H. Richardson came to examine the plan.[74] The foundation work for the third Pinebank began in the fall of 1869. By January 1870 ornamental bricks had arrived from England, and construction commenced in April—all during the months when Perkins and his brother Charles

FIG. 50 Josiah J. Hawes, *The Museum of Fine Arts, Boston*, 1876. Photograph, 16.8 × 21.6 cm (image). Collection of the Boston Athenæum

were busily organizing the MFA.[75] Sturgis's personal connections to these men contributed, at least in part, to his and Brigham's selection as the architects for the MFA's first building.

By the fall of 1871, estimates had come in from the architects. To the dismay of the trustees, the figures were too high: the lowest estimate, for constructing only the St. James Avenue side of the building, came to $261,265 (including commission). The $260,000 the Building Committee had, which was meant to pay for the entire building, would barely cover one quarter of it! Worse yet, it soon became apparent that even that small fraction of the proposed plan would cost more than the available amount. In late September, the board voted to erect "four sevenths only of the portion of the building fronting on St. James Avenue" unless an additional $400,000 were raised by subscription by February 1, 1872.[76] Sadly, this goal was not met. In the spring of 1872 the discouraged trustees saw few choices but to settle for a much reduced plan, that is, to build, for the time being, only slightly more than half of the St. James Avenue side. The curtailed building would contain the entrance hall and only one wing to the west, measuring 119 by 62 feet, a small percentage of the initially proposed dimensions of 210 by 300 feet.[77]

The beginning of construction was further delayed by the need to remove the temporary building that had stood on the museum's lot. Sometime after July 1872 the structure was demolished, and the museum's foundation was dug and 1,490 piles driven in.[78] In April 1874 the site was finally ready for construction to commence aboveground.[79] By then, however, the museum's financial standing had worsened even further. The cost had continued to climb, and the financial panic of 1873 meant

FIG. 51 Shaw and Lord, *The Museum of Fine Arts, Boston*, 1880 or 1881. One-half of a stereograph. Collection of the Boston Athenæum

FIG. 52 Baldwin Coolidge, *Museum of Fine Arts, Boston, Copley Square Location*, ca. 1902. Museum of Fine Arts, Boston. Photograph © 2013 Museum of Fine Arts, Boston

that some of the subscribed funds were not forthcoming. Two great urban fires—Chicago's in 1871 and Boston's in 1872—had also cut into the local pool of available contributions.[80] In January 1874 the Building Committee conceded that the museum was "unable to finish even the four seventh[s] of the front on St. James Avenue" and

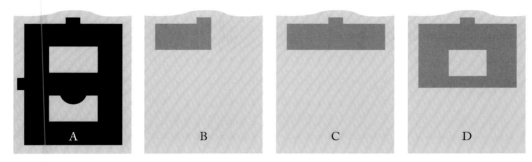

FIG. 53 The first building of the Museum of Fine Arts, Boston. The original plan (in black) and the building's changing shapes between 1876 and 1909 (in darker gray) on the museum's lot (in lighter gray); the northern perimeter of the lot faced what became Copley Square in 1883. A. The plan proposed by Sturgis and Brigham, 1871; B. At the museum's opening, 1876; C. After the first expansion of 1878–1879; and D. After the second expansion of 1888–1889. *Diagram by Alice Platt*

was reduced to asking the full board "whether they are to proceed with the erection of any part of the building this year . . . if so, with how much of it."[81] Reluctantly, the trustees decided to draw from the $100,000 permanent fund, set aside in 1871 presumably for acquisitions, in order to proceed. In the meantime, the original building deadline of May 1873 (as stipulated by the city in 1870) had come and gone, and a new target date was set for May 1876.[82]

When the museum finally opened, in 1876, only the northwest corner of the building had been constructed (fig. 50). Even after two subsequent expansions, first in 1878–1879 to complete the St. James Avenue frontage to the east (fig. 51) and in 1888–1889 (opening in 1890) to the south along Dartmouth Street (fig. 52), the building represented just over half of the original 1870 plan (fig. 53). Further expansion southward along Dartmouth Street, which would have created the main façade envisioned in the original plan, never happened, and the southern third of the museum's lot remained empty.[83] Instead, the northern flank of the museum building as seen from Copley Square became the MFA's most recognizable face until the institution moved in 1909 to its current location on Huntington Avenue.

The Montpensier Exhibition, 1874–1876, and the Quincy Adams Shaw Exhibition, 1875

While the museum's building project proceeded ponderously, the Committee on the Museum continued to mount exhibitions at the Athenæum. By 1874 the two institutions worked on their exhibitions in virtual unison with only a titular formality of separation. The museum's exhibitions at the Athenæum had largely retained a similar character and contents since 1872, but in 1874 and 1875 the predominance of archaeo-logical specimens and decorative arts was interrupted by two exhibitions of paintings.

At the beginning of 1874 Charles Perkins formed a joint committee of six museum and Athenæum trustees, of whom, predictably, two served both institutions.[84] This committee's function was to consider the possibility of borrowing from Antonio María d'Orléans, duc de Montpensier (1824–1890), fifth son of King Louis-Philippe of France and brother-in-law of Queen Isabella II of Spain, his collection of fifty-five paintings for exhibition. The duke's collection was thought to be particularly strong in paintings by the Spanish masters of the sixteenth and seventeenth centuries. Some of the pictures had been in the Galerie Espagnole that his father had installed at the Louvre in 1838—containing over five hundred Spanish paintings—and purchased by the duke after the gallery closed, in 1849, following Louis-Philippe's abdication the previous year.[85] In the 1870s Spain was in the middle of a civil war between the devoutly Catholic Carlists and the more liberal government. The duke, fearing anarchy, had already moved his collection from his Sevillian palace, San Telmo, to Gibraltar, with plans for its eventual exhibition at the Royal Academy of Arts in London. The death of the popular British artist Sir Edwin Landseer (1802–1873), however, neces-sitated a memorial exhibition at the academy, forcing the duke's pictures to remain at Gibraltar. When the museum trustees in Boston heard of the exigency—reportedly from the Bostonian Arthur Codman, who had recently passed through the Spanish port—they immediately applied to the duke for the honor of borrowing the collec-tion.[86] With Boston's long-established taste for Old Master paintings, the trustees jumped at the chance to exhibit what were thought to be authentic specimens. The royal provenance no doubt heightened the allure. The duke's pictures included twenty-one Spanish works that were attributed to Juan Valdès Leal (1630–1694), Bartolomé Esteban Murillo, Jusepe de Ribera (1591–1652), Diego Rodríguez de Silva y Velázquez (1599–1660), and Francisco de Zurbarán (1598–1664), with eight thought to be by such Italian and Flemish artists as Jacopo Bassano (ca. 1510–1592), Salvator Rosa (1615–1673), and Frans Snyders (1579–1657). The rest consisted of twenty-six works by the "modern" French artists favored by Louis-Philippe, such as François Granet (1777–1849), Henri Lehmann (1814–1882), and Tony Johannot (1803–1852).

The duke consented to the loan, with the proviso that Boston raise $30,000 to guarantee the collection against loss or damage. Within a week, the newly formed Montpensier Committee raised the required amount from sympathetic friends, without drawing a cent from the institution's funds.[87] Letters and telegrams were dispatched to and from Gibraltar, and in March the Athenæum offered the museum the use of the entire third floor for one year, free of rent. The terms were extremely generous: so that the proceeds of the exhibition could be maximized, no free tickets were to be issued; and should there be any money left after expenses, the profit was to be given to the museum. The Athenæum even replaced, at its own cost, the wooden entrance door to the galleries with an iron gate to ensure greater security and paid almost $3,000 for "draping the walls and tenting the ceilings of the two galleries" slated for the exhibition.[88] Moreover, when a delay in the shipment made it impossible to open the Montpensier exhibition on May 1, as had originally been scheduled, the Athenæum readily accepted the hasty request from Charles Perkins to use one of the rooms to display the recent bequest to the MFA from the late Senator Charles Sumner. (Sumner had died on March 11, 1874, only days after congratulating the museum trustees on securing the Montpensier loan.[89]) In addition, many well-placed friends of the members of the Montpensier Committee assisted the transatlantic crossing of the collection: U.S. Treasury Secretary William Richardson granted an extended duty-free period for the paintings from Spain; the American consul at Gibraltar, Horatio Sprague, personally oversaw the embarkation of the crated collection; and the Cunard Line provided free freight from Gibraltar to Boston.[90]

In 1874 events unfolded on the Athenæum's third floor in a convoluted sequence. At the beginning of the year, two rooms on that floor housed the museum's exhibition, and the Athenæum's own displays occupied the other two. On May 23 the Athenæum's Fine Arts Committee vacated one of the two rooms to offer it to the Sumner exhibition (of 132 items), removing the twenty-nine paintings (all owned by the Athenæum) from the room and hanging them on the walls of the building's majestic Sumner staircase.[91] The Athenæum's exhibition in the remaining room—of fifty-four paintings, a combination of Athenæum holdings and loans—closed on August 1. The Athenæum's 1874 exhibition was the smallest in its history, and no dedicated catalogue was printed for it; instead, when one for the Sumner exhibition was published in early summer, it also listed the works exhibited by the Athenæum in "Room 4, and on the Staircase."[92]

The closing of the Athenæum's one-room exhibition in August 1874 was probably overshadowed by the imminent arrival of the Montpensier pictures, and it unceremoniously marked the end of the Athenæum gallery exhibitions, the first of which had been held in 1827 under the stewardship of Thomas Handasyd Perkins, great-uncle of both Edward and Charles Perkins. At the end of the year, Fine Arts Committee chairman Edward Perkins described the quiet end of the enterprise that had exerted, at one point, a significant influence on the fine arts in Boston:

> "Athenæum Exhibition" has thus after a period of 47 years . . . of great usefulness and honor come to its close. The fine arts have been fostered and encouraged until an Institution has been founded devoted exclusively to their cultivation and destined (as we trust) to carry on the work of artistic education and refinement of taste, to the highest point of attainment. The time is propitious for the removal of the Fine Arts Department. The Athenæum needs this building for the exclusive use of its rapidly increasing Library, and is impatiently awaiting the moment when the galleries can be shelved for books.[93]

Without fanfare, the Athenæum's Fine Arts Committee gave up exhibitions, which had once been one of its most significant functions.[94]

On September 15 the Montpensier pictures finally arrived in Boston, and the museum's exhibition opened at the Athenæum on September 22, occupying all four rooms on the third floor; it remained there at least until June 1876.[95] One room housed the Montpensier collection, with a few additional European paintings lent by local patrons expressly for this occasion. The other three rooms contained the Cesnola and Way collections, decorative arts, and a handful of paintings. To the delight of both institutions' trustees, the Montpensier exhibition was extremely popular. Despite the 50¢ admission fee, which was double the usual price, the number of visitors to the gallery was so large that a third ticket seller had to be hired.[96] The first nineteen weeks of the show's run saw 17,503 visitors—an average of more than 900 per week—and the subsequent thirteen months brought almost 200 viewers a week.[97]

The exhibition elicited a great deal of press coverage, yet the reviews were mixed. Admirers lauded the show as a coup for America—"an event of almost epochal art importance in this country"—because the canvases were believed to be authentic, not copies.[98] One of the most vocal advocates for the collection, Charles Perkins, declared ecstatically that the MFA had "first among American institutions exhibited to the citizens of the United States a fine collection of pictures by the old masters than any hitherto seen in this country. *Hoc erat in votis* [This was among my prayers]."[99] Others cast doubt on the authenticity and quality of some of the works on view. A writer for *Scribner's Monthly*, for example, complained (perhaps with a degree of competitive feeling from rival New York) that "we have all been deceived in the Montpensier Collection," for he found many of the paintings to be either copies or of low quality, even while he accepted the authenticity of some of them.[100] Henry James praised the works by Murillo and Zurbarán but dismissed the majority of the canvases as "the sort of ware that forms the rough padding of large European collections and is generally consigned to the friendly twilight of corridors and staircases."[101] To the cosmopolitan James, the "submissive hush" that permeated the Athenæum gallery was particularly irritating because it signified, in his opinion, a blind and excessive American reverence for Old Master paintings with little regard for their actual quality.

In reality, despite the hopeful attributions of some of the works on view, a number of the Old Master paintings in the exhibition were genuine, among them five canvases by Zurbarán: four large pictures constituting the Childhood of Christ series—*The Annunciation*, *The Adoration of the Shepherds*, *The Adoration of the Magi*, and *The Circumcision* (1638–1639, 1638; figs. 54–57)—and *A Monk Praying* (1631–1640; Collection of Marqués de Valdeterrazo, Madrid). Also genuine was a picture by Murillo, *The Virgin of the Swaddling Clothes* (ca. 1655–1660; private collection), as was *Cato of Utica Tearing out His Entrails* (ca. 1660; Art Gallery of Hamilton, Ontario), then thought

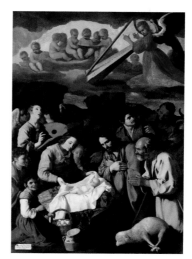

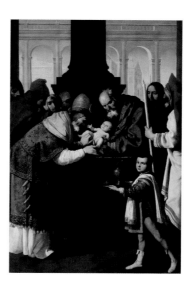

to be by Ribera and now attributed to his Italian pupil Luca Giordano (1634–1705).
They all had the illustrious pedigree of having been acquired in Spain in the 1830s
for Louis-Philippe's Galerie Espagnole.[102] That these original paintings from the
Spanish Golden Age came to Boston in 1874 was as surprising as it was significant.
In nineteenth-century America, innumerable pictures were attributed to Murillo, long
the preferred Spanish painter in England and the United States, but only a few of
them were authentic, whereas works attributed to Zurbarán were extremely rare in
American exhibitions.[103] The Montpensier exhibition demonstrated the museum's
incipient desire to display original works of fine art—not copies or objects of decorative

arts—even though it could not afford to acquire them. In retrospect, by bringing these remarkable original works to Boston, the exhibition marked a shift in the city's attitudes about Old Master paintings: Bostonians, who had earlier been content with copies, were beginning to wish to view, or even own, original works.

In 1875, the first year when all of the Athenæum's third-floor gallery rooms were occupied by the Museum of Fine Arts, an exhibition of the collection of the Bostonian Quincy Adams Shaw (1826–1908) opened in April.[104] Of the twenty-nine pictures, three were by Italian Renaissance masters and the majority of the rest were Barbizon landscapes, by Corot, Troyon, Rousseau, and others, including seven by Millet (fig. 58). (One painting by William Morris Hunt, *Bugle Call*, was among them.) Shaw was sailing to Paris in the early summer of 1875 to attend the posthumous sales of Millet's work following the master's death in January. Before leaving Boston, Shaw placed his collection of Barbizon paintings in the museum's exhibition at the Athenæum.[105]

A somewhat later convert to the Barbizon School, Shaw made a spectacular fortune in copper mining that would make him, at his death in 1908, "the richest man in New England."[106] After seeing some Barbizon works at the 1867 Exposition Universelle in Paris, he began buying, under Hunt's guidance, paintings, pastels, and drawings by Millet and his associates. By the late 1870s he owned at least fifty-four works by the French artist, eventually forming one of the largest aggregates of Millet's oeuvre anywhere.[107] A buyer of French pictures as well as Renaissance art, Shaw lent many important works of art to the MFA beginning in 1875 and, after his election as a trustee in 1877, made numerous gifts to the museum during his lifetime. His benefaction continued even after his death in 1908, most notably when, in 1917, his heirs donated to the MFA, according to his wishes, a large segment of his extensive collection: nineteen pieces of Italian Renaissance sculpture in marble and terra-cotta, as well as twenty-six paintings, twenty-seven pastels, two etchings, and one etching washed in watercolor by Millet.[108] In part thanks to this gift, the Museum of Fine Arts, Boston, owns the largest aggregate of the works by the French master outside Paris.

The exhibition of the Shaw collection in 1875—the year of both Millet's and Corot's deaths—was the first substantial presentation of Barbizon paintings by the museum. Before 1876, many Boston collectors of paintings had either not lent to the museum's installations or withheld their more progressive paintings. (Brimmer, for example, lent none of his Millets before 1876.) The Shaw exhibition was thus an anomaly, but it nevertheless signaled the beginning of the more serious participation by Boston collectors of advanced taste at the museum. The small kernel of change planted in 1875 would grow, after 1876, into a greater presentation of Barbizon paintings (and, later, those by the Impressionists) by the MFA.[109] Eventually, many works by the Barbizon and Impressionist masters that had made their way into Boston collections before 1900 would come, either as loans or gifts, to the museum.

FIG. 58 Enrico Meneghelli, *Picture Gallery of the Boston Athenæum*, 1876. Oil on canvas, 33.2 × 53.7 cm. Collection of the Boston Athenæum, Purchase, 1876. Most prominent in the foreground are Paolo Veronese, *Marriage of Saint Catherine* (ca. 1550–1560; The Detroit Institute of Arts) and Gustave Brion, *Coming out of Church* (1859?), both from the Quincy Adams Shaw collection

PARTNERSHIP IN ACQUISITIONS: CASTELLANI PURCHASE

The museum's founding in 1870 fundamentally changed the function of the Athenæum's Fine Arts Committee in the area of acquisitions. After 1870, the committee ceased to collect for the Athenæum and instead acquired almost entirely for the MFA.[110] The Committee on the Museum, responsible for filling the museum's future galleries but short on funds, naturally turned to its counterpart at the Athenæum for help with acquisitions, and the Fine Arts Committee willingly spent its own money on purchases for the museum, often eagerly following Charles Perkins's recommendations. As a result, most of the Athenæum's purchases in the 1870s and early 1880s were decorative arts and plaster casts.

Before 1876, the lack of sufficient space for storage or exhibition precluded major purchases, and the Fine Arts Committee bought relatively few objects. In 1874 the Fine Arts Committee accepted Perkins's suggestion that his mentor and friend, the French sculptor Baron Henri de Triqueti (1803–1874), act in Europe as the "art agent" of the Athenæum. The committee spent $3,293.50 on the four objets d'art that Triqueti had selected in France for the faraway Athenæum: three Limoges enamels purported

FIG. 59 Cinerary urn, Roman, 1st century A.D., with 18th- and 19th-century restorations to the lid. Marble, 49 × 32.5 × 32.5 cm. Collection of the Boston Athenæum, Purchase, 1874

FIG. 60 Cloisonné vase, Chinese, Qianlong era (1735–1796). Cloisonné with copper, brass, and enamel, 42.5 × 25.1 × 25.1 cm. Collection of the Boston Athenæum, Purchase, 1875

to be from the sixteenth century but clearly of nineteenth-century manufacture, and a marble Roman cinerary urn from the first century A.D. (fig. 59).[111] The following year, the Fine Arts Committee acquired at auction three pieces of Chinese cloisonné (fig. 60) that had belonged to a local China trade firm before its bankruptcy.[112] Crafted in eighteenth-century Beijing, probably in the imperial workshop of the discerning Qianlong emperor, the cloisonné vases and duck demonstrated masterful skills in a medium that fascinated the West in the late nineteenth century. In addition, the Fine Arts Committee purchased a considerable number of reproductions on paper, especially the chromolithographs of Old Master paintings published by the Arundel Society of London and photographs of Old Master drawings, paintings, and architecture by the French photographer Adolphe Braun (1812–1877).[113] Most of the objects purchased during this period briefly joined the MFA's displays at the Athenæum before 1876, but they were clearly intended to help fill the new museum's galleries in the Back Bay.

Ironically, the largest of the Athenæum's acquisitions for the museum was born out of the most shocking of all the setbacks experienced by the young institution: the near-total loss of the Lawrence collection of arms and armor, the earliest material impetus for the MFA's creation. On the evening of November 9, 1872, fire broke out in

FIG. 61 F. Shaw (active late 19th century), *The Boston Fire: A View of Boston from across the Harbor in East Boston*, 1876. Oil on canvas, 45.7 × 76.2 cm. Collection of the Boston Athenæum, Gift of Mr. and Mrs. Herbert W. Pratt, 1986

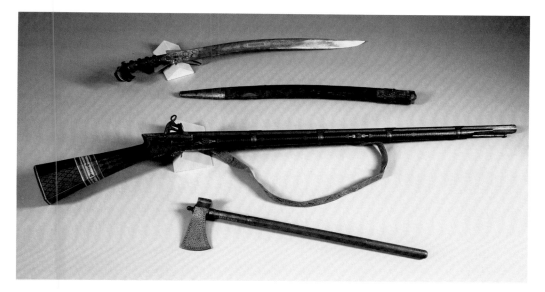

FIG. 62 Weapons from the original Lawrence collection, three of the twenty-eight that survived the Great Fire of 1872. Gun, Iranian, probably early 19th century; battle axe, Indian; and sword and scabbard, Turkish, 18th–19th century. Collection of the Boston Athenæum, Bequest of Colonel Timothy Bigelow Lawrence, 1869

a section of downtown Boston and quickly spread. By the time the fire subsided a day and a half later, it had consumed more than seventy acres of the neighborhood that had been densely packed with businesses and warehouses (fig. 61). Losses were staggering in monetary as well as artistic terms. The Lawrence collection had been stored in a warehouse in the burned district and "dissolved into fiery vapor" (as did its inventory). On hearing of the loss, Mrs. Lawrence reportedly uttered, "There is no armor against fate."[114] The only survivors were the twenty-eight weapons that had been at the Athenæum, as part of the museum's exhibition there (fig. 62).

Luckily, the entire collection was insured, and the Athenæum trustees soon resolved to devote the insurance money to the formation of a new Lawrence collection.[115] This new collection would be, the trustees hoped, as impressive a presence as the original Lawrence collection would have been, making the Athenæum's contributions unmistakably visible while pleasing and celebrating the generous Mrs. Lawrence. In the fall of 1875, when it finally appeared likely that the museum would open the following summer, the Athenæum's Fine Arts Committee discussed "the desirability of giving as great importance as possible to the Lawrence Collection."[116] The yet unformed collection was to occupy the "Lawrence Room" at the future museum, a gallery devoted to the display of decorative arts, joining the twenty-eight weapons from the original Lawrence collection and other loans from the Athenæum.[117] In the fall of 1875 the committee contemplated with genuine enthusiasm how to open the new museum "with éclat" the following summer.[118] The Lawrence Fund, the insurance money recovered from the loss of the original collection, would be devoted to that felicitous purpose, and the committee eagerly searched for suitable objects.[119] Once again, it was the museum's Charles Perkins who recommended a purchase to the Athenæum, this time from the Italian dealer Alessandro Castellani.

Alessandro Castellani (1823–1883; fig. 63) and his brother Augusto inherited the Roman jewelry shop of their father, Fortunato Pio Castellani, and made the firm famous in the middle decades of the nineteenth century for its meticulous copies of Etruscan, Greek, and Roman artifacts as well as for its own classically inspired designs.[120] Castellani jewelry in the archaeological style was considered de rigueur among ladies of fashion, and its popularity among royalty and the aristocracy only intensified the fad. Alessandro himself was of theatrical temperament and of sometimes dubious honesty, and his life was full of showy drama. Jailed in 1853 for a political reason, he is said to have feigned mental illness to escape prison and was exiled from Rome in 1860, which effectively ended his career as the chief artistic force of the family firm. He spent the 1860s in Paris and London as the flamboyant promoter of Castellani jewelry, charming his way into the circles of the rich and famous as well as of connoisseurs and scholars. Soon Alessandro's wares began to extend beyond Castellani products to include antiquities and other objects gathered in Italy. Rome was then a fertile ground for the antiquities trade, and Alessandro was one of its chief players, capitalizing on his extensive connections and the cachet of a native expert, which he assiduously cultivated. Dubbed "Alexander the Great of the *bibelots*," he "stayed at the grandest hotels, this too an element of the *mise-en-scène* he so excelled in, confirming with this luxury the dignity of his person and the distinction of his wares."[121] By 1870 Castellani was well known on both sides of the Atlantic for his diverse inventory of all things Italian, old and new, authentic and spurious, including many well-crafted artifacts recently sold off by increasingly cash-strapped Italian noble

FIG. 63 *Alessandro Castellani*, n.d. From *Catalogue des objets d'art antiques....* (Paris, 1884), frontispiece. Courtesy of Special Collections, Fine Arts Library, Harvard University

families and churches. Castellani did a brisk business at international expositions, and didactic museums illustrating examples of applied arts—such as the South Kensington Museum—were his particularly willing clients.

In the summer of 1875, one year before the Philadelphia Centennial Exposition, Castellani contacted Charles Perkins and Martin Brimmer in Boston, almost certainly in full knowledge of the young museum's South Kensingtonian leanings. Before long Perkins was at the Athenæum, recommending to the Fine Arts Committee a large purchase from the Italian *marchand-collectionneur*.[122] The name of Alessandro Castellani was already familiar to the Athenæum. The 1868 purchase by the South Kensington Museum of his collection of Italian jewelry must have been known to the cognoscenti in Boston, and the MFA's exhibitions at the Athenæum had since 1872 included Thomas Gold Appleton's collection of more than forty Greco-Italian painted ceramic vases that had been discovered, reportedly, "by Alessandro Castellani in Etruscan and Campanian Tombs."[123] Even while Castellani was making a series of successful sales, however, a whiff of doubt had already begun to attach itself to his reputation, and the authenticity of some of his merchandise was called into question.[124] The museum in Boston, however, was blithely unaware—or unconvinced—of such simmering suspicion, and Perkins recommended the collection with high praise: "It may be safely said that nothing approaching the Castellani collections, in the beauty, rarity, and value of the objects which they contain, has ever been seen in this country."[125]

In the fall of 1875 the Athenæum's Fine Arts Committee was initially reluctant to accept Perkins's proposal because the collection cost more than the $8,000 then available in the Lawrence Fund. But Perkins was soon back at the Athenæum, this time with three other museum trustees—Brimmer, Loring, and Robert William Ware—to persuade the committee to reconsider. Perkins reminded the committee of the brotherly relations between the Athenæum and the museum, assured the committee that the objects would appreciate in value more rapidly than cash in a bank, and invoked the generosity of Mr. and Mrs. Lawrence. Perkins proved effective, and the committee immediately voted to purchase the items. Perkins worked out the terms of the sale with Castellani, and after months of negotiation the Italian agreed to send his crates to Philadelphia via Boston, where the Athenæum would exercise the right of first refusal after inspecting their contents. The delighted Castellani declared to Edward Perkins, with his characteristic ebullience, that he had formed his collection for Boston "con Amore" and looked forward to visiting Boston: "To see Boston has been the dream of my life, and to pay a visit to my old and new friends there!"[126]

In the early summer of 1876, the shipment reached the museum's newly completed building in the Back Bay, just one month before its scheduled opening. The crates were followed by Signor Castellani himself, who arrived on June 17 and promptly arranged the contents of the crates for inspection.[127] The trustees of both institutions approved the wares, Mrs. Lawrence was delighted with them, and the Athenæum's Fine Arts Committee voted on July 3—the day of the MFA's opening ceremony—to purchase the entire collection for $8,000.[128] Once purchased, the Castellani collection became a part of the new Lawrence collection at the museum, joining the maiolicas, furniture, and oak paneling that Mrs. Lawrence herself had purchased for the institution, and a portion of this collection was placed in the vaguely baronial Lawrence Room (fig. 64).[129] After this success in Boston, Castellani went on to exhibit a large number of "Italian antiquities"—marbles, bronzes, personal ornaments, and maiolica—at the Centennial Exposition in Philadelphia. Apparently both the museum and the Athenæum were enamored of Castellani and his wares: visiting the exposition in November, the Athenæum's Edward Perkins purchased even more objets d'art on behalf of the Athenæum, some of them from Castellani, as did the museum's curator, Charles G. Loring, for his institution. Many of the two institutions' trustees also traveled individually to the fair and bought objects to add to the new galleries. Apparently pleased, the Italian dealer presented to the Athenæum an inscribed copy of the catalogue of his exhibition in Philadelphia.[130]

The Athenæum purchased from Castellani in July 1876 a total of thirty objects in bronze and other metals, nineteen articles of carved wood, and thirty-one Italian silk textiles, hangings, and embroideries, and a few more items in Philadelphia. These Italian objects conformed to the South Kensingtonian prescription—to teach by example—that the young institution espoused. Although they varied in age and quality, most were created with substantial skill and attention to design. The metalworks, predominantly from Italy and Spain, ranged in age from the fifteenth to the eighteenth centuries; most of them were religious accoutrements—chalices, processional crosses, reliquaries—which had been deaccessioned from churches and monasteries. Among the selection was a seventeenth-century sculpture in gilt bronze, *Ecce Homo (Torso of*

FIG. 65 Northern Italian or southern German, *Ecce Homo (Torso of Christ),* ca. 1650–1700. Gilt bronze, 31.1 × 24.1 × 7.6 cm. Carnegie Museum of Art, Purchase, Gift of Vira I. Heinz. Image © 2012 Carnegie Museum of Art, Pittsburgh

FIG. 66　Cartouche
depicting a scene
from ancient history,
surrounded by putti
and scrolls, n.d. Carved
wood, 52 × 58.5 × 7.5 cm.
Collection of the Boston
Athenæum, Purchase,
1876

FIG. 67　Chalice veil,
Italian, 18th century.
Silk woven with strips
of gold, embroidered
with gold threads and
coils, and edged with
gold lace, 72.1 × 71.4 cm.
Collection of the Boston
Athenæum, Purchase,
1876

FIG. 68 Letter pouch, Italian, 17th century. Silk embroidered with silk, silver, and gold thread, red fringe, and pink silk lining, 50 × 25.4 cm (open). Collection of the Boston Athenæum, Purchase, 1876

Christ), from either northern Italy or southern Germany, made at a considerable expense for either a church or private devotion by a wealthy individual (fig. 65). The articles in wood were an eclectic assortment, comprising furniture, frames, bas-reliefs (fig. 66), and fragments of carved interior decorations, some of them a century or two old and others of more recent manufacture. The Italian textiles included many ecclesiastical vestments such as chasubles and copes as well as altar frontals and chalice veils, all with elaborate decorations. A chalice veil, embroidered with gold in high relief on violet silk woven with strips of gold, most likely came from a set of splendid ceremonial vestments that were made in eighteenth-century Italy for an unknown church (fig. 67), and the embroidered letter pouch, thought to date from the seventeenth century, demonstrates remarkable craftsmanship as well (fig. 68). The museum trustees were frank to admit that these items were "a part of the past . . . though in no sense art" and "associated with *dilettanti* collectors." The trustees nevertheless believed that the pieces were eminently suitable for the museum's educational mission, for they were "objects of the greatest importance to industrial interests."[131]

To help the MFA's Committee on the Museum, the Athenæum's Fine Arts Committee not only spent its own money but also allowed the museum—especially in the person of Charles Perkins—a remarkable degree of control over its purchases. In their shared zeal, the two committees operated almost as one, making joint decisions about acquisitions and heeding surprisingly little who in fact benefited from the purchases.

EVENTS OF 1876

In early 1876, as construction of the museum's building entered its final stages, the Committee on the Museum began the long-awaited task of selecting objects from the Athenæum's art collection for deposit at the new institution. After years of intimate collaboration both physical and philosophical, the museum's committee was by then thoroughly familiar with the Athenæum's art collection. By February the committee had compiled a list, and the Athenæum trustees swiftly approved it.[132]

During the spring and early summer of 1876, the members of the Committee on the Museum busily prepared for the opening. To outfit the new building, the committee had to make hundreds of timely decisions about wall colors, display cases, furniture, shades, lights, hanging fixtures, and more. The picture rods installed in January were found in June to be "insufficient" and had to be replaced with those "covered with brass."[133] The committee had to supervise "putting up plain gas pipe 1 inch to be painted in harmony with the walls,"[134] while debating about the prices of admission (25¢) and of season tickets ($10 for one season ticket plus ten single tickets).[135] All the while, the committee had to decide where to place each and every object in the new galleries—and to oversee the physical labor involved in the installation. As late as May, the committee asked that the museum's central staircase be changed from circular to straight, probably to ensure greater ease of displaying artworks around it.[136] To carry out the enormous task of "fitting up of the Museum," including "the transportation to the building & arrangement therein of works of art . . . [and] the cost of transportation from Europe & for repairs of casts for the Museum," the committee was allotted a modest $12,000.[137] Even with the additional $3,000 granted for the purpose in July, the committee was hardly well funded. As Boston's first art museum prepared for its historic opening under these tight fiscal constraints, the deposit of the Athenæum's art collection was undoubtedly an immense help, as was the Athenæum's $8,000 purchase from Castellani.

Throughout this process, the Athenæum's extraordinary casualness in all its dealings with the museum was of singular value to the younger institution. In the spring of 1876, for example, the Athenæum added to its list of museum-bound loans a number of wooden pedestals that had been stored in the basement presumably since the closing of the statuary gallery in 1868. In a typically relaxed manner, James Elliot Cabot, a trustee of both institutions, called these pedestals technically a loan, not a gift, but admitted that "there [was] little probability that they [would] ever be recalled."[138] When dealing with the Athenæum, the museum often found it unnecessary to put in writing the exact terms of the arrangements. Even the most important agreements were simply reported orally at meetings, and formality was observed only to the extent that the minutes of meetings recorded the fact of these verbal presentations.[139]

In contrast, the MFA's negotiations with Harvard for the deposit of the Gray Collection of Engravings were far more formal, sometimes even difficult. Formed by Boston's early nineteenth-century polymath Francis Calley Gray and given posthumously to Harvard in 1857 by his nephew William Gray (who also gave, the following year, an endowment to be used for the collection), the collection comprised more than four thousand prints, the bulk of which were engravings after works by the representative European painters of the Renaissance and Baroque periods.[140] Harvard had long lacked suitable facilities for the collection's display, and the engravings were deemed, even before the MFA was incorporated, a likely candidate for deposit there. Yet in early 1876, as the museum's opening approached, the museum's board had to appoint Charles Perkins and George Washington Wales to "a committee to wait upon Mr. [William] Gray"—who was on the museum's board representing Harvard—and formally ask that the collection be deposited at the museum. After complex negotiations, an agreement between the Museum of Fine Arts and Harvard, signed in May 1876, spelled out the terms of the seven-year loan in exacting detail with many stipulations. Monetarily, Harvard consented to give the museum, for the care and exhibition of the engravings, only the income from the endowment for the collection but refused to pay any more. Harvard further required that the MFA hire a curator solely for the care of the Gray collection and to cover the cost of its transport to the Back Bay.[141] No similar conditions existed between the museum and the Athenæum, at least not as of 1876.

Difficulties of a different kind befell another institutional deposit promised to the museum, this one from the Massachusetts Institute of Technology. When the MFA opened in 1876, there was simply not enough space for the hundreds of architectural casts that MIT had promised to deposit at the new institution. Only after the museum's first expansion, in 1878–1879, did a gallery called the Architectural Room appear at the east end of the enlarged first floor; it housed the six hundred plaster casts of architectural elements and carvings, chiefly from Lincoln Cathedral in England, that had been lent by MIT's architecture department.[142] Purchased in Europe in 1866–1867 by William Robert Ware, the department's first chair, the casts had been part of the rapidly growing architectural study collection in his department, along with books, drawings, and photographs. MIT's deposit of these casts at the new museum, just one block away from the school, was in part a space-saving measure for the school but mainly a neighborly gesture of cooperation, similar to the Athenæum's attitude to the museum.

Another neighbor, the Boston Public Library (on Boylston Street until its move in 1895 to its current location facing Copley Square), however, did little for the museum by way of loans. In 1869 the library had received from Thomas Gold Appleton, a library trustee, the collection formed by the Roman Catholic cardinal Antonio Tosti of more than ten thousand European engravings.[143] Toward the end of 1869, the library's president, William W. Greenough, was an early and active participant in the movement to establish the museum and promised to deposit the Tosti collection there. But, for one reason or another, the Tosti prints never went to the museum.[144]

Finally, in late May, the museum's new building in the Back Bay was nearly complete, and the Committee on the Museum began to install the works of art. On Saturday, June 3, 1876, the Athenæum's third-floor gallery, by then occupied entirely by the museum, closed for the last time.[145] Soon thereafter, the Athenæum's Fine Arts Committee undertook the monumental task of transporting the selected portion of its art collection from Beacon Street to the new museum.[146]

The long-awaited opening of the museum's building was to coincide with the nation's centennial birthday, July 4, 1876. The day before, at 12:15 in the afternoon, an outdoor public ceremony was held in front of the museum. As morning fog cleared to let the sun shine on the gathered crowd, a host of dignitaries acknowledged the contributions made to the museum by its "happily adopted relations": the Athenæum, Harvard, MIT, the Boston Public Library, and the American Social Science Association.[147] In the last—and perhaps the most emotional—speech of the day, Charles Callahan Perkins singled out the Athenæum for the extraordinary role it had played:

> The trustees of the Museum owe this public expression of their gratitude . . . to the trustees of the Athenæum, who have never failed in their generous support of the Museum. All that they had of value in the way of art objects they placed at our disposal. . . . for five years they have allowed us to occupy their picture-gallery, without price, as a cradle in which we could nurse our growing infant, until it had become too large to be confined within such narrow bounds.[148]

The rest of Perkins's celebratory address confirmed the MFA's expansive founding vision. While the museum aspired to grow "to be a rival . . . of the great industrial museums at Kensington and Vienna," Perkins also proclaimed it "a place dedicated to the enjoyment and profitable instruction of all who enter it."[149] "Hither will come," he happily predicted,

> the "myriad sons of toil" for relaxation and refreshment; the archaeologist to study ancient monuments and inscriptions; the painter to find material for the backgrounds of his pic-

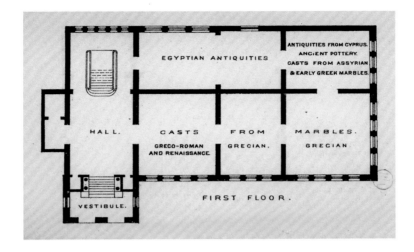

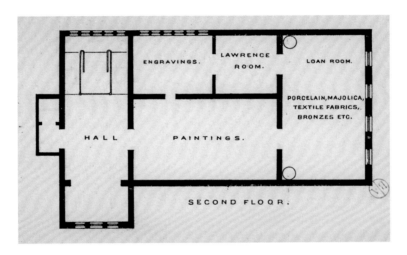

tures, and stuff for the robes of his fair sitters; the designer to take hints for patterns from mediaeval brocades and Oriental enamels and porcelain; the poet to take inspiration from masterpieces of art; the musician to seek fresh ideas for melodious utterance.[150]

Finally, after six years of travails, Perkins declared the Museum of Fine Arts open.

At that time, the museum contained, befitting its all-encompassing aim, a wide range of objects: archaeological artifacts, paintings, prints, sculpture, plaster casts, decorative arts, and more. Two galleries housed archaeological specimens from Egypt, Cyprus, and Assyria, while two others were devoted to decorative arts objects in porcelain, maiolica, textile, bronze, and glass. Plaster casts numbered eighty-one in 1876 and occupied three galleries, and paintings filled the large skylit gallery as well as the landing on the second floor (fig. 69). Most of the contents of the museum's former

FIG. 70 Vincent Brooks, after Mrs. Higford Burr, *The Giotto Chapel, Padua, in 1306.* London: Arundel Society, 1856. Chromo-lithograph, 73 × 80.6 cm (sheet). Collection of the Boston Athenæum, Purchase, 1871

exhibitions moved from the Athenæum to the new building, joining the long-promised institutional deposits as well as other loans and gifts. Compared with the substantial number of loans, however, the museum's collection in 1876 was modest: apart from the more than five hundred Cypriot objects from the Cesnola collection and the close to five thousand Egyptian items from the Way collection, the museum's own holdings numbered only a few hundred.[151]

Among the many institutional and private loans, the Athenæum's was the largest: fifty-six paintings (eighteen by American and thirty-eight by European artists), six marble sculptures, twenty plaster casts, the Dowse collection of fifty-two watercolor copies of Old Master paintings, seven miniatures, fifty-one chromolithographs published by the Arundel Society (fig. 70), more than five hundred photographs by Adolphe Braun of Old Master paintings, drawings, and sculptures (fig. 71), and almost all of the Athenæum's holdings in the decorative arts, including those that the Fine Arts Committee had purchased since 1870 expressly for the MFA.[152] Even more important than the quantity, though, were the quality, celebrity, and strategic placement of the Athenæum's deposits, which made a particularly strong visual impact at many locations within the museum. In the handsome entrance hall and staircase, five of the eight marble sculptures belonged to the Athenæum (fig. 72): *Orpheus and Cerberus* by Thomas Crawford, *Will-o'-the-Wisp* (ca. 1856; BA) by Harriet Hosmer (1830–1908), *Carthaginian Girl* (1863; BA) by Richard Saltonstall Greenough, *Canephora* (n.d.; BA)

FIG. 71 Adolphe Braun, *Florence, Michel-Ange. Twilight. Aurora. Monument of Lorenzo de Medici. Church of San Lorenzo*, n.d. Carbon photograph, 65.1 × 47.9 cm (mount). Collection of the Boston Athenæum, Purchase, probably 1872

FIG. 72 T. E. Marr, *Museum of Fine Arts, Boston, Copley Square Location*. Entrance Hall, 1902–1903. Museum of Fine Arts, Boston. Photograph © 2013 Museum of Fine Arts, Boston

FIG. 73 T. E. Marr, *Museum of Fine Arts, Boston, Copley Square Location.* Painting Gallery (Allston Room), 1902–1903. Museum of Fine Arts, Boston. Photograph © 2013 Museum of Fine Arts, Boston

by Émile Wolff (1802–1879), and a marble copy of the Venus de' Medici (n.d.; BA).[153] Upstairs, the large hall was made equally splendid by thirty-four paintings of which twelve belonged to the Athenæum, including the large and impressive *King Lear* by Benjamin West, *The Sortie Made by the Garrison of Gibraltar* by John Trumbull, two Roman views by Giovanni Paolo Panini, and *The Golden Age* (ca. 1695–1705; BA) by Gregorio Lazzarini (1653–1730), as well as such famous Athenæum icons as the portraits of George and Martha Washington by Gilbert Stuart (fig. 73).

Although it opened in a size much smaller than the original plan, the Museum of Fine Arts finally had its own physical presence for all to see. This was its "modest yet brilliant beginning," wrote Thomas Gold Appleton with apparent pride and bright hope for the future.[154] Before the end of 1876, average daily attendance reached more than two hundred on weekdays and an astounding twelve hundred on "free" Saturdays.[155]

Across town, at the Athenæum on Beacon Street, paintings and sculptures still adorned many rooms. After the exodus, however, the art collection was essentially ornaments, no longer central to the Athenæum's cultural mission. By closing the gallery and transferring much of its art collection, the Athenæum had irrevocably abandoned one of its original aims, to foster the fine arts in Boston by collecting and exhibiting works of art. In the summer of 1876 the Library Committee took possession of the now empty third floor, and Edward Clarke Cabot began drafting plans for refitting it as a library.[156] Finally, after ten years, the ominous 1866 decree by the Athenæum's Standing Committee—that one purpose of the Athenæum's art collection was to "adorn & dignify its halls, & render them more attractive to the stranger, and more interesting and dear to the daily visitor"—had come true.

At the end of 1876, the Athenæum's Edward Perkins reflected on the transfer of much of the Athenæum's art collection to the MFA, a momentous task accomplished by his committee. Proud of the past, resigned to the present, and still hopeful of the future, Perkins nevertheless betrayed a modicum of sadness:

> The Museum which has thus become the Depository of the Athenæum F. A. Collections "present and to come," is carrying on the work which has been done here for nearly 50 years, but with greater facilities and higher aims. The relation of the two institutions is intimate, the Athenæum being represented in the Museum board by 3 and in the Museum Committee by 2 of its Trustees. It is therefore confidently believed that the [Athenæum's] Proprietors will not lose their interest in the Fine Art Dept. because it is no longer under the roof-tree of the Athenæum. In no other way than by removal could the conflicting wants of the Galleries and the extension of the Library have been so happily reconciled.[157]

Three months later, on March 19, 1877, a formal contract spelling out the terms of the Athenæum's deposits at the museum was signed by both parties.[158]

CHAPTER FIVE

After 1876: Changing Directions

$\mathscr{I}$N JULY 1876 the Museum of Fine Arts finally proclaimed its physical presence with its richly polychrome building in the Back Bay. By late November the trustees no longer felt it necessary to place regular advertisements in the city's newspapers, satisfied that the public had duly "become familiar with the Museum."[1] In 1877, the first full year of operation, almost 160,000 people visited the MFA. On weekdays, an average of 60 visitors quietly strolled in the galleries, but on Saturdays, when the 25¢ admission fee was waived, the crowd swelled to almost 3,000.[2]

Once in its own building, the MFA naturally attracted more gifts and loans from those eager to have their possessions on display at one of Boston's newest cultural landmarks. These objects were not all artistic masterpieces; in fact, they varied considerably in media and quality. Nevertheless, within a few short years, the trustees' initial difficulty in filling the galleries turned into the exact opposite. In early 1878 President Brimmer lamented that "the crying want of the Museum is want of space."[3] That spring, the museum's first expansion began, to complete the northern façade eastward along St. James Avenue, and the enlarged institution opened in July 1879. In the new building, almost the entire first floor was devoted to plaster casts and the Cypriot and Egyptian antiquities, while most of the second floor featured paintings, engravings, and decorative arts (fig. 74). The increased floor space also meant that the museum was now able to mount changing temporary exhibitions, which, consisting almost entirely of loans, were a relatively inexpensive way to generate interest. The first three special exhibitions took place in 1879: the Gray engravings with additional loans (chiefly from Charles Eliot Norton and Charles Perkins); a display of contemporary American paintings, held jointly with the Boston Art Club; and a memorial installation of William Morris Hunt's work, to mark his death earlier in the year. The following year, five special exhibitions were held.[4] Yet even though the building was bigger, it was hardly large enough to accommodate all of the functions envisioned in 1870, lacking, for example, a lecture hall. Soon, the galleries were again full of gifts,

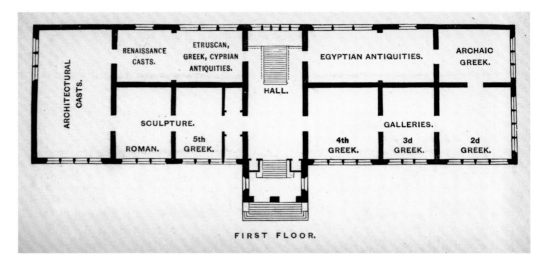

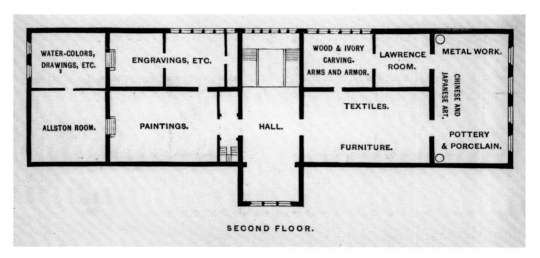

FIG. 74 Floor plans of the Museum of Fine Arts, Boston, after the first expansion of 1878–1879. From *Museum of Fine Arts, Boston. Fourteenth Catalogue of the Collection. . . .* (Boston, 1879), n.p.

loans, and the growing number of plaster casts. By 1883 the trustees had decided on yet another expansion, which took place in 1888–1889 (fig. 75).[5]

Even though funds for the two expansions were raised relatively quickly, the rest of the museum's income remained meager.[6] The disproportionately large numbers of nonpaying visitors on weekends did nothing to enrich the coffers, and significant gifts and bequests of money were slow to arrive. Despite the trustees' public pleas for more funds, the museum's deficit remained high—several thousand dollars each year—into the 1890s. This insolvency affected all of the museum's operations to some extent, but

FIG. 75
Floor plans
of the
Museum of
Fine Arts,
Boston, after
the second
expansion of
1888–1889.
From
*Museum of
Fine Arts
Bulletin* 1
(March
1903): n.p.

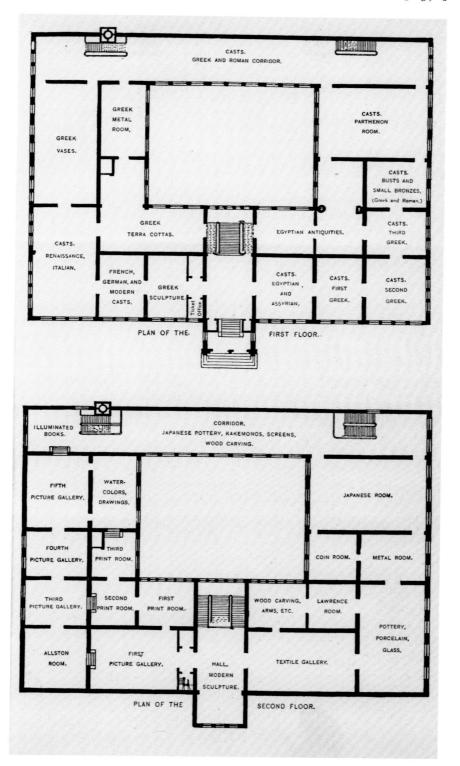

the lean finances put a particular damper on acquisitions. In 1880, for example, Martin Brimmer deplored the institution's "ill-deserved reputation of being a wealthy corporation, able to use the frequent opportunities which are offered to make valuable purchases for its collections."[7] At an auction in London in 1881, Charles Perkins "sighed and wished for more of money to spend for our Museum."[8] Many of Boston's available donors had given to the two expansions, and the curator, Charles G. Loring, ruefully remarked, in 1888, that "Boston has been pretty well drained."[9]

The museum's poverty in the face of its continuing physical expansion—an awkward phase of the growth process—prompted, for one thing, a reassessment of its founding vision, especially its commitment to industrial art education. When, in October 1876, the board furnished Loring with $2,000 to spend on purchases at the Centennial Exhibition in Philadelphia, the selections were, still, "to be made with reference to the advancement of artistic design in the industries of Massachusetts."[10] Toward the end of the 1870s, however, as the fervor for industrial art education waned in the city and the state, support for the museum's commitment to that particular educational role also began to diminish. "The best pictures and marbles," not specimens of art industry, were the incontestable "prizes" for art museums,[11] wrote Brimmer in 1880. By 1883 the bright hope of 1870 for the MFA's broad purpose was clearly in eclipse: that year the Committee on the Museum admitted that the institution had been founded "upon a very broad basis" and, "if we had one limited and sharply defined purpose, there would be no difficulty."[12] Instructed to "prepare a scheme for the regular increase of the collections,"[13] the committee signaled a clear shift in the museum's acquisition priorities: "[the] primary intention is to collect and exhibit the best obtainable works of genius and skill; . . . the application of the Fine Arts to industry, and the illustration of the Fine Arts by archaeology, are both within its province, but . . . neither of these is its first object."[14]

Nevertheless, without adequate funds, the committee had little choice but to concede that the museum "must rely principally on the liberality of others for original works of art and . . . spend the greater part of the money available for purchases in buying reproductions."[15] In fact, the MFA had done just that: by 1883 it had spent approximately $18,000 on reproductions (95 percent of the sum on plaster casts) as opposed to only about $7,800 on non-reproductions (66 percent of it on decorative arts).[16] During its first decade of operation in the new building, even as a growing number of paintings arrived as gifts and loans, the Museum of Fine Arts largely retained its earlier character as a repository of plaster casts, decorative arts, and curiosities.

COLLABORATION IN ACQUISITION

After 1876 the Athenæum's Fine Arts Committee was relieved of the physical care of its art collection (much of which had been moved to the MFA) and of the need to provide shelter for the homeless museum. Besides the maintenance of some paintings and sculptures that still resided on Beacon Street, the committee's only duty was to spend the modest income that continued to accrue in several of its funds. (As required, the committee also inspected the Athenæum's deposits at the museum annually and reported their condition to the Athenæum's board.) That the money should be devoted largely to the same purpose as before—making purchases for the Museum of Fine Arts—apparently merited no particular discussion in 1876, and until the late 1880s all of the Fine Arts Committee's purchases of works of art were for the other institution, none for its own. As the Committee on the Museum gratefully acknowledged, the Athenæum's assistance was indeed a proof of "the combined good-will and hearty co-operation of the Trustees of the Athenæum, in all that tends to increase the value of the collections at the Museum."[17] The museum may have left its "cradle," but the Athenæum's ministrations to it continued.

The first of the Athenæum's acquisitions for the MFA after 1876 took place the following year, when it purchased, from the Berlin Museum, twenty-four plaster casts of sculptures excavated by the German government from the Temple of Zeus at Olympia.[18] Conducted between 1875 and 1881, the German excavations left the originals in Greece—in the museum built in Olympia to house them—and took home only the documentation and casts of the unearthed objects.[19] (In a major departure from earlier procedure, this marked the beginning of modern archaeological practice.) The Germans were allowed to reproduce the casts for sale, which was eagerly anticipated by didactic institutions on both sides of the Atlantic. Built in the fifth century B.C., the Temple of Zeus provided one of the earliest instances of mature classical Greek temple architecture. Art historians deemed the figures on the temple's exterior—in the pediments and metopes—particularly important examples of the Early Classical period, showing the naturalism and balance that would mature into the later masterpieces of Greek figurative sculpture. In 1877, when the Berlin Museum offered plaster casts of the temple's pediments and metopes for sale, the Athenæum purchased, for $450, the first twenty-four from the series for the museum.[20] In the ensuing years, the museum would spend its own money to acquire many more from the Olympia series (fig. 76).

In the larger scheme of things, however, the Athenæum's purchase of the Olympia casts was overshadowed by the museum's total expenditure on plaster casts in the 1870s and 1880s. During this period, the MFA ordered shiploads of casts from both institutional and commercial sources in Dresden, Berlin, Paris, Rome, Athens, and London.[21]

The international vogue for building encyclopedic cast collections had only escalated since midcentury with the medium's increased availability, and museums in both Europe and the United States aspired to assemble—although none succeeded completely—a comprehensive gallery of casts of all the acknowledged sculptural masterpieces. In Boston, the museum's cast collection had begun with the thirteen purchased, in 1874, with the proceeds from the sale of Charles Sumner's bequests and the twenty-one deposited by the Athenæum in 1876. More casts came thereafter, and by 1879 more than six hundred examples were on view. In fact, by that time, the museum was ordering so many casts in rapid succession from different sources that the Committee on the Museum discussed ways to keep better track of the innumerable orders and receipts.[22] The number peaked at more than one thousand in the early 1890s, making the MFA's collection one of the largest in the world, third only to those at the museums in Berlin and Strasbourg.[23]

Like the Olympia casts, most of the Athenæum's acquisitions for the museum after 1876 were relatively inexpensive: James McNeill Whistler's French Set of twelve etchings (with decorated wrapper) was purchased in 1879 for less than $200; a Gobelins tapestry, in 1879, for $84.82; and an assortment of decorative objects—a pair of Satsuma vases, enameled candlesticks, and a chalice—and a polyptych that Edward Perkins procured in 1884 during his visit to Cannes, France, for $287.37.[24] For the Committee on the Museum, the primary benefit of its close relationship with the Fine Arts Committee lay not so much in the actual dollar amount it spent as in its dependability as an

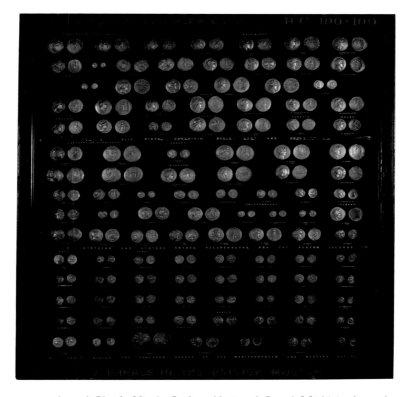

FIG. 77 (LEFT) Claude-Nicolas Ledoux (designer); Joseph Méthivier (carver). Carved panel from the Hôtel de Montmorency, Paris, ca. 1770. Painted and gilt oak, 365.7 × 81.3 cm. Museum of Fine Arts, Boston, Museum purchase with funds by exchange from a Gift of Mr. and Mrs. Cornelius C. Vermeule III, 1975.802. Photograph © 2013 Museum of Fine Arts, Boston

FIG. 78 (ABOVE RIGHT) "Electrotypes of Greek Coins—B.C. 190–100. Originals in the British Museum," ca. 1880. Frame number six, containing 220 coins, in a set of seven. 76 × 76 cm (frame). Collection of the Boston Athenæum, Purchase, 1881

always willing partner to the museum's committee, which constantly had to finagle funding for acquisitions during these financially lean early years.

As the 1880s wore on, however, the Athenæum's contributions began to be made more often in the form of joint purchases. Instead of buying objects and depositing them at the museum, the Athenæum simply split the costs with the other institution, a method that facilitated purchases of greater value. In 1879, for example, the Athenæum and the museum jointly acquired eight carved eighteenth-century panels from the Hôtel de Montmorency in Paris, which had been exhibited by the museum since 1872, first at the Athenæum and then in the Back Bay (fig. 77). Each institution paid $2,000 for four of the eight panels, but all eight were placed on view at the museum.[25] Likewise, in 1881 the two institutions jointly purchased framed reproductions of ancient coins from the British Museum (fig. 78).[26] The MFA could afford only two of the seven sets that were available, so Charles Perkins consulted the Fine Arts Committee, which in turn handed Perkins, who was about to sail to England in February 1881, the money to purchase the remaining five frames.[27] Although on paper the Museum of Fine Arts owned two framed sets and the Athenæum five, all seven were displayed at the museum.

In these purchasing maneuvers, the institutional boundaries between the respective committees of the museum and the Athenæum grew even less clear than before. The talk of joint purchases took place not only at committee meetings but also privately, among the members who sat on the two committees. In 1883, for example, the two committees were working together to buy for the museum with the Athenæum's money several contemporary engravings (by Francis Seymour Haden [1818–1910], Hubert von Herkomer [1849–1914], and others). After many men from both institutions separately visited the commercial gallery of Noyes and Blakeslee, which was offering the prints for sale, Edward Perkins had to ask Loring whether he had taken some prints "for [the] Art Museum or on approval for [the] Athenæum."[28] The Athenæum's annual large orders of Adolphe Braun's photographs, many of which were immediately lent to the museum, also generated a quantity of confused correspondence that ricocheted among individuals from the two institutions, each requesting or giving recommendations, decisions, or payments.[29] The final vote at committee meetings was often a mere gesture, confirming the casual but extensive negotiations that had already occurred.

Perhaps the most complex of the joint purchases came, in 1886, with the acquisition of two stone Etruscan sarcophagi (fig. 79). Unearthed in 1845–1846 in Vulci, an Etruscan city north of Rome, the sarcophagi date to about 330–300 B.C. and 300–280 B.C. The sides of each coffin are decorated with figures in relief while each of the lids bears the image of a recumbent, embracing couple. The two objects were exhibited in 1883 in Boston by James Jackson Jarves at the Foreign Fair, Boston's attempt at a world's fair (but "foreign" because it excluded American products).[30] Not having sold, the massive coffins were moved a few blocks in 1884 to the museum for display.[31]

The sarcophagi were natural candidates for acquisition by the MFA, but funds were not forthcoming until a year later, when the Athenæum's Fine Arts Committee pledged $2,000 toward Jarves's asking price of $10,000 "on condition that one of the two shall be assigned to the Athenæum as its property."[32] Nonetheless, both institutions dillydallied, probably because the price was too high. Another year passed with no progress, and when Jarves demanded resolution of the matter in the spring of 1886, the museum hastily allocated $1,000 on the condition that the Athenæum produce the $2,000 it had pledged. To its embarrassment, however, the Fine Arts Committee had not actually raised the money.[33] Under pressure from the museum, the Fine Arts

Committee reluctantly obtained from the full board an advance of $2,000. Yet with only $3,000 having been pledged, the matter again stood in abeyance for several months.[34] In late 1886 a gift of $6,000 from Mrs. Gardner Brewer almost covered the shortfall.[35] Finally, with the remaining $1,000 raised by subscription, the museum and the Athenæum jointly purchased the sarcophagi.[36] Although the Athenæum contributed only one-fifth of the purchase price for the pair, it claimed full ownership of one of the sarcophagi. The museum issued an official receipt for the loan of the Athenæum's sarcophagus on January 18, 1887.[37]

The last of the Athenæum's museum-bound acquisitions occurred in 1889, when the Fine Arts Committee contributed $2,000 toward the purchase of ten Dutch paintings from the San Donato collection. This magnificent collection of fine and decorative arts had been formed earlier in the century by the Russian industrialist Nicholas Demidoff and his son Anatole N. Demidoff at their Villa San Donato, near Florence.[38] At the collection's sale in 1880, the Bostonian Stanton Blake purchased, through Jarves, ten Dutch paintings—four genre scenes, three landscapes, and three still lifes—and two sculptures. Although a few of the canvases bore hopeful attributions, others were genuine, including those by Frans Snyders, David Teniers the Younger, Gabriel Metsu (1629–1667), and Jan van Huysum II (1682–1749), and remain in the museum's collection.[39] When Blake placed the objects on loan at the MFA in 1881, it immediately laid plans for a subscription campaign to raise $25,000 to purchase them. The Athenæum's Fine Arts Committee pledged the sum of $2,000 toward the purchase "on condition that a picture or pictures of that value be assigned to the Athenæum as its property."[40] As before, little happened for a while, until 1889, the year of Blake's death.[41] This time, with a gift of $10,000 from Francis Bartlett—who would soon become a trustee and major donor to the institution—the Museum of Fine Arts bought the group in October 1889.[42] Making good on the promise from 1881, the Athenæum's Fine Arts Committee paid the $2,000, and the Athenæum was duly allotted one of the San Donato pictures, a view of Dordrecht by Jacob van Strij (1756–1815), then attributed to Aelbert Cuyp.[43]

Cooling Relationship

Even as the two committees continued to collaborate, there were subtle signs toward the end of the 1870s that the Athenæum's other trustees and committees were growing more critical of the Fine Arts Committee's purchases for the museum. For each purchase that the committee wished to make jointly with the other institution, the Athenæum was increasingly anxious to obtain official title to what it had paid for. In 1879, for example, after the committee reluctantly voted to spend $2,000 for four of the eight Montmorency panels on the condition that they become the Athenæum's property, Edward Perkins, the Fine Arts Committee chairman, alluded to the pressure placed on his committee in his apologetic letter to Loring: "Don't think [us] as grasping for the Committee as you know *cannot give away money but must have a quid pro quo*."[44]

If the Athenæum's relationship with the Museum of Fine Arts remained cordial, it was logical for the Athenæum as a whole to question the wisdom of continuing to spend its money on objects that went straight to the Back Bay, without stopping even temporarily on Beacon Street. Over time, the physical separation of the two institutions in 1876 inevitably brought subtle changes to their relationship. Furthermore, as the museum grew in size and stature, it became increasingly obvious that the Athenæum was but one of many donors and lenders, no longer the single most important partner. By the mid-1880s, the relative importance of the Athenæum's loans to the museum had diminished, and the Athenæum's institution-wide zeal to help the museum had unmistakably begun to cool.

A contentious exchange that took place in 1885 regarding the Athenæum's deposits of photographs at the MFA was emblematic of this subtle transition. Since 1876 the Athenæum had lent to the museum an increasing number of Braun's images of Old Master paintings, drawings, and architecture.[45] They were placed in the third-floor photography room, probably in portfolios, together with the Gray Collection of Engravings and other flat materials, under the care of the curator of the Gray collection. But in May 1885 the Athenæum proprietors collectively lodged a complaint with the Committee on the Museum: they objected to having to pay admission to view the Braun photographs.[46] The museum immediately granted free admission to any Athenæum proprietors who came to see the items deposited by the Athenæum. It soon turned out, however, that the complaint was less about free admission than about the inability to see the photographs when no staff member was present. In response, the museum agreed to hire attendants for the photography room to ensure uninterrupted access.[47]

The complaint about access may have come from a few dissenting Athenæum proprietors, but it nevertheless posed a pointed question: Should the Athenæum have a say in the management of its deposits at the museum, even to the extent of affecting the latter institution's staffing? Although amicably resolved, the episode revealed that the Athenæum was increasingly critical of the fundamentally vague status of its deposits at the museum. Agreed on in fits of enthusiasm—in principle in 1870 and officially in 1877—the arrangement was clearly becoming, with each passing year, difficult to sustain. Moreover, during the fifteen years that had passed since the Museum of Fine Arts was established, the Athenæum's memory of its own internal circumstances that had led to the museum's birth in the first place had begun to fade. In 1886 an Athenæum proprietor made the startling suggestion that that institution should "hold an Exhibition of works of art as in former days, at the Athenæum Gallery." The proposal, of course, was swiftly voted down because it was "impracticable, as the Collections of the Athenæum are exhibited at the Art Museum where they may be seen & no galleries exist here for that purpose."[48] The fact that such a proposal was made at all spoke volumes about how perceptions had changed with the passage of time since 1870.

While the Athenæum simply had no room to accommodate the return of any of its paintings and sculptures, flat materials were another matter, since they took up less space. Indeed, in the 1880s, the two institutions wrangled, in a progressively more fractious tone, about the Athenæum's Braun photographs and Arundel Society chromolithographs that were at the museum in the Back Bay. When, for example, the Athenæum librarian, Charles Ammi Cutter, complained in 1882 that the Arundel prints at the museum were underutilized, Loring contradicted him and tried to keep them, ending his rebuttal defensively: "But if [the prints] are needed in Beacon St— our claim falls."[49] By 1885 the Braun photographs were in fact "wanted at the Library for the use of the Proprietors,"[50] and the museum immediately sent back the requested 444 images of the Hermitage in St. Petersburg, while retaining several hundred others. The negotiations leading up to this solution were confused and contentious, with too many people from both institutions voicing their opinions.[51] Communication between the Athenæum and the museum was growing less smooth, no longer amicable.

Death of Charles Callahan Perkins

Were it not for one crucial event that occurred in 1886, however, the cooling of the relationship between the Athenæum and the museum would not have led to the precipitous end of their collaboration: the death of Charles Callahan Perkins. In the late summer, Perkins was visiting his elder son, Edward Clifford Perkins, and his family in Windsor, Vermont, an idyllic village nestled on the western bank of the Connecticut River.[52] On August 25, Perkins went for an afternoon ride with William Maxwell Evarts (Edward's father-in-law and a U.S. senator from New York) and a young lady. When a broken bit in the bridle drove the horses wild, control of the carriage was lost. The phaeton careened around a sharp corner, and Perkins, thrown against a stone wall, was killed instantly. The other two survived with minor injuries. Perkins was sixty-three years old.[53]

Perkins's death was a shocking blow to his family, friends, and the public at large, and a flurry of letters and eulogies crisscrossed New England and beyond. Public outpouring of sympathy, in recognition of Perkins's many contributions to Boston, was overwhelming:

> A man of ripened culture, familiar with the art centres of the Old World as with the streets of his native Boston. . . . He had brought home from Europe a purpose and hopefulness, and discerned the wants and capabilities of his native city and country. There was nothing in his tone of that dyspeptic discontent with everything American which is the only thing so many Americans ever bring home from Europe.[54]

Perkins had lent his hand to innumerable artistic enterprises of his native city as a patron, scholar, organizer, trustee, lender, donor, and advocate. His obituaries ran long with lists of the philanthropic causes he had supported, and many resolutions were passed and hymns sung in his memory.[55] "I had no idea how much he was valued & respected in Boston and it is a consolation indeed that he is so much appreciated," wrote Perkins's sister, Sarah Cleveland, even as she grieved over her brother's sudden departure.[56] Of the many cultural institutions he had served, it was said that if the Museum of Fine Arts was "his object, it was also his recompense."[57] The shepherding of the museum through its early years had proven an ideal occupation for Perkins, a task to which he had brought, with ample passion, his knowledge, experience, skills, wealth, and social connections. "If ever there had been a man," a close friend bemoaned, who would "not die a violent death, but . . . sink to rest after an industrious, innocent, well-spent life, surrounded by sorrowing family and friends, it would have been Charlie."[58] But fate denied Perkins such comfort, and the stark violence of his death almost eclipsed the memory of his accomplished, striving life. Years later, Henry James recollected: "A master of all amenities, and accomplished student of Italian art . . .

Charles Perkins lives for us again . . . in the unforgotten harshness of premature and accidental death."[59]

Despite all his erudition in things related to art, Perkins had nevertheless believed in the social function of art, as had many in his generation. Art was a means to elevate taste and thereby improve the quality of material and spiritual life of the people. As Perkins wrote in 1869, art's

> humblest function is to give enjoyment to all classes; [its] highest, to elevate men by puri-fying the taste and by acting upon the moral nature; [its] most practical, to lead by the creation of a standard of taste in the mind to improvement in all branches of industry . . . [and] in all objects made for daily use.[60]

Eager to make the museum in Boston a vehicle whereby art's reforming function could reach the whole of society, Perkins envisioned an institution remarkably dem-ocratic in its aim: "All educated persons will agree that nations as well as individuals should aim at that degree of aesthetic culture which, without passing the dividing line between general and special knowledge, will enable them to recognize and appreciate the beautiful in nature and in art."[61] Perkins himself personified the expansive ideal of the "cultivated gentleman"—a cultural prescription of an earlier time—as a learned person engaged in the multiple arenas of connoisseur, critic, and patron. Even in Perkins's lifetime, however, such a model had begun to face a challenge from what the historian Thomas L. Haskell has called "the late-nineteenth-century imperative . . . to specialize,"[62] an imperative that would have labeled Perkins, with disdain, an "amateur."

Perkins's tenure at the Museum of Fine Arts, from 1870 to 1886, coincided with the institution's first chapter under the heady influence of the South Kensington idea. Among the founding trustees, Perkins had contributed to the museum in capacities more numerous than had any others, performing work that modern museums divide into many administrative and curatorial positions. At the time of his death, however, Perkins's brand of art museum—a didactic repository of reproductions dedicated to public art education and improvement of industrial design—already showed signs of its eventual decline. As the most vocal proponent of the South Kensington idea, Perkins had likely faced a growing amount of internal tension with his colleagues about the museum's direction. This may explain, at least in part, why the MFA remained relatively silent about Perkins's death, while many other cultural organiza-tions in the city mourned it publicly. In contrast, the deaths of museum president Martin Brimmer and curator Charles Loring, in 1896 and 1902, respectively, occa-sioned much appreciative institutional memorializing, and long tributes to them were published in the museum's annual reports. Moreover, each death was followed by the acquisition of a significant work of art in honor of the men's long and devoted service:

after Brimmer's, *The Entombment of Christ* (1848; MFA) by Eugène Delacroix (1798–1863) was purchased; in Loring's memory, the museum received from the trustee Denman Waldo Ross a portrait of William Lock of Norbury (1790; MFA) by Sir Thomas Lawrence (1769–1830).[63] Furthermore, in 1905 the trustees commissioned the Boston artist Edmund Charles Tarbell (1862–1938) to paint a posthumous portrait of Loring (1905; MFA).

Other factors contributed to Perkins's relative posthumous obscurity. For one thing, his death came earlier than those of most of the other founders, before, that is, the museum had risen to a position of influence supported by affluence. Identified undeservedly only with the early museum's didactic focus, Perkins did not receive the recognition that was due one of the institution's chief architects. Also, because he did not have a university post and a following that that would have generated—as did, for example, his contemporary Charles Eliot Norton—much of Perkins's learning and ideas did not survive him. Further, an outspoken commentator on art and art education during his life—unlike his colleagues Brimmer and Loring, who only infrequently commented on art in public—Perkins was an easy target for criticism, precisely because of his copious output. Finally, Perkins's title of honorary director, an unsalaried post but one of central importance, confused later generations as to his role in the institution's early history. For all these reasons, Perkins—an incorrigible idealist and an indefatigable organizer—disappeared into oblivion after his death, as did the memory of his tireless efforts on behalf of the MFA.

In 1886 the records of the Committee on the Museum remained mute on Perkins's death for two months. Only in October did a terse line break the silence: "Mr. Cabot was chosen Chairman, in place of Mr. Perkins deceased."[64] For the Athenæum's Fine Arts Committee, Perkins's death meant the severing of its closest tie to the younger institution. Members of the committee still sat on the Committee on the Museum, and the new committee chairman, James Elliot Cabot, had long been on the boards of both institutions. Without Perkins's zeal and influence, though, the intimate cooperation between the two committees all but ended.[65]

Changes at the Museum after 1886

Like water that gushes over a broken dike, Perkins's death made irrevocable the changes that had already been afoot at the museum. Within six months of his death, the museum's board amended its bylaws for the first time since 1876. The office of honorary director, which Perkins had held since its creation in 1876, was abolished.[66] Loring, who as curator had overseen—with Perkins—the museum's entire collection, was given the new title of director. In place of a single curator, several professional curators were to attend to segments of the collections in their respective areas of specialization. To be sure, a few specialist curators had been at the museum before 1886. The Gray Collection of Engravings had had a part-time curator, as required by Harvard, since 1876, first in the person of Erastus Brainard (or Brainerd), succeeded the following year by Edward H. Greenleaf. During Greenleaf's leave of absence, in 1885, Sylvester Rosa Koehler took the position on a temporary basis, and in the same year Edward Robinson (1858–1931) became assistant curator of classical archaeology.[67] It was not until 1887, though, that the first two departments were established—the Department of Prints and the Department of Classical Archaeology (renamed the Department of Classical Antiquities in 1888)—with Koehler and Robinson as their respective founding curators.[68] The professionalization of the museum's staff had begun, as had the gradual division of its collections into departments.

In retrospect, the advent of professional staff at the Museum of Fine Arts reflected, in large measure, the growing emphasis that was placed during the late nineteenth century on the specialist rather than the generalist, on the professional rather than the amateur. Both Koehler and Robinson had received training in their respective disciplines before they arrived at the museum.[69] As professionals, their allegiance was not so much to Boston but to their fields of expertise, and their academic knowledge and professional skills were transferrable to other cities and collections. Their curatorial performance threw into sharp relief the older practice at the museum, whereby amateur trustees who happened to know something about art lent their knowledge to their local institutions. Perkins had been in some ways an exception, possessing specialized knowledge of Italian sculpture as well as a record of European publications, but nevertheless he was a self-trained scholar and functioned at the museum as a generalist.

As specialist curators rose in position and influence, the Committee on the Museum, which was essentially a group of generalist trustees, gradually lost its control over the institution's curatorial operations. More departments came into being: the department of Japanese art in 1890 and that of Egyptian art in 1902. In areas without departments, "keepers" were designated to take care of specific areas of the collection: the first keeper of paintings, for example, was appointed in 1902.[70] By 1903 the museum's annual report plainly conceded: "The Committee on the Museum makes no report for the past year, referring to the reports of the Director and those in charge of the various collections."[71] The committee's function, once central to the museum, had effectively been absorbed by a host of burgeoning curatorial departments. Institution-wide, too, the staff was beginning to carry out more of the day-to-day operations than ever before. In 1894, as if to mark this shift, the corporate name was changed from "the Trustees of the Museum of Fine Arts" to "the Museum of Fine Arts."[72] In 1902, for the very first time, the annual report listed the names of staff members in addition to those of trustees. And in 1903 the bimonthly *Museum of Fine*

Arts Bulletin was expressly created by the staff, not the trustees. That same year, Edward Robinson became director, the first time that a non-trustee assumed the position.

The late 1880s also saw signs of the museum's later rise to affluence. Although the institution was still burdened by yearly deficits and the considerable strain of the two building expansions, gifts and bequests of money—quite a few from deceased early supporters—began to increase the amount of funds available for acquisitions.[73] In 1899 the MFA recorded its first budgetary surplus, and at the dawn of the new century, Loring confidently declared that the institution possessed "collections of no mean value, with ampler means."[74] As funds grew, the museum was able to contemplate acquiring original works of art. In time, this new capability would lead to significant revisions of the institution's purpose and collecting focus.

In the Department of Classical Antiquities, this development unfolded in what later historians have come to call the "battle of the casts."[75] In the late 1880s the department began to acquire original works of great rarity and aesthetic value. Not surprisingly, when the Greek originals began to arrive at the museum, they gave rise to a heated controversy over the merit of plaster casts, which so far had formed the bulk of the department's holdings.

The chief criticism leveled against the plaster casts was that they were poor mechanical imitations, devoid of the aesthetic merit that the originals possessed. Those in favor of originals relied on their direct sensory appeal to invoke a standard of beauty, whereas the older view depended on an exhaustive display of examples to give visual instruction. Original works of antiquities inspired an aesthetic response, the argument went, whereas plaster casts merely taught. In Boston and elsewhere, the aestheticism of the fin de siècle was beginning to challenge the didacticism of midcentury. Much later, in 1912, Arthur Fairbanks, the museum's third director, described the epiphany felt by many in the 1890s: "What a revelation it was when the original Greek sculpture began to appear in the Museum. The casts became mere plaster without a soul and we recognized the magic of the craftsmen's hands, the beauty of texture and the nobility of form."[76] To be sure, around the turn of the century, some trustees continued to believe in the usefulness of plaster casts; one of them even asked if "an original statue [was] in any way more valuable than [a] cast."[77] The growing presence of the original works of antiquities—plus a new generation of trustees and staff as well as the institution's improving finances—pushed the issue to the fore, pitting the older attitude against the newer ethos.

In the mid-1890s a fierce debate unfolded just as the decade of spectacular acquisitions for the department began. Robinson, curator of classical antiquities and, after Loring's death in 1902, director, continued to believe in the pedagogical usefulness of plaster casts, but he faced growing opposition from those who embraced the cult of the original. Among them were the Bostonians Samuel Dennis Warren and Edward

Perry Warren, siblings and scions of a paper-manufacturing fortune. Samuel, a museum trustee since 1883, became the president of the board in 1901; his younger brother Edward collected classical antiquities from his home in Lewes, England, and supplied some of them to the museum in Boston.[78] In addition, two relatively new staff members vocally opposed Robinson: Benjamin Ives Gilman (1852–1933), who joined the museum in 1893 and became assistant director in 1902;[79] and Matthew Stewart Prichard (1865–1936), an English aesthete and classical scholar from Edward Warren's circle in Lewes, who assumed the newly created post of secretary to the director in 1902.[80] Gilman and Prichard charged that casts facilitated only a "scientific education" in the history of art, whereas the real education of art was "a spiritual training."[81] "Joy not knowledge is the aim," Prichard famously declared.[82] Eventually, the proponents of the original won the battle. A final break came in 1904, when the Committee on the Museum voted to discontinue further purchases for the cast collection. The institution had accepted the new hierarchy that placed plaster casts—and all other reproductions—far below originals. In frustration, Robinson resigned in 1905, after twenty years of service.[83]

Although a tempest in one department, the controversy and its aftermath nevertheless signaled an important shift in the museum's overall purpose in the early twentieth century. By rejecting casts and other forms of reproductions in favor of originals, the Museum of Fine Arts had essentially transformed its aim, intended audience, and manner of display. The new museum expected visitors to experience aesthetic pleasure, to become "the lover of the beautiful."[84] The early institution had sought to address the society at large—artists, artisans, teachers, industrial workers, and the general public—but the new museum wished instead "to create the amateur" out of, presumably, a narrower, culturally receptive portion of the public.[85] Under the new ethos, a smaller number of works of art, selected for their aesthetic superiority—as opposed to every piece belonging to the institution, as before—would be displayed and interpreted by trained curators. If the original museum had hoped to give its visitors, in the words of Charles Perkins, a "degree of aesthetic culture which, without passing the dividing line between general and special knowledge, will enable them to recognize and appreciate the beautiful in nature and in art,"[86] the new museum no longer hesitated to pass "the dividing line"; in fact, it consciously aspired to cross it.

Changed Institutions:
The Museum of Fine Arts and the Boston Athenæum

In the meantime, in 1899 the museum trustees had begun to search for a new site for the institution, and after purchasing a twelve-acre lot farther west on Huntington

Avenue, sold its land and building on Copley Square in 1902. (The museum continued to occupy the building until 1909.) By 1906, when the plans for the new building (designed by the Boston architect Guy Lowell [1870–1927]) were finalized, the Museum of Fine Arts was a changed institution. Its earlier didactic focus had been replaced by the ambition to collect original works of art of great rarity and outstanding aesthetic worth. It now envisioned itself as a temple of aesthetic contemplation, rather than a school of mass education. As the older, didactic ideal faded away, so did its founding generation: among its earliest trustees, Martin Brimmer died in 1896, Charles Loring in 1902, and at least eight others in the interval. By the early twentieth century, the changing of the guard was complete; as Loring observed in 1901, "the Museum . . . passes into the control of a younger generation."[87]

Other changes were also afoot. For one thing, the new bylaws adopted in 1906 clarified the division of curatorial authority over the collections. The ambiguous sharing of curatorial responsibilities practiced since the museum's early years—when Perkins led the Committee on the Museum and Loring was the curator—had become untenable in an institution with much larger collections and staff.[88] The new bylaws eliminated most of the former duties of the Committee on the Museum, leaving it with only a supervisory role over acquisitions and other expenditures.[89] Most significantly, the amended bylaws relieved the trustees of the "detailed supervision of the administration with which they [had] charged themselves since the foundation of the Museum."[90] With this change, the museum's administration was officially transferred from the trustees to the staff.

Having gained power, curators also set in motion, in 1906, a series of new measures. They introduced a new system of accession numbers for the museum's entire holdings and published the first of the illustrated *Handbook*s, which featured selected masterpieces from the collection rather than an exhaustive listing of every item belonging to the institution. Although several of the most outspoken proponents of originals soon left the museum, the new ideals that they had planted early in the century had taken root.[91] Never again would the Museum of Fine Arts question its focus on collecting original works of art, and curators would long be assured a paramount position as specialist arbiters of aesthetic standards, acquiring objects and interpreting them for their audience.

The building plan announced in 1906 manifested, on the one hand, all these changes taking place at the museum and, on the other, its struggle to come to terms with them (fig. 80). With its footprint projected to be almost triple that of the old structure in Copley Square, the new museum was not only divided into departments but also spatially separated into one floor of original works of art—aesthetic masterpieces—and another of reproductions and other didactic materials, adapting the two-tiered program advocated by Gilman.[92] With the confidence born of its new

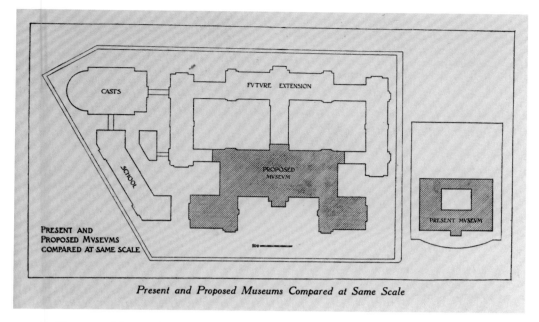

Present and Proposed Museums Compared at Same Scale

FIG. 80 "Present and Proposed Museums Compared at Same Scale." From *Museum of Fine Arts Bulletin* 4 (June 1907): 31

affluence, the MFA even hoped that it would eventually relegate its "collections of mechanical imitations" to more expressly didactic institutions—such as university museums—while itself becoming a collection of originals, "like the Louvre."[93] To be sure, the plan of 1906 retained some of the objects collected under its old aim— examples of applied arts in the Lawrence Room, for instance—and called for a separate hall for plaster casts, located away from the main building. Now, however, the specimens of industrial arts were no longer the central focus, and, as plaster casts fell further out of favor, the "basilica of casts" was never built. The museum had clearly renounced its role as a "public treasury of art" that was managed "as if primarily an agency of popular education."[94] Instead, the chief focus was squarely on the wonder of the original, the power to inspire: "the future Museum promises the city a new agency of spiritual well being; not dedicated to discipline of mind or direction of conscience, like a school or a church, but, like the shrine of the Muses whence it takes its name, sacred to the nurture of the imagination."[95]

In 1907 ground was broken on the museum's Huntington Avenue site. The deadline for completion of the new building was set for 1909.

Meanwhile, at the Athenæum on Beacon Street, the late nineteenth century was also a period of significant transformation, particularly for the Fine Arts Committee. The shrinking of the committee's spheres of influence—a process that had begun in

1868 with the closing of the sculpture gallery—essentially continued during the 1870s and 1880s, even as the committee energetically assisted the young Museum of Fine Arts for several of those years. The Athenæum's annual exhibitions ended in 1874, and much of its art collection left Beacon Street for the museum in 1876. Even its last form of assistance to the MFA—acquisition of objects for immediate deposit there— soon diminished to mere contributions of money, finally ending altogether in 1889. The death of Charles Perkins in 1886 dealt an irrevocable blow to the collaboration between the two institutions, and the subsequent deaths of the committee's four long-serving members—George Washington Wales in 1896, Samuel Eliot in 1898, Edward Newton Perkins in 1899, and James Elliot Cabot in 1903—propelled the alliance into twilight.

Most significantly, however, the shift in the museum's overall direction brought the collaboration to a close. As the museum shed its early identity as a didactic repository of reproductions and applied arts, many of the Athenæum's loans to it—plaster casts, copies of paintings, chromolithographs, photographs, and examples of the decorative arts—lost the centrality they had once enjoyed. Early in the new century, a considerable number of the Athenæum's deposits were "permanently withdrawn from exhibition" and either returned to Beacon Street or, along with some of the museum's own holdings, sent to a warehouse.[96] What had once been eagerly borrowed were now mere burdens, and with this downgrading came the inevitable question of cost. Robinson asked if the Athenæum might shoulder part of the storage fees; the Athenæum declined.[97]

As it happened, during these same years, the Athenæum was also contemplating a move to a new site. Although the entire building had been devoted to books since 1876, the library had once again run out of space. In 1901 the Athenæum purchased a lot on Arlington Street in the Back Bay, but attachment to the Beacon Street location proved too strong, and, after a highly public controversy, the decision to move was reversed in 1903.[98] Instead, the Athenæum decided to maximize the usable space in the existing building. Thus, possessing neither the desire nor the space for the return of its possessions from the museum, the Athenæum deposited some of the returned items—as well as other unwanted canvases from within the building—at schools and churches, with no expectation of their ever returning to Beacon Street.[99] Other objects were quietly sold to dealers.[100] The ebbing of the Athenæum's interest in art was palpable; in 1904, for example, when the institution transferred to the Worcester Art Museum a marble statue (*Shipwrecked Mother and Child*, by Edward Augustus Brackett [1818–1908]) that had long been on deposit at 10½ Beacon Street, Charles Knowles Bolton, the Athenæum's librarian since 1898, remarked aptly: "its removal reminds us that the Athenæum, once the art centre of Boston, no longer strives for eminence in a field so well occupied by the Museum of Fine Arts."[101]

The Fine Arts Committee's only duties—besides caring for the small art collection that still remained at the Athenæum—lay in the acquisition of visual reference materials such as books and photographs. Yet even the purchase of art books was increasingly carried out by the all-powerful Library Committee, and by the early twentieth century the Fine Arts Committee's reports had conceded that "the work of the committee has been more particularly described by the Librarian's Report."[102] The Athenæum stopped its subscription to the Arundel Society prints in 1897 but continued to purchase Braun photographs well into the twentieth century. By 1911 the photographs numbered more than thirty thousand, and the management of this elephantine compendium was clearly a problem.[103] In 1912, unwilling to add further to this bulk but unsure of its options, the Fine Arts Committee was reduced to begging the proprietors for some advice "as to future purchases."[104]

Finally, in 1914, in the midst of the first major renovation of the Beacon Street building, the Athenæum's bylaws were amended so that the Fine Arts Committee would no longer be required to present its report at the institution's annual meetings. In proposing the amendment, Charles Bolton soberly spelled out the effective end of the Fine Arts Committee as it had existed:

> Before the establishment of the Museum of Fine Arts the Athenæum maintained an Art Gallery, and the reports of the committee in charge were an important contribution to the history of the work of the Athenæum. At present the report is little more than a formality since the Librarian's printed report contains a review of the work of your Committee.
> I suggest therefore that the By-laws be amended so that Article 6 of Chapter I will instruct the Art Committee to present a report to the Proprietors whenever in their judgment it is desirable.[105]

By then, more than forty years had passed since the Museum of Fine Arts had been founded.

The museum moved into its new building in 1909, and the Athenæum completed its renovation—by adding two floors, among other things—in 1915. By the second decade of the century, the museum and the Athenæum had each shed its old identity and defined its new purpose. The details of the stormy battles fought earlier—particularly at the MFA—were gradually forgotten, since many of their protagonists had exited the stage.

In the natural development of institutions, old ideals are routinely replaced by new directions. In the museum's case, the process also entailed revisions of the institution's past. During the "battle of the casts," Gilman and Prichard asserted that the MFA's intention had always been to collect only original works of art. As we have seen, however, the early museum had clearly chosen to spend its limited funds on reproductions rather than on originals in order to achieve its didactic goals. Even when, in 1883, the

Committee on the Museum renounced parts of the institution's initial South Kensingtonian aspirations—"the application of the Fine Arts to industry"—the committee still believed, given the museum's continuing poverty, that it "should spend the greater part of the money available for purchases in buying reproductions."[106] A short generation later, Gilman and Prichard asserted that the museum's primary aim had always been "to collect and exhibit works of art," which, in their view, excluded all reproductions.[107] Seeking to strengthen their argument, they presented a revised version of the museum's early years. In 1905, when William Robert Ware, a museum trustee from 1875 to 1881, reminded Gilman and Prichard of the founders' modest wish to build a gallery of reproductions, the pair vehemently contradicted the old man. No such view had ever been recorded in "any utterance of our Board known to [them], whether oral, written, or printed," they protested.[108] Moreover, the pair dismissed the growth of the museum's cast collection as an episode "without essential connection with [the museum's] general plan" and concluded, with breathtaking certitude, that "to retain the cast collection would become a breach of the contract of the Corporation with the Commonwealth that created it."[109]

A generation after the Museum of Fine Arts was established, with its ideals shifting and most of the founding trustees gone, the memory of its initial ambition and travails was fast receding into the past. The passage of time always brings change, sometimes even partial erasure of the past. At the museum, however, an active revision of its earliest years had begun.

EPILOGUE

*I*N TOTAL, the Boston Athenæum deposited more than twelve hundred items at the Museum of Fine Arts, Boston.[1] This sizable loan clearly expressed the Athenæum's desire to help the young museum; this desire also prompted the Athenæum to offer its gallery, funds, and eager support to the other institution, especially during the latter's first six years.

What were the sources of this closeness? Self-preservation, on both sides, was certainly one. The museum, which began with no collection, no building, and modest funds, needed to depend on the kindness of others. On the part of the Athenæum, the Fine Arts Committee, its fate within its own institution becoming more and more tenuous in the late 1860s, wished to preserve at least a portion of its function in the proposed museum. Moreover, the Athenæum and the museum were siblings, sharing parentage and values, in the family of cultural and educational organizations that Boston's elite founded and funded with increasing zeal in the nineteenth century. Among the many institutions that made up this family, the Athenæum and the museum were particularly close because of their shared interest in art.

In reality, however, the museum's founding purpose incorporated a number of cultural prescriptions of midcentury origin about the role of art in society. The transatlantic impulse to link art and industry was one of these imperatives; the democratizing urge to make art available to a wider audience was another. These, and others, of the museum's aspirations were in fact quite different from the Athenæum's overall purpose, which had its roots in earlier times. But because the Fine Arts Committee, having effectively been severed from the main body of the Athenæum, had by the late 1860s lost much of its vision and vigor, it eagerly embraced even the newer ideas that defined the founding vision of the MFA. As it happened, this institutional relationship was reinforced further by the personal closeness between the brothers Edward Newton Perkins of the Athenæum and

Charles Callahan Perkins of the museum. Finally, as post–Civil War America sought to strengthen its support for art, the growing competition among American cities to establish institutions of art—or, more precisely, institutions of art education—united the two Boston entities all the more strongly in their joint endeavor.

By the end of the nineteenth century, however, the collaboration had run its course. When, after 1900, the focus of the Museum of Fine Arts shifted from the didacticism of its early years to the acquisition and display of the original and the rare, many crucial parts of its earlier history were selectively ignored, as was the Athenæum's close former association with it. Much of the Athenæum's contribution to the MFA had been intangible and was therefore the more easily forgotten. As for the Athenæum's tangible offerings—loans—to the museum, they might have been remembered better and longer if they had taken the form of the kinds of objects that are today deemed worthy of the great institution that the Museum of Fine Arts has become. Instead of such objects—say, a rare ancient Greek vase, a painting by Jean-François Millet, or a screen from the Edo period in Japan—the Athenæum purchased mostly plaster casts and decorative arts, which the younger institution had desired in its early years but which sat, after 1900, increasingly outside its new collecting focus.

A small number of the Athenæum's deposits at the museum began to return as early as the late 1880s, but the majority stayed at the museum into the twentieth century. As the MFA changed and taste shifted in the new century, many of the physical signs of the Athenæum's once ardent desire to help the young institution came to feel increasingly like an inconvenient inheritance. As the twentieth century wore on, some of the Athenæum's objects remained on view, and a few categories of objects even rose in their value to the museum, such as nineteenth-century American works. The rest of the Athenæum's deposits, however, became irrelevant to the museum for one reason or another and disappeared, one by one.

Much of the oak paneling of the Lawrence Room, for example, was pronounced to be "modern" or fake soon after the museum moved to its new building in 1909. The room remained at the museum until 1930, but when the Athenæum, still the legal owner, was asked that year to take back the room's panels and fittings, it quietly sold them to a dealer. Most of the reproductions clearly fell outside the museum's new aesthetic ambition, and many of the once coveted copies of Old Master paintings were sold, given away, or returned to the Athenæum. As for the plaster casts, the sad end came in 1933, when the museum disposed of the Athenæum's forty-five casts with its permission; those belonging to the Athenæum were "not wanted at the [Athenæum] Library."[2] Toward midcentury, at the height of modernism, few people saw any aesthetic, educational, or historical merit in preserving plaster casts, and the MFA was in the process of discarding many of the casts that had once been the centerpiece of its Copley Square building.[3] At about the same time, the twenty-eight surviving examples of Islamic and Indian weapons—the only remnants of the original Lawrence collection—were deemed too ethnological and returned without fanfare, in 1942, to the Athenæum. Lacking purpose in a library, they were immediately placed on long-term deposit at the Peabody Museum in Salem, Massachusetts. Only the key to the storeroom on Pearl Street, where much of the original Lawrence collection burned in 1872, remained at the Athenæum.

As for the Castellani collection, after several decades in storage, some of the carved wooden pieces—many of which are now thought to be modern forgeries—were returned quietly to the Athenæum in 1953, and most of the Italian bronze objects were sold at auction in the 1970s. In that decade, the Athenæum's financial exigencies also forced the sale of many of the institution's iconic nineteenth-century American paintings and other objects, some of them, ironically, to the Museum of Fine Arts. Only the Castellani textiles, still owned by the Athenæum, have remained at the museum, attesting to the aspirations that had guided both institutions in the 1870s.

In 1928, more than half a century after the museum opened in the Back Bay, the Athenæum installed in its building a plaque describing its history. On it was engraved a sentence that claimed, with some inaccuracy, that the Athenæum gallery formed "*the* nucleus" of the Museum of Fine Arts.[4] As we have seen, however, it is clear that the Athenæum's gallery had been only one of many nuclei. By the time the museum mounted, in 1947, a special exhibition of the Athenæum's deposits there, "Boston Athenæum in the Museum of Fine Arts," these essentially permanent loans were a long-settled historical fact requiring few explanations, unquestioned as to their original purpose and meaning.[5] By then, the museum and the Athenæum had each evolved into an institution distinctly different from the other, each with collecting areas and audiences of its own. The details of the once close connection between the two had been all but forgotten.

At several crucial moments, the Athenæum played a critical role in bringing the MFA into existence and ensuring its survival. Beyond the ample logistical support that the Athenæum gave the nascent museum, the historical importance of the Athenæum's contribution lies in its function as a kind of bridge. As the museum's earliest institutional partner, the Athenæum was a bridge in Boston between the art gallery of early nineteenth-century origin that upheld standards of taste for the privileged few to the educational institution that sought to make art available—and useful—to a much larger segment of the population. In addition, the Athenæum, founded on the all-encompassing Enlightenment ideal of learning, brought into existence an institution that increasingly embraced a more specialized, compartmentalized form of knowledge. With this shift came the rise of the specialist in place of the generalist. Even while the paternalistic civic-mindedness of Boston's elite continued to support the city's innumerable cultural institutions—of which the museum was one—the actual running of the organizations shifted from the hands of the local amateur doing good for his native city into those of the cosmopolitan professional with specialized training. Further, because of its timing in history, the collaboration of the Athenæum and the museum also made manifest the transformation of America's attitude toward art, from one insecure about its thin aesthetic soil—so that virtually any art was welcomed—to one confident of its taste, knowledge, and immense purchasing power. Finally, by helping the museum survive in its early years, the Athenæum played a role in enabling the MFA's later shift in focus from the didacticism of mid-nineteenth-century origin to the aestheticism of the twentieth century. The museum's transformation was part of the larger evolution of the form and ethos of the art museum in nineteenth-century Europe and America, from a privileged agent of taste to a more egalitarian site of education, and eventually to a temple of beauty dedicated to the collecting and display of masterpieces as well as scholarship.

The Athenæum's contribution to the Museum of Fine Arts, however, must be viewed in its proper place: the Athenæum can make only a modest claim to having laid a foundation for the eventual success of the museum. In its collaboration, the Athenæum was guided not so much by a clear vision as by kindly goodwill toward the newest member of the city's cultural family, while at the same time navigating through its own evolution and the period's changing ideas about art, education, and art museums. At each crucial juncture, the trustees of the Athenæum and the MFA acted to the best of their judgment and within the constraints of their circumstances. Not surprisingly, all of their dreams did not come true. But the humble museum they launched survived and prospered. Without fully seeing the historical significance or the future consequences of their actions, this group of generous Bostonians nevertheless brought the museum into this world "with éclat."

The Incorporators of the Museum of Fine Arts, Boston, 1870

The incorporators are listed in alphabetical order.

"Other Institutional Affiliations" lists organizations with which each incorporator associated himself. If an individual was an officer or a lecturer at an institution, these capacities are indicated in the parentheses following the organizations' names.

"Corporation member" at Massachusetts Institute of Technology is equivalent to "trustee" at other institutions.

For sources consulted in addition to those given for individual incorporators, see the list at the end of the appendix.

JOHN TISDALE BRADLEE
Boston, MA 1837–1908 Boston, MA
No academic degrees

John Tisdale Bradlee was a wealthy cotton merchant who retired at a young age.

Hailing from an old New England family, he prepared for a career in business at Boston's Chauncy Hall School. In his youth, he engaged in the Southern trade as a merchant and shipper of cotton, which was so profitable that he was able to retire from active business in his twenties, in the early 1860s. He married Sarah Elizabeth Goddard in 1861 and built two contiguous houses on the desirable waterside of Beacon Street (just west of the Public Garden). He was active in local politics in the 1860s, remained president of the New England National Bank for almost five decades, and served on the boards of several charitable and cultural institutions. Other details of his life, however, are difficult to ascertain.

In 1870 the thirty-three-year-old Bradlee was the youngest member of the MFA's founding board. His enormous wealth and involvement in municipal politics likely recommended him to the body. He resigned from the board in 1883.

BA: proprietor, 1896–1908
MFA: trustee, 1870–1883

OTHER INSTITUTIONAL AFFILIATIONS
Boston City Hospital (president); Boston Public Library (trustee); Home for Aged Men (president); Mount Auburn Cemetery Corporation (president, trustee); New England National Bank (president)

PUBLIC OFFICES HELD
Boston Common Council (1864); Boston Board of Aldermen (1869)

SELECTED SOURCES
Oliver Ayer Roberts, *History of the Military Company of the Massachusetts, Now Called the Ancient and Honorable Artillery Company of Massachusetts, 1637–1888*, 3 vols. (Boston: A. Mudge, 1895–1901), 3:313–314; obituary, *Boston Evening Transcript*, May 15, 1908.

MARTIN BRIMMER
Boston, MA 1829–1896 Boston, MA
Harvard University A.B. 1849

Martin Brimmer was a much-admired philanthropist, legislator, and art collector.

He was a scion of an illustrious Boston family distinguished for its public service and involvement in the arts. He was named for his father, who was a state representative (1838–1839) and mayor of Boston (1843–1844); his uncle George Watson Brimmer was a noted collector and philanthropist (and a founding member of the Athenæum's Fine Arts Committee). In 1860 Martin Brimmer married Mary Ann Timmins of Boston.

After graduation from Harvard, Brimmer went to Europe for study and travel, returning to Boston in 1853. From then on, he assumed a prominent role in his native city's philanthropy, politics, and culture, a path befitting his pedigree, social position, and interests. He was a benefactor of innumerable cultural, educational, and charitable organizations, ranging from older, well-established institutions such as Harvard and the Athenæum to more recent, reformist enterprises such as the Boston Provident Association, which offered financial aid to the city's poor, and the Boston Cooperative Building Company, which provided affordable housing to the working class. In the 1850s and 1860s he was also active in politics: he supported the New England Emigrant Aid Company, a Massachusetts organization that sought to keep Kansas a free territory by promoting emigration to it, and also served in the state legislature. But his lasting interest remained art. One of the first Americans to collect the work of the French Barbizon painters, especially Jean-François Millet, Brimmer was a friend and patron to many artists as well as an enthusiastic student of archaeology, particularly of Egypt.

Brimmer's considerable stature in Boston as a philanthropist, connoisseur, and guardian of the city's cultural tradition made him the preëminent choice to serve as the MFA's first president.

BA: proprietor, 1849–1896; trustee, 1854–1861
MFA: trustee and president, 1870–1896

OTHER INSTITUTIONAL AFFILIATIONS
American Academy of Arts and Sciences; Boston Cooperative Building Company (president); Boston Farm School (director); Boston Provident Association (director); Harvard University (fellow, overseer); Massachusetts General Hospital (trustee); Massachusetts Historical Society; Massachusetts Institute of Technology; New England Emigrant Aid Company (executive committee, treasurer); Perkins Institution for the Blind (president); Provident Institution for Savings (trustee), Trinity Church (vestryman)

PUBLIC OFFICES HELD
Massachusetts representative (1859–1861); Massachusetts senator (1864); presidential elector (1876)

SELECTED SOURCES
Samuel Eliot, "Memoir of Martin Brimmer," *Proceedings of the Massachusetts Historical Society*, 2nd ser., 10 (April 1896): 586–595; George Silsbee Hale, "Memoir of Hon. Martin Brimmer, A.B.," *Publications of the Colonial Society of Massachusetts* 3 (January 1897): 337–347; Edward Waldo Emerson, "Martin Brimmer," in

The Early Years of the Saturday Club, 1855–1870, ed. Emerson (Boston: Houghton Mifflin Company, 1918), 366–375; Mark Anthony DeWolfe Howe, *John Jay Chapman and His Letters* (Boston: Houghton Mifflin Company, 1937), 56–57; Wayne Andrews, "Martin Brimmer: The First Gentleman of Boston," *Archives of American Art Journal* 4 (October 1964): 1–4.

CHARLES WILLIAM ELIOT

Boston, MA 1836–1926 Mount Desert Island, ME

Harvard University A.B. 1853, M.D. and LL.D. 1909 (both honorary)

Charles William Eliot was a scientist, educator, and Harvard University's president from 1869 to 1909.

He was a scion of an old and distinguished Boston family. His father, Samuel Atkins Eliot, was a state representative (1834–1837), mayor of Boston (1837–1839), and treasurer of Harvard University (1842–1853). His mother, Mary Lyman, was the daughter of the wealthy merchant Theodore Lyman and sister of Theodore Lyman Jr., also mayor of Boston (1834–1836). In 1858 Eliot married Ellen Derby Peabody, daughter of the minister of King's Chapel; after her death in 1869, he married, in 1877, Grace Mellen Hopkinson of Lowell, Massachusetts.

After his graduation from Harvard, Eliot chose teaching as his profession. He taught mathematics and chemistry at Harvard from 1858 to 1863 before spending two years in Europe, where he investigated its educational systems and furthered his training as a chemist. When he returned to Boston, he taught analytical chemistry at the newly established Massachusetts Institute of Technology from 1865 to 1869. Both Eliot and the school's founder and president, William Barton Rogers, recognized the need to reform higher education, especially to reconcile the perceived gap between the traditional academic endeavor based on classical studies and the real world of commerce and industry. In 1869 Eliot was appointed president of Harvard, a position he would keep for the next four decades. A superb administrator, he transformed Harvard from a provincial college into a modern, national university, committed to academic excellence, research, and preparing its students for active future.

Eliot resigned from his MIT professorship in July 1869 and became Harvard's president in October, four months before the MFA's incorporation. He brought to the museum not only his intellectual and social stature and educational vision but also Harvard's unequivocal support for it. He became the longest-serving member of the founding board. Among fellow incorporators was his first cousin Samuel Eliot.

BA: proprietor, 1858–1926

MFA: trustee, 1870–1926

OTHER INSTITUTIONAL AFFILIATIONS

American Academy of Arts and Sciences; American Social Hygiene Committee (president); Carnegie Foundation for the Advancement of Teaching (trustee); Harvard Musical Association; Harvard University (president, overseer); Lowell Institute (lecturer); Massachusetts Historical Society; Massachusetts Institute of Technology (professor); National Committee for Mental Hygiene (vice president); National Education Association (president); Rockefeller Foundation (trustee)

SELECTED SOURCES

"William Charles Eliot," *Proceedings of the Massachusetts Historical Society*, 3rd ser., 60 (1926–1927): 2–15; Edward H. Cotton, *The Life of Charles W. Eliot* (Boston: Small, Maynard, and Company, 1926); Theodore W. Richards, "Charles William Eliot," in *Later Years of the Saturday Club, 1870–1920*, ed. Mark Anthony DeWolfe Howe (Boston: Houghton Mifflin Company, 1927), 3–13; Henry James, *Charles W. Eliot, President of Harvard University, 1869–1909* (Boston: Houghton Mifflin Company, 1930); Hugh Hawkins, *Between Harvard and America: The Educational Leadership of Charles W. Eliot* (New York: Oxford University Press, 1972).

SAMUEL ELIOT

Boston, MA 1821–1898 Beverly Farms, MA

Harvard University A.B. 1839, A.M. 1842; Trinity College (Hartford, CT) A.M. 1857 (honorary); Columbia College LL.D. 1863 (honorary); Harvard University LL.D. 1880 (honorary)

Samuel Eliot was a widely admired historian, educator, reformer, and philanthropist.

He was a scion of an old and distinguished Boston family that had produced many scholars and politicians. His grandfather had endowed the Eliot professorship of Greek literature at Harvard, and his uncle Samuel Atkins Eliot was mayor of Boston (1837–1839). On his mother, Margaret Boies Bradford's, side, he was a descendant of William Bradford, the second governor of the Plymouth Colony. In 1853 he married Emily Marshall Otis of Boston.

After graduation from Harvard in 1839 and travel in Europe in 1841–1844, Eliot spent a decade writing books on the histories of Rome and the United States, which were published in the early 1850s. Devout, reform-minded, and independently wealthy, Eliot devoted the rest of his life to philanthropy, especially to the field of education. He was both a teacher and an administrator. He taught disadvantaged children and adults in Boston before becoming, in 1856, a professor of history at Trinity College in Hartford, Connecticut; he later served as the college's president. After his return to Boston in the late 1860s, he held several public offices in the city's educational agencies, including that of the headmaster of Boston Girls' High and Normal School, the superintendent of Boston Public Schools, and a member of the Boston School Committee. Endowed with wealth, social position, sense of duty, and oratorical gift—in an era that clearly appreciated these attributes—Eliot was also trustee and benefactor of an astonishing number of philanthropic, educational, and cultural organizations.

Eliot brought to the MFA's founding board his considerable stature and wealth as well as his wide influence in the city's educational community. Among the MFA incorporators Eliot could count his first cousin Charles William Eliot and his cousin and close friend from youth Charles Callahan Perkins.

BA: proprietor, 1859–1898; trustee, 1866–1898; president, 1880–1889
MFA: trustee, 1870–1898

OTHER INSTITUTIONAL AFFILIATIONS
American Academy of Arts and Sciences; American Social Science Association (president); Boston Episcopal Charitable Society (president); Church of the Advent (corporation member, vestryman); Harvard Musical Association; Harvard University (lecturer, overseer); Lowell Institute (lecturer); Massachusetts General Hospital (trustee, board chairman); Massachusetts Historical Society (member-at-large of the council); Massachusetts School for the Feeble Minded (president); Perkins Institution for the Blind (trustee, president); St. Paul's School, Concord, NH (trustee); Trinity Church (vestryman); Trinity College, Hartford, CT (professor, president)

PUBLIC OFFICES HELD
Headmaster, Boston Girls' High and Normal School (1872–1876); superintendent of Boston Public Schools (1878–1880); Boston School Committee (1885–1888)

SELECTED SOURCES
Henry Williamson Haynes, "Memoir of Samuel Eliot, LL.D.," *Proceedings of the Massachusetts Historical Society*, 2nd ser., 13 (March 1900): 105–126; Barrett Wendell, "Samuel Eliot," *Proceedings of the American Academy of Arts and Sciences* 34 (June 1899): 646–651; Michael Wentworth, *"Aye, fold thy mantle round thy tiny form . . . ,"* in his *Look Again: Essays on the Boston Athenæum's Art Collections* (Boston: Boston Athenæum, 2003), 153–157.

GEORGE BARRELL EMERSON

Wells, ME (then part of Massachusetts) 1797–1881 Brookline, MA

Harvard University A.B. 1817, LL.D. 1859 (honorary)

George Barrell Emerson was a widely respected educator and naturalist, a lifelong teacher who was instrumental in the state's education reforms of the early to mid-nineteenth century.

Born in Maine the son of a Harvard-trained physician, Emerson graduated from Harvard in 1817. After college, he began his long teaching career as the first headmaster of the newly founded English Classical School (later renamed the English High School). He married twice. His first wife was Olivia Buckminster, whose brother was the Reverend Joseph Stevens Buckminster, one of the Athenæum founders. After her death, Emerson married, in 1834, Mary Rotch Fleeming of New Bedford, Massachusetts, who was an aunt of Benjamin Smith Rotch, a fellow MFA incorporator.

One generation older than most of the other MFA incorporators, Emerson was at once a classical scholar, educator, and scientist, with a particular interest in botany. Dedicated to education, especially public education of all people, Emerson was active in a variety of educational reforms: he was an associate of Horace Mann, the founding secretary of the state's board of education; was involved with the establishment of MIT; and, after the Civil War, took part in the Educational Commission that sought to educate former slaves. He was also a respected botanist, having conducted extensive fieldwork of New England flora and served as the founding president of the Boston Society of Natural History. His was a career that successfully straddled the fields of science, education, and institution building, and he knew many of nineteenth-century Boston's illustrious figures.

In 1870 the seventy-three-year-old Emerson was the oldest among the MFA incorporators. His stature as teacher and scientist, as well as his long experience in organizing and managing educational institutions, likely recommended him to the MFA's founding board.

BA: proprietor, 1845–1881

MFA: trustee, 1870–1876

OTHER INSTITUTIONAL AFFILIATIONS

American Academy of Arts and Sciences; American Institute of Instruction (president); Boston Society of Natural History (founding member, president); Harvard Musical Association; King's Chapel (warden, vestryman); Lowell Institute (lecturer); Massachusetts Historical Society; Massachusetts Institute of Technology (corporation member); Perkins Institution for the Blind (trustee)

PUBLIC OFFICE HELD

Boston School Committee (1847–1848)

SELECTED SOURCES

"George B. Emerson," *Proceedings of the American Academy of Arts and Sciences* 16 (May 1880–June 1881): 427–429; Robert C. Waterston, "Memoir of George Barrell Emerson, LL.D.," *Proceedings of Massachusetts Historical Society* 20 (1882–1883): 232–259.

WILLIAM ENDICOTT JR.

Beverly, MA 1826–1914 Boston, MA

Williams College A.M. 1868 (honorary); Harvard University A.M. 1888 (honorary)

William Endicott Jr. was a wealthy merchant, known for his business sagacity and moral integrity, who developed extensive connections with prominent Bostonians during his long life.

Born into an old New England family as a son of a respectable dry goods merchant in Beverly, Massachusetts, Endicott was bright but could not attend Harvard for health reasons and chose a career in business. In 1857 he married Annie Thorndike of Boston.

Endicott rose quickly in business and became, in 1851, a partner in the firm of C. F. Hovey and Company in Boston, an importer and retailer of dry goods. With offices in New York and Paris, the firm's store in downtown Boston became an innovator in department-store-style merchandising. As Endicott's wealth grew, he served many of the city's financial, cultural, and charitable institutions as trustee and treasurer. He also took active interest in politics, local and national, even though he held no political office. (Although he was not an abolitionist himself, he lent money to the abolitionist William Lloyd Garrison and participated in the effort to keep Kansas free of slavery.) He considered himself a simple businessman, but he was well-traveled, intelligent, and interested in the arts, and associated closely with many of Boston's cultural leaders. He received honorary master's degrees from Williams College and Harvard University, and was elected a member of the Saturday Club—whose membership consisted of Boston's leading intellectuals—a rare distinction for a man of commerce.

Endicott brought to the MFA's founding board his proven fiscal acumen, wealth, and connections with both the commercial and intellectual communities of Boston.

BA: proprietor, 1859–1914
MFA: trustee, 1870–1907; president pro tempore, 1896–1901

OTHER INSTITUTIONAL AFFILIATIONS
Boston Children's Hospital (trustee); Harvard Musical Association; Harvard University (overseer); Industrial School for Crippled and Deformed Children (vice president); King's Chapel (vestryman); Massachusetts General Hospital (trustee); Massachusetts Historical Society; Massachusetts Institute of Technology (treasurer, corporation member); New England Historic Genealogical Society (president); New England Trust Company (president); Perkins Institution for the Blind (trustee, treasurer); Provident Institution for Savings (trustee); Suffolk Savings Bank (president)

SELECTED SOURCES
Obituary, *Boston Evening Transcript*, November 7, 1914; Henry Lee Higginson, [Tribute], *Proceedings of the Massachusetts Historical Society*, 2nd ser., 48 (November 1914): 76–78; Robert S. Rantoul, "Memoir of William Endicott," *Proceedings of the Massachusetts Historical Society*, 2nd ser., 48 (January 1915): 243–252; "William Endicott, Jr.," in *Later Years of the Saturday Club, 1870–1920*, ed. Mark Anthony DeWolfe Howe (Boston: Houghton Mifflin Company, 1927), 201–204.

HENRY PURKITT KIDDER
Boston, MA 1823–1886 New York, NY
No academic degrees

Henry Purkitt Kidder was a wealthy investment banker influential in the city's business community. He was also an avid art collector.

Son of a fish and meat inspector, Kidder was educated at the English High School in Boston and thereafter achieved success by dint of his business acumen and hard work. He married twice: in 1847 he wed Caroline Whitmarsh Archbald of Hopkinton, Massachusetts; and in 1883 Elizabeth Huidekoper of Meadville, Pennsylvania.

After stints at a grocery store and a railroad company, in 1843 he joined the banking office of Nathaniel Thayer, where Kidder's talent and dedication led to his meteoric rise. In 1858 he became a partner and in 1865, with several partners, established his own banking and investment concern, Kidder, Peabody and Company. The firm prospered and became, in 1886, the American representative of Baring Brothers and Company of

London. One of Boston's leading businessmen, he also took an active interest in the arts and was benefactor to a remarkable range of cultural, educational, and philanthropic organizations, serving many of them as trustee and treasurer. His stature and influence in Boston were such that, in 1881, he became the first non-graduate ever to be elected to Harvard's Board of Overseers. An ardent art collector with large means, he owned European prints, contemporary French and American paintings (Bonnat, Corot, Diaz, Inness, and Troyon, among others), and Greek and Etruscan antiquities. He exhibited many of these works at the MFA, and a number of them later entered the museum's collection.

Kidder brought to the MFA's founding board his financial acumen as well as considerable influence in the city's business community. His personal wealth, public spirit, and sizable art collection also likely recommended him to the board.

BA: proprietor, 1857–1886
MFA: trustee and treasurer, 1870–1886

OTHER INSTITUTIONAL AFFILIATIONS
Adams-Nervine Asylum (president); American Academy of Arts and Sciences (treasurer); American Unitarian Association (president); Boston Art Club; Children's Mission (president); Harvard Musical Association; Harvard University (overseer); Massachusetts General Hospital (trustee); Massachusetts Institute of Technology (corporation member); Young Men's Christian Association (board chairman)

SELECTED SOURCES
"Henry Purkitt Kidder," *Proceedings of the American Academy of Arts and Science* 21 (May 1885–May 1886): 527–532; "Henry P. Kidder's Will," *New York Times*, February 7, 1886.

OTIS NORCROSS
Boston, MA 1811–1882 Boston, MA
No academic degrees

Otis Norcross was a prosperous merchant and local politician who exerted a powerful influence on local politics and other municipal affairs. He was mayor of Boston in 1867.

Born the son of a successful dry goods merchant, he was educated at the English High School in Boston. In 1835 he married Lucy Ann Lane of Boston.

Having begun his commercial career at a young age, Norcross inherited the firm of Otis Norcross and Company when his father died in 1827. An importer and dealer of ceramics, glassware, and pottery, the company thrived under the partnership of Norcross and other family members. Widely respected for his integrity, fiscal acumen, and public spirit, he helped establish several charitable institutions for the disadvantaged and helped organize the city's effort to deliver medical care to the poor. He held many public offices in the 1860s, and in those capacities he was involved with the filling of the Back Bay and other endeavors to improve the city physically. He retired from active business in 1867 but continued to participate in the city's affairs and served as a trustee and treasurer to many philanthropic institutions.

Norcross brought to the MFA's founding board his extensive connection to, and influence on, the city's political structure and business community. He was instrumental in securing a parcel of land for the MFA in the Back Bay.

BA: proprietor, 1872–1882
MFA: trustee, 1870–1882

OTHER INSTITUTIONAL AFFILIATIONS
Boston City Hospital (president); Boston Society of Natural History; Home for Aged Men; Home for Aged Women; Massachusetts Hospital Life Insurance Company (vice president); Massachusetts Institute

of Technology (corporation member); Mount Auburn Cemetery Corporation (trustee); New England Historic Genealogical Society; New England Trust Company (president); Young Men's Christian Association (treasurer)

PUBLIC OFFICES HELD
House of Industry, South Boston (director, 1856); Boston School Committee (1858–1861); Boston Board of Aldermen (member, 1862–1865; chairman, 1864–1865); mayor of Boston (1867); Massachusetts Governor's Council (1869); Boston Overseers of the Poor (treasurer)

SELECTED SOURCES
Mayors of Boston: An Illustrated Epitome of Who the Mayors Have Been and What They Have Done (Boston: State Street Trust Company, 1914), 27–29; *Boston Evening Transcript*, September 6, 1882.

FRANCIS EDWARD PARKER
Portsmouth, NH 1821–1886 Boston, MA
Harvard University A.B. 1841, LL.B. 1845

Francis Edward Parker was a brilliant and cultivated trust lawyer whose clients and associations included many prominent Bostonians and the institutions they supported.

He was born in Portsmouth, New Hampshire, the son of a Unitarian minister; his mother was a daughter of the state's chief justice. He never married.

After graduation from Harvard and European travel, Parker studied law at Harvard and began his legal career with James Elliot Cabot (a fellow MFA trustee, representing the Athenæum). Parker then worked with Richard Henry Dana Jr., a well-connected and prominent lawyer, before establishing himself as an independent attorney specializing in the management of trust estates. He quickly achieved professional prominence and financial success. Known as a man of intellectual sophistication, taste, and moral conviction, he developed close relationships with many members of Boston's upper class. He was benefactor to both high-minded cultural institutions (such as the Athenæum and Harvard) and many of the charitable societies of Boston that catered to the disadvantaged. He was an original member and longtime officer of the Boston Provident Association, a private charitable organization founded in 1851 to give monetary aid to the city's poor, and served as an elected member of the Boston Overseers of the Poor in the 1860s. He served one term as a state senator in 1865 but thereafter declined all public offices.

Parker brought to the MFA's founding board not only his legal expertise and wealth but also his broad knowledge of the city's wealthy individuals and its cultural institutions.

BA: proprietor, 1856–1886; trustee, 1856–1876
MFA: trustee, 1870–1885

OTHER INSTITUTIONAL AFFILIATIONS
Boston Provident Association (vice president); Harvard University (overseer); Massachusetts Historical Society; Provident Institution for Savings (trustee, vice president)

PUBLIC OFFICES HELD
Boston School Committee (1855–1858, 1861); Boston Overseers of the Poor (1864–1867); Massachusetts senator (1865)

SELECTED SOURCES
"Funeral of Francis E. Parker," *Boston Evening Transcript*, January 21, 1886; "Tributes to Francis E. Parker," *Proceedings of the Massachusetts Historical Society*, 2nd ser., 2 (February 1886): 208–216; Edward Bangs, "Memoir of the Hon. Francis Edward Parker," *Proceedings of the Massachusetts Historical Society*, 2nd ser., 3 (February 1887): 247–252.

CHARLES CALLAHAN PERKINS

Boston, MA 1823–1886 Windsor, VT

Harvard University A.B. 1843, A.M. (no date)

Charles Callahan Perkins was a well-known critic, patron, and connoisseur of both the visual and musical arts. He was also a philanthropist active in establishing and supporting organizations dedicated to those arts.

He was a scion of a wealthy mercantile family known for its patronage of Boston's cultural institutions in the first half of the nineteenth century. The family's involvement was particularly deep with the Boston Athenæum: his grandfather James Perkins and great-uncle Thomas Handasyd Perkins were two of the most significant benefactors to the institution. In 1855 he married Frances Davenport Bruen of New York and Newport, Rhode Island.

After his graduation from Harvard, Perkins spent about two decades in Europe (in three installments) before returning to Boston in 1869. Throughout his life, his chief interests remained the fine arts and music. He initially studied those disciplines in various European capitals, but he never succeeded in establishing himself as a professional painter or composer. Instead, his greatest distinction lay in his work as an art historian: in the late 1860s he was awarded the *Légion d'honneur* by the French government and made the first American member of the Académie des Beaux-Arts, both on the merit of his publications on the history of Italian sculpture. In addition, he made valuable contributions to his native city by organizing and supporting several institutions of art and music. A connoisseur as well as a reformer, he also took an active part, in both official and private capacities, in the state's effort to reform art education during the 1870s and 1880s.

A well-established art historian with European credentials, Perkins brought to the MFA's founding board his long-standing passion for establishing an institution of art in Boston, his extensive knowledge of art history, and his considerable social standing and connections in both Boston and abroad, all of which made him the leading visionary among the incorporators. Samuel Eliot, also an incorporator, was his cousin.

Perkins's life is discussed in greater detail in chapter 2.

BA: proprietor, 1845–1886

MFA: trustee, 1870–1886; honorary director, 1876–1886

OTHER INSTITUTIONAL AFFILIATIONS

Académie des Beaux-Arts, Institut de France; American Academy of Arts and Sciences; American Social Science Association; Boston Art Club (president); Handel and Haydn Society (president); Harvard Musical Association (director, vice president); Harvard University (lecturer); Lowell Institute (lecturer); Massachusetts Historical Society (member-at-large of the council); Trinity College, Hartford, CT (lecturer)

PUBLIC OFFICE HELD

Boston School Committee (1872–1884)

SELECTED SOURCES

Samuel Eliot, "Tribute to Charles C. Perkins," *Proceedings of the Massachusetts Historical Society*, 2nd ser., 3 (October 1886): 59–61; Martin Brimmer, "Charles Callahan Perkins," *Proceedings of the American Academy of Arts and Sciences* 22 (May–December 1886): 534–539; Samuel Eliot, "Memoir of Charles Callahan Perkins, A.M.," *Proceedings of the Massachusetts Historical Society*, 2nd ser., 3 (February 1888): 223–246; "Charles Callahan Perkins," in *Later Years of the Saturday Club, 1870–1920*, ed. Mark Anthony DeWolfe Howe (Boston: Houghton Mifflin Company, 1927), 17–20.

WILLIAM BARTON ROGERS

Philadelphia, PA 1802–1882 Boston, MA

College of William and Mary LL.D. 1859 (honorary);

Harvard University LL.D. 1866 (honorary)

William Barton Rogers was a geologist and educator from Virginia who founded the Massachusetts Institute of Technology in 1861 and served as its first president.

His was a family of scientists: his father was professor of natural philosophy and chemistry at the College of William and Mary, and all four of his sons became prominent scientists. After attending the college (although it is unclear if he received a degree at this point), Rogers began his career as a professor: first of chemistry and physics at William and Mary and later of natural philosophy at the University of Virginia. From 1835 to 1848 he was state geologist of Virginia. Dissatisfied with the condition of higher education in science, however, Rogers and his brother Henry devised, in 1846, a plan to establish a polytechnic school that would emphasize practical knowledge, laboratory practice, and research as important components of scientific studies. The brothers proposed the plan to the Lowell Institute in Boston, but no school materialized at that time.

In 1849 he married Emma Savage of Boston; she was a daughter of James Savage, a wealthy banker and well-known antiquarian. The couple moved to Boston in 1853. A respected scientist, dedicated teacher, and inspiring orator, Rogers remained an independent scientist while continuing his efforts to reform higher education in science. The school Rogers envisioned eventually won strong support from the city's business community that was eager to establish, on the newly created land of the Back Bay, a school that would bring benefit to industry. With Rogers at the helm, the Massachusetts Institute of Technology was chartered in 1861 and opened its doors in 1865. MIT's curriculum emphasized practical application of scientific knowledge, specialization, and technological innovation, presenting a new model for the teaching of science.

In the winter of 1869–1870 Rogers was in Philadelphia, recuperating from ill health. (He officially resigned from the institute's presidency in May 1870 but returned to the post in 1879.) But his stature in Boston as the founder of an innovative educational institution, as well as his commitment to educational reform that would make knowledge useful, likely made him an important addition to the MFA's founding board.

BA: No official affiliation

MFA: trustee, 1870–1882

OTHER INSTITUTIONAL AFFILIATIONS

American Academy of Arts and Sciences (corresponding secretary); American Social Science Association (president); Association of American Geologists and Naturalists (chairman); Boston Society of Natural History; Lowell Institute (lecturer); Massachusetts Institute of Technology (founder, president); National Academy of Science (president); Perkins Institution for the Blind (trustee); Thursday Evening Scientific Club (president)

SELECTED SOURCES

"William Barton Rogers," *Proceedings of the American Academy of Arts and Sciences* 18 (May 1882–May 1883): 428–438; Henry S. Prichett, "William Barton Rogers," in *Later Years of the Saturday Club, 1870–1920*, ed. Mark Anthony DeWolfe Howe (Boston: Houghton Mifflin Company, 1927), 99–102; Julius A. Stratton and Loretta H. Mannix, *Mind and Hand: The Birth of MIT* (Cambridge, MA: MIT Press, 2005); A. J. Angulo, *William Barton Rogers and the Idea of MIT* (Baltimore: Johns Hopkins University Press, 2009).

BENJAMIN SMITH ROTCH
New Bedford, MA 1817–1882 Milton, MA
Harvard University A.B. 1838, A.M. 1870

Benjamin Smith Rotch was a wealthy philanthropist and amateur painter.

He came from a prosperous family of whalers and bankers in New Bedford, Massachusetts. After graduation from Harvard, he and his brother William founded the New Bedford Cordage Company, which flourished as a supplier of ropes and lines to ships and boats. He served as a state representative in 1843 and 1844.

In 1846 he married Annie Bigelow Lawrence of Boston, who was a daughter of Abbott Lawrence, a textile magnate and prominent philanthropist. Rotch accompanied his father-in-law when Lawrence was appointed the United States minister to Great Britain in 1849, and Rotch and his family eventually spent five years in Europe, mostly in Paris. In Europe he visited galleries, studied oil painting, and befriended artists such as the American painter William Morris Hunt. After he returned to Boston in the mid-1850s, Rotch devoted himself to the fine arts as a connoisseur, philanthropist, and amateur painter. He exhibited his landscape paintings at the Athenæum gallery, lent support to several of the city's cultural institutions, and gained influence in the city as an authority on matters of artistic taste.

A man of fortune known for his aesthetic interests, Rotch was also the only member of the Lawrence family among the MFA's incorporators: he was brother-in-law of Timothy Bigelow Lawrence, whose 1869 bequest to the Athenæum had instigated the movement to found the MFA.

BA: proprietor, 1868–1882; trustee, 1868–1882
MFA: trustee, 1870–1882

OTHER INSTITUTIONAL AFFILIATIONS
Boston Art Club (trustee); Harvard University (overseer); Massachusetts Institute of Technology; Perkins Institution for the Blind (trustee)

PUBLIC OFFICE HELD
Massachusetts representative (1843–1844)

SELECTED SOURCES
Obituary, *Boston Evening Transcript*, August 31, 1882; John M. Bullard, *The Rotches* (New Bedford, MA, 1947), 413–414; Harry L. Katz, *A Continental Eye: The Art and Architecture of Arthur Rotch* (Boston: Boston Athenæum, 1985), 2–8.

SOURCES CONSULTED

BIOGRAPHICAL DICTIONARIES

Appleton's Cyclopaedia of American Biography. 6 vols. New York: D. Appleton and Company, 1888–1889.

Cyclopaedia of American Biography. 5 vols. New York: Press Association Compilers, Inc., 1915–1928.

The Biographical Dictionary of America. 10 vols. Boston: American Biographical Society, 1906.

Who's Who in New England. Vol. 1. Chicago: A. N. Marquis and Company, 1909.

Dictionary of American Biography. 20 vols. New York: Charles Scribner's Sons, 1928–1936.

American National Biography. 24 vols. New York: Oxford University Press, 1999.

INSTITUTIONAL RECORDS AND HISTORIES

American Academy of Arts and Sciences, *Book of Members, 1780–2005*. Cambridge, MA: American Academy of Arts and Sciences, 2005.

Annual Catalogue of the Officers and Students, and Programme of the Course of Instruction, of the School of the Massachusetts Institute of Technology.

Annual Report of the Perkins Institution and Massachusetts School for the Blind.

Annual Report of the School Committee of the City of Boston.

Annual Report of the Trustees of the Cemetery of Mount Auburn.

Foote, Henry W. *Annals of King's Chapel from the Puritan Age of New England to the Present Day*. Boston: Little, Brown, 1882–1940.

Massachusetts General Hospital Memorial and Historical Volume, Together with the Proceedings of the Centennial of the Opening of the Hospital. Boston: Griffith-Stillings Press, 1921.

Membership files, Harvard Musical Association Library.

The Parish of the Advent in the City of Boston, A History of One Hundred Years, 1844–1944. Boston: Parish of the Advent, 1944.

Proceedings of the American Academy of Arts and Sciences.

Thayer, Eli. *The New England Emigrant Aid Company and Its Influence, through the Kansas Contest, upon National History*. Worcester, MA: Published by Franklin P. Rice, 1887.

Trinity Church in the City of Boston, Massachusetts: 1733–1933. Boston: Wardens and Vestry of Trinity Church, 1933.

Tucker, Louis Leonard. *The Massachusetts Historical Society: A Bicentennial History, 1791–1991*. Boston: Massachusetts Historical Society, 1995.

Whitehill, Walter Muir. *The Provident Institution for Savings in the Town of Boston, 1816–1966*. Boston: Provident Institution for Savings, 1966.

The Year-Book of the Unitarian Congregational Churches.

NOTES

ABBREVIATIONS

The following abbreviations and short titles are used for the two major institutions under discussion, frequently cited manuscript sources, and published works.

INSTITUTIONS

BA: Boston Athenæum

MFA: Museum of Fine Arts, Boston

MANUSCRIPT SOURCES

ASSA Records
>American Social Science Association Records. Manuscripts and Archives. Yale University Library

BA Fine Arts Committee Records
BA Letters
BA Proprietors Records
BA Trustees Records
>Boston Athenæum Archive

Cleveland-Perkins Family Papers
>Cleveland-Perkins Family Papers. Manuscripts and Archives Division. The New York Public Library. Astor, Lenox and Tilden Foundations

MFA Building Records
MFA Committee on the Museum Records
MFA Director's Correspondence
MFA Early Organizational Material
MFA General Correspondence
MFA General Organizational Material
MFA Trustees Minutes
>Museum of Fine Arts, Boston, Archives

MFA Register of BA Loans
MFA Register of Casts
MFA Register of Purchases, 1876–1906
> Museum of Fine Arts, Boston, Department of Conservation and Collections Management

Ward-Perkins Family Papers
> Ward-Perkins Family Papers. Mss 129. Department of Special Collections. Davidson Library.
> University of California, Santa Barbara

Published Works

Perkins, "American Art Museums"
Perkins, Charles Callahan. "American Art Museums." *North American Review* 111 (July 1870): 1–29.

Perkins, *Art Education in America*
Perkins, Charles Callahan. *Art Education in America: Read before the American Social Science Association at the Lowell Institute, Boston, Feb. 22, 1870.* Cambridge, MA: Riverside Press, 1870.

Perkins, *Art in Education*
Perkins, Charles Callahan. *Art in Education: Reprinted from the Second Volume of the Journal of the American Social Science Association.* New York: Nation Press, 1870.

Proceedings
Proceedings at the Opening of the Museum of Fine Arts: with the Reports for 1876. Boston: Alfred Mudge and Son, 1876.

Quincy, *History*
Quincy, Josiah. *The History of the Boston Athenæum, with Biographical Notes of Its Deceased Founders.* Cambridge, MA: Metcalf and Company, 1851.

Slautterback, *Designing the BA*
Slautterback, Catharina. *Designing the Boston Athenæum: 10½ at 150.* Boston: Boston Athenæum, 1999.

Swan, *Athenæum Gallery*
Swan, Mabel Munson. *The Athenæum Gallery, 1827–1873: The Boston Athenæum as An Early Patron of Art.* Boston: Boston Athenæum, 1940.

Whitehill, *MFA*
Whitehill, Walter Muir. *Museum of Fine Arts, Boston: A Centennial History.* Cambridge, MA: Harvard University Press, 1970.

NOTES TO INTRODUCTION

1. BA Fine Arts Committee Records, October 18, 1875.

2. Ibid. The sum of $8,000 in 1876 was equivalent to $168,000 in 2010, using the Consumer Price Index. http://www.measuringworth.com/uscompare.

3. Whitehill, *MFA*, 1–2.

4. Swan, *Athenæum Gallery*, 173–174; and Whitehill, *MFA*, 1–22, 27–30.

5. Martin Burgess Green, *The Problem of Boston: Some Readings in Cultural History* (New York: W. W. Norton, 1966); Ronald Story, *The Forging of an Aristocracy: Harvard and the Boston Upper Class, 1800–1870* (Middletown, CT: Wesleyan University Press, 1980); Paul DiMaggio, "Cultural Entrepreneurship in Nineteenth-Century Boston: The Creation of an Organizational Base for High Culture in America," *Media, Culture and Society* 4 (January 1982): 33–50; Peter Dobkin Hall, *The Organization of American Culture, 1700–1900: Private Institutions, Elites, and the Origins of American Nationality* (New York: New York University Press, 1982); and Robert F. Dalzell Jr., *Enterprising Elite: The Boston Associates and the World They Made* (Cambridge, MA: Harvard University Press, 1987).

6. For an example of the first charge, see a comment by Matthew Stewart Prichard, a later staff member of the museum: "A few families had a special cult for [the museum], regarded it as their appanage . . . [and] their family tomb," quoted in Whitehill, *MFA*, 212; for the second, see Frank Jewett Mather, "An Art Museum for the People," *Atlantic Monthly* 100 (December 1907): 729–740, and John Cotton Dana, *The Gloom of the Museum* (Woodstock, VT: Elm Tree Press, 1917); and for the third, John Kouwenhoven, *Made in America: The Arts in Modern Civilization* (Garden City, NY: Doubleday, 1948).

7. For one, the historian Neil Harris countered the prevailing twentieth-century views of the museum's origin by demonstrating, in a 1962 article, the central role that education had played in the institution's founding vision. Harris, "The Gilded Age Revisited: Boston and the Museum Movement," *American Quarterly* 14 (Winter 1962): 545–566.

8. Oliver Wendell Holmes, *Elsie Venner: A Romance of Destiny* (Boston: Houghton, Mifflin and Company, 1861), 17, 24. According to Holmes, the "Brahmin caste of New England" consisted of the "races of scholars among us, in which aptitude for learning, and all these markers of it . . . are congenital and hereditary," although they were sometimes "blended with connections of political influence or commercial distinction." The text had appeared as "The Professor's Story" in monthly installments in the *Atlantic Monthly* from January 1860 to April 1861.

9. John P. Marquand, *The Late George Apley* (Boston: Little, Brown, and Company, 1937), 181.

NOTES TO CHAPTER ONE

1. For an analysis of the evolution of athenaeums from the ancient to the modern times, see Richard Wendorf, "Athenæum Origins," in *The Boston Athenæum Bicentennial Essays*, ed. Wendorf (Boston: Boston Athenæum, 2009), 3–32.

2. Quincy, *History*; *The Athenæum Centenary: The Influence and History of the Boston Athenæum from 1807 to 1907* (Boston: Boston Athenæum, 1907); *Anthology Society: Journal of the Proceedings of the Society Which Conducts the Monthly Anthology and Boston Review, October 3, 1805, to July 2, 1811* (Boston: Boston Athenæum, 1910); Lewis P. Simpson, ed., *The Federalist Literary Mind: Selections from the Monthly Anthology, and Boston Review, 1803–1811, Including Documents Relating to the Boston Athenæum* ([Baton Rouge]: Louisiana State University Press, 1962); Kenneth E. Carpenter, "America's Most Influential Library?" in Wendorf, *Bicentennial Essays*, 33–68; and Katherine Frances Wolff, *Culture Club: The Curious History of the Boston Athenæum* (Amherst: University of Massachusetts Press, 2009).

3. *Monthly Anthology and Boston Review* 4 (November 1807): 598.

4. The future "Repository of Arts" was envisioned as containing "models of new and useful machines . . . drawings, designs, paintings, engravings, statues, and other objects of the fine arts, and especially the productions of our native artists," while the "Museum" would house "specimens from the three kingdoms of nature, natural and artificial curiosities, antiques, coins, medals, vases, gems, and intaglios." John T. Kirkland, "Memoir of the Boston Athenæum, with the Act of Incorporation, and Organization of the Institution (1807)," in Quincy, *History*, 28.

5. For comparisons of the two athenæums, see Ronald Story, "Class and Culture in Boston: The Athenæum, 1807–1860," *American Quarterly* 27 (May 1975): 178–199.

6. The founders consisted of the fourteen original members of the Anthology Society and five others who were elected before 1807.

7. The Athenæum issued additional shares in 1822, 1826, 1844, 1845, 1850, and 1854, bringing the total up to the current 1,049.

8. For the terms of annual subscription, see Kirkland, "Memoir," 29; for those of life subscription, see "Terms of Subscription to the Boston Athenæum," May 8, 1807, in Quincy, *History*, 42.

9. See a set of bylaws issued in 1808 (original document in the BA Archive), cited in Quincy, *History*, 48–53; and "Rules and Regulations of the Boston Athenæum," January 20, 1815, BA Archive.

10. Quincy, *History*, 179. Reportedly, two-thirds of the original 150 proprietors were active businessmen. Story, "Class and Culture in Boston," 182. For Boston's mercantile elite's support for cultural institutions in the first half of the nineteenth century, see also Ronald Story, *The Forging of an Aristocracy: Harvard and the Boston Upper Class, 1800–1870* (Middletown, CT: Wesleyan University Press, 1980); and Robert F. Dalzell Jr., *Enterprising Elite: The Boston Associates and the World They Made* (Cambridge, MA: Harvard University Press, 1987).

11. *Monthly Anthology and Boston Review* 4 (November 1807): 601.

12. Kirkland, "Memoir," 31.

13. Ibid., 32–34.

14. See Katherine Frances Wolff, "Whose Library?" in Wendorf, *Bicentennial Essays*, 125–150.

15. Kirkland, "Memoir," 31 and 35.

16. The earliest recorded discussion on circulating some of the Athenæum's books—albeit among only "such proprietors and life share-holders as pay five dollars per annum for the privilege"—took place in early 1826, just as the trustees considered absorbing the city's other libraries (such as the Boston Medical Library and the Massachusetts Scientific Library). The proprietors voted to allow book circulation on March 18, 1826. Quincy, *History*, 94–95.

17. Ibid., 57.

18. A "gift" was given to the Athenæum, whereas a "deposit" was placed physically at the Athenæum without the transfer of ownership.

19. "Anthology Reading-Room and Library (1807)," quoted in Quincy, *History*, 12. The number of books in 1822 is from Quincy, *History*, 72. In the 1820s the Athenæum was the third-largest library in America, after the City Library in Philadelphia and the Harvard University Library, each holding 30,000 volumes. Martin Green, *The Problem of Boston: Some Readings in Cultural History* (New York: W. W. Norton, 1966), 51.

20. In 1817 Captain Henry Austin gave the Athenæum a "brick from the Tower of Babel taken 1816 with an inscription in the Persepolitan character; with some reeds used in the construction of the wall," February 28, 1817, BA Donation Book. Austin apparently gave several fired bricks with cuneiform inscriptions to several American institutions, including the Athenæum. See William B. Dinsmoor, "Early American Studies of Mediterranean Archaeology," *Proceedings of the American Philosophical Society* 87 (1943): 70–104.

21. Benjamin Codman to [William Smith Shaw], November 13, 1817, BA Letters.

22. The Athenæum was at Joy's Building (on Congress Street) in 1807, at Scollay's Building (at the corner of Tremont and Court Streets) from 1807 to 1809, and at the Rufus Amory House (on Tremont Street and overlooking the King's Chapel Burying Ground) from 1809 to 1822.

23. For discussions of the Athenæum on Pearl Street and the gallery, see Quincy, *History*; Swan, *Athenæum Gallery*; Slautterback, *Designing the BA*; Michael Wentworth, "Artists and the Athenæum in the Early 19th Century," in his *Look Again: Essays on the Boston Athenæum's Art Collections* (Boston: Boston Athenæum, 2003), 13–37; and David B. Dearinger, "Collecting Paintings and Sculpture for the Boston Athenæum," in Stanley Ellis Cushing and Dearinger, *Acquired Tastes: 200 Years of Collecting for the Boston Athenæum* (Boston: Boston Athenæum, 2006), 32–63.

24. Quincy, *History*, 70.

25. Charles Bullard Fairbanks, "Daybook, July 2, 1847–August 28, 1848," BA Archive. Quoted in Wentworth, *Look Again*, 53.

26. *Boston Evening Transcript*, September 2, 1893. The reference to the breeze from the water is in Henry Lee, memorial broadside to Sarah Paine Perkins Cleveland (granddaughter of James Perkins), 1893, Cleveland-Perkins Family Papers, box 6, folder 13.

27. The receipt of the Thorndike collection of casts was recorded the Athenæum's "Donation Book" on December 30, 1823. More than a year earlier, the BA Trustees Records had mentioned, on October 14, 1822, a collection of casts at the Athenæum and referred to it on January 8, 1823, by Thorndike's name. The Athenæum's portrait of Perkins by Stuart was a replica of the smaller original that the artist had painted for the Perkins family earlier the same year. Both versions were painted after the merchant's death in August 1822.

28. Other pieces of sculpture and paintings had entered the Athenæum's collection before 1822: for example, a marble bas-relief of a horse from Pompeii was given in 1812, and a portrait of the Hawaiian king Kamehameha I in 1818. By contemporary standards these were not considered specimens of fine art, and the catalogues of the gallery exhibitions (after 1827) did not list them.

29. The full-scale casts were of the Apollo Belvedere, the Belvedere Torso, and the Laocoön (Vatican Museum, Rome); the Venus de' Medici (Galleria degli Uffizi, Florence); the Capitoline Venus (Capitoline Museum, Rome); and the Borghese Gladiator, Diana the Huntress, and Hermaphrodites (Musée du Louvre, Paris); the small-scale casts were of the Discobolus (National Museum of Rome), the Apollino (Galleria degli Uffizi, Florence), and the Capitoline Antinous (Capitoline Museum, Rome).

30. Ralph Waldo Emerson to John B. Hill, July 3, 1822, in Ralph L. Rusk, ed., *The Letters of Ralph Waldo Emerson*, 6 vols. (New York: Columbia University Press, 1939), 1:119–120.

31. "Lecture Hall/Gallery Circular," March 6, 1823. Reproduced in Slautterback, *Designing the BA*, 96.

32. Ibid.

33. BA Trustees Records, April 10, 1826.

34. BA Trustees Records, November 11, 1850. Trustees informally discussed this naming possibility with Mrs. James Perkins (widow of the donor of his mansion in 1822) in 1839, when they sought her general permission for the Athenæum to consider moving to another site.

35. Abel Bowen, *Bowen's Picture of Boston* (Boston: Otis, Broaders and Company, 1838), 37.

36. BA Trustees Records, March 20, 1827.

37. Thomas Perkins was a founder of the Massachusetts General Hospital and the Asylum for the Insane (later renamed McLean Hospital), both in 1811, and an incorporator, in 1829, of the New England Asylum for the Blind. The last institution was renamed the Perkins Institution for the Blind after Perkins gave one of his houses to it, in 1832.

38. Swan, *Athenæum Gallery*, 18.

39. For example, for the first annual exhibition in 1827, the Fine Arts Committee hired William Harris Jones as manager. Listed as an "artist" in the *Boston Directory*, Jones was also a dealer and sold to the Athenæum, in 1828, a portrait attributed to Annibale Carracci, one of the first paintings purchased by the Fine Arts Committee. In late 1827, after the close of the first exhibition in July, Jones also brought to the Athenæum gallery a temporary installation of John Vanderlyn's *Panorama of Versailles* (1818–1819; The Metropolitan Museum of Art, New York).

40. In the second edition of the catalogue, *A Catalogue of the First Exhibition of Paintings, in the Athenæum Gallery: Consisting of Specimens, by American Artists, and a Selection of the Works of the Old Masters;*

From the Various Cabinets in This City and Its Vicinity (Boston: Press of William W. Clapp, 1827), 134 paintings were by living artists, and 165 by—or, mostly, after—the Old Masters.

41. *Columbian Centinel*, May 16, 1827.

42. Swan, *Athenæum Gallery*, 33. In the early years, the exhibitions ran for only about two months in early summer. The plan was to rent out the gallery the rest of the year to individuals and organizations.

43. For descriptions of Boston's early "museums," see Walter K. Watkins, "The New England Museum and the Home of Art in Boston," *Bostonian Society Publications*, 2nd ser., 2 (1917): 101–130; and Lillian B. Miller, *Patrons and Patriotism: The Encouragement of the Fine Arts in the United States, 1790–1860* (Chicago: University of Chicago Press, 1966), 112–113.

44. Watkins, "The New England Museum," 125–127. Displays devoted solely to paintings had also appeared in some of the city's all-purpose exhibition rooms: in 1821, for example, the frame maker and dealer John Doggett showed a collection of small-size (and mostly copies of) Old Master paintings at his Repository of Arts on Market Street. *Descriptive Catalogue of Original Cabinet Paintings, Now Arranged in the Gallery, Doggett's Repository of Arts. . . .* (Boston, 1821).

45. Kirkland, "Memoir," 35.

46. BA Trustees Records, April 10, 1826.

47. BA Trustees Records, March 20, 1827.

48. The paintings were *James Perkins* (1822; BA) and *William Smith Shaw* (1826; BA), both commissioned by the Athenæum from Gilbert Stuart; Gilbert Stuart, *John Adams* (ca. 1815; originally thought to be a copy after Stuart by his nephew, Gilbert Stuart Newton; BA), gift of the estate of William Smith Shaw, 1826; Gilbert Stuart Newton, after Gilbert Stuart, *Fisher Ames* (ca. 1815; BA), provenance unknown; Jonathan Mason Jr., after Gilbert Stuart, *George Washington* (n.d.; unlocated), gift of the artist; Charles Robert Leslie (1794–1859), after Sir Thomas Lawrence, *Benjamin West* (1818; BA), gift of Henry Pickering, 1824; and unidentified artist, after Murillo, *Jacob and Rebecca at the Well* (n.d.; unlocated), gift of William Foster, 1824. Sculpture: a bust of John Adams (1819; BA) by J. B. Binon (French, active in Boston, 1818–1820), gift of the artist, 1819; the Thorndike casts; and Raimondo Trentanove (1792–1832), *Marble Bust of Washington* (1824; location unknown), purchase by subscription, 1824. This count excludes the many three-dimensional objects of antiquarian nature— plaster gems, medals, and coins—that had entered the Athenæum's collection before 1827.

49. The committee made its first purchase, the Carracci portrait, in February 1828 for $100. Trumbull's *Sortie* cost $2,000; Neagle's *Pat Lyon*, $400; West's *King Lear*, $600; and *Franklin* after Duplessis—then thought to be by Jean-Baptiste Greuze (1725–1805) but now known to be by Jean Valade (1710–1787)—$200. BA Trustees Records, February 12 and June 30, 1828.

50. Stuart's Washington portraits were sold in the 1970s, after a century's deposit at the MFA. Of the four Panini pictures—*Interior of St. Peter's, Rome*; *View of St. Peter's Square with the Departure of the Duc de Choiseul*; *Interior of an Imaginary Picture Gallery with Views of Ancient Rome*; and *Interior of an Imaginary Gallery with Views of Modern Rome*—the second and third were exchanged in 1837 for other paintings and are now in the collections, respectively, of the Duke of Sutherland, Mertoun House, Melrose, Scotland, and the Staatsgalerie Stuttgart, Germany. The first picture remains in the collection of the Athenæum, while the last was sold to the MFA, after a century's stay there, in the 1970s. For a detailed history of the four canvases, see Hina Hirayama, "*Interior of St. Peter's, Rome*," in Cushing and Dearinger, *Acquired Tastes*, 194–197.

51. BA Proprietors Records, January 5, 1829.

52. BA Proprietors Records, January 3, 1831.

53. [William Tudor], "An Institution for the Fine Arts," *North American Review* 2 (January 1816): 153–164.

54. BA Trustees Records, December 13, 1826.

55. BA Trustees Records, April 9, 1827.

56. Seth Bass to the Trustees, "Schedule of the Books and other Property belonging to the Boston Athenæum," July 11, 1825, BA Letters.

57. BA Trustees Records, April 11, 1825.

58. BA Trustees Records, May 12, 1829.

59. In 1831 the Fine Arts Committee held a contest with two cash prizes, one for landscapes and the other for history paintings. Alvan Fisher won the first place in landscape with *The Freshet*, and Robert Walter Weir (1803–1889) won in history painting with *The Antiquary*.

60. BA Proprietors Records, January 7, 1839.

61. William T. Andrews to the Trustees, December 30, 1842, BA Letters.

62. Quincy, *History*, 156.

63. From 1845 to 1848, for example, the committee invited the Boston Artists' Association—founded in 1841 under the leadership of Chester Harding, with Washington Allston as its first president—to participate in the Athenæum's annual exhibitions and to share the profit. The association wished to apply its portion of the proceeds to "the support of a school for drawing from casts and from life," while the Athenæum hoped that the association's participation would bring to its exhibitions new works and visitors. Quincy, *History*, 166–167. The association also offered drawing classes for local artists. In 1850 the association established the New England Art Union for the promotion of the fine arts. Many prominent Bostonians initially lent support to the union, but it was disbanded in 1851. Leah Lipton, "The Boston Artists' Association, 1841–1851," *American Art Journal* 15 (Autumn 1983): 45–57.

64. In 1848 the "paintings, busts, &c., including *Orpheus [and Cerberus]*" were worth $19,921.63, whereas the books were valued at $65,257.77. Quincy, *History*, 184.

65. By early 1844 the Athenæum had bought a piece of land on Tremont Street for its future building. An architectural competition was held, and the existing building on the site demolished, but the Athenæum then decided to sell the land and to purchase the lot at its current location on Beacon Street. See Slautterback, *Designing the BA*, 19–31.

66. BA Proprietors Records, May 2, 1845. In 1845 interest on $6,000 would have been about $300.

67. Wolff, "Whose Library?"

68. For details of this debate, see ibid., 123–148; Josiah Quincy, *An Appeal in Behalf of the Boston Athenæum, Addressed to the Proprietors* (Boston: John Wilson and Son, 1853); and George Ticknor, *Union of the Boston Athenæum and the Public Library* (Boston: Dutton and Wentworth, 1853).

69. Quoted in *Athenæum Centenary*, 46.

70. Story, "Class and Culture in Boston," 192. Story identified the Quincys, the Adameses, the Shaws, the Perkinses, the Lowells, the Grays, and the Appletons.

71. Oscar Handlin, *Boston's Immigrants, 1790–1865: A Study in Acculturation* (Cambridge, MA: Belknap Press of Harvard University Press, 1959), 51–52, 243.

72. BA Proprietors Records, January 7, 1850.

73. *Boston Evening Transcript*, January 22, 1848.

74. "Eliot's *Sketch of Harvard College*," *North American Review* 68 (January 1849): 106.

75. Quoted in *Athenæum Centenary*, 38.

76. BA Proprietors Records, January 5, 1852.

77. Edward N. Perkins [to the *Daily Advertiser*], [September 1851], BA Letters.

78. Edward A. Crowninshield to the Trustees, "Report of the Fine Arts Committee," December 31, 1856, BA Letters.

79. Edward A. Crowninshield to James Robb, February 16, 1854, BA Letters.

80. Quoted in *Athenæum Centenary*, 45.

81. The Michelangelo cast was purchased by the sculptor Horatio Greenough, probably in Florence, in the early 1830s and subsequently given to his patron, Thomas Handasyd Perkins. Perkins deposited the cast at the Athenæum in 1838; it became the Athenæum's property in 1854 after Perkins's death. The pedestal for the cast was designed by Edward Clarke Cabot and followed the original in the Medici Chapel at San Lorenzo in Florence. Cabot's drawing for the pedestal survives in the BA Archive.

82. BA Proprietors Records, January 3, 1853.

83. Edward N. Perkins [to the *Daily Advertiser*], [September 1851], BA Letters.

84. For the Fine Arts Committee's opinion, see Edward N. Perkins to Thomas G. Cary, March 8, 1852, BA Letters. For the trustees' rejection, see BA Proprietors Records, January 3, 1853.

85. Slautterback, *Designing the BA*, 38, 40.

86. BA Proprietors Records, March 28, 1850.

87. BA Proprietors Records, February 28, 1850; Quincy, *History*, 212.

88. BA Proprietors Records, January 1, 1855.

89. BA Trustees Records, February 9, 1853.

90. Charles Eliot Norton to the Trustees, "Instructions and Suggestions of the Library Committee," January 16, 1854, BA Letters.

91. William I. Fletcher, "Some Recollections of the Boston Athenæum, 1861–1866," *Library Journal* 39 (August 1914): 580–581. BA Proprietors Records, January 14, 1867.

92. BA Proprietors Records, January 2, 1860.

93. BA Trustees Records, March 13, 1854.

94. William T. Andrews to the Trustees, "Report of the Committee on Fine Arts Fund," November 13, 1854, BA Letters.

95. "Treasurer's Report," BA Proprietors Records, January 5, 1857.

96. BA Trustees Records, December 10, 1855.

97. Quincy, *An Appeal in Behalf of the Boston Athenæum*, 15.

98. The five members were James Elliot Cabot, Benjamin Smith Rotch, Christopher Toppan Thayer, George Washington Wales, and Edward Newton Perkins, chairman. The number of trustees on the committee increased from three to four in 1862, and to five in 1866.

99. BA Trustees Records, February 10, 1862. Allston Hall, at 118 Tremont Street, occupied part of the Studio Building, built about 1860, and was used for shows and other public purposes. Donald C. King, *The Theatres of Boston: A Stage and Screen History* (Jefferson, NC: McFarland and Company, 2005), 55.

100. BA Trustees Records, October 13, 1862.

101. BA Proprietors Records, January 5, 1863.

102. BA Trustees Records, January 12, 1863.

103. "Fine Arts. Athenæum Gallery of Fine Arts," *Dwight's Journal of Music* 19 (May 4, 1861): 38.

104. BA Proprietors Records, January 14, 1864.

105. The gallery housed the National Sailors' Fair after the closing of the Athenæum's annual exhibition. BA Trustees Records, September 12, 1864.

106. BA Trustees Records, March 19, 1866.

107. Ibid., December 17, 1866.

108. BA Proprietors Records, January 4, 1864.

109. Ibid., January 8, 1866.

110. Ibid., January 4, 1864.

111. Ibid., January 8, 1866.

112. Charles S. Storrow to the Trustees, "Report of the Standing Committee," March 19, 1866, BA Letters.

113. BA Proprietors Records, January 8, 1866.

114. Ibid.

115. BA Proprietors Records, January 14, 1867.

116. Ibid.

117. For a discussion of this proposal and Cabot's plan for the proposed art gallery, see Slautterback, *Designing the BA*, 60–61. Cabot had been on the Fine Arts Committee from 1857 to 1860 and in 1862 but not in 1866, around the time he made the drawing.

118. BA Trustees Records, March 19, 1866. The original members of this new committee were Samuel Eliot (Library Committee), Francis Edward Parker (chairman, Library Committee), Francis E. Parkman (Library Committee), and Edward N. Perkins (chairman, Fine Arts Committee).

119. "Reports of the Committee on the Library and of the Committee on the Fine Arts of the Boston Athenæum. Submitted at the Annual Meeting of the Proprietors, January 8, 1867," BA Proprietors Records, January 14, 1867.

120. William Frederick Poole to the Trustees, February 17, 1868, BA Letters.

121. "Report of the Committee of Proprietors," dated March 1, 1867. BA Proprietors Records, March 4, 1867.

122. *Boston Daily Evening Transcript*, March 5, 1867.

123. BA Trustees Records, May 18, 1868.

124. William Frederick Poole to the Trustees, February 17, 1868, BA Letters.

125. The reason for Poole's sudden departure is not known; his biographer speculates that it was caused by the birth of Poole's seventh child and first son. William Landram Williamson, *William Frederick Poole and the Modern Library Movement* (New York: Columbia University Press, 1963), 41–43. Poole was a significant figure in the history of American libraries, best remembered for his *Poole's Index to Periodical Literature* (1853–1882). After leaving the Athenæum, Poole became the librarian of the Cincinnati Public Library (1869–1873), the Chicago Public Library (1873–1887), and the Newberry Library (1887–1894). See ibid.; and William H. Jordy, "The Beaux-Arts Renaissance: Charles McKim's Boston Public Library," in *American Buildings and Their Architects: Progressive and Academic Ideals at the Turn of the Twentieth Century* (Garden City, NY: Anchor Press/Doubleday, 1976), 324–326.

126. *First Annual Report of the Trustees of the Peabody Museum of American Archaeology and Ethnology* (Cambridge, MA: John Wilson and Son, 1868), 6.

127. Massachusetts Institute of Technology, *Report of the President . . . Massachusetts Institute of Technology, 1871–1872* (Boston: A. A. Kingman, 1872), 49.

128. "Special Meeting of the Proprietors [submitted] February 25, 1867," BA Proprietors Records, January 13, 1868. The meeting had been held on February 4, 1867.

129. BA Proprietors Records, January 13, 1868.

130. Little is known about Henry Harris, except that he had lived in Boston and died on May 23, 1867, at age seventy-nine. *Boston Daily Evening Transcript*, May 25, 1867.

131. On T. B. Lawrence, see Abbott Lawrence, *T. Bigelow Lawrence* (Boston: privately printed, 1869).

132. Augustus Thorndike Perkins, *Losses to Literature and the Fine Arts by the Great Fire in Boston* (Boston: David Clapp and Son, 1873), 7–9. In addition to weapons, the Lawrence collection included "carved furniture and Majolica." MFA Trustees Minutes, March 17, 1870.

133. Helen Hartman Gemmill, *The Bread Box Papers: A Biography of Elizabeth Chapman Lawrence* (Bryn Mawr, PA: Dorrance and Company; Doylestown, PA: Bucks County Historical Society, 1983), 104.

134. The collection was shipped from Florence to Boston in 1870. Ibid., 178–179.

135. BA Trustees Records, November 13, 1869. The date of Mrs. Lawrence's offer of $25,000 to the Athenæum, in November 1869, refutes Gemmill's claim (*The Bread Box Papers*, 184–187) that Mrs. Lawrence promised the amount to Martin Brimmer as a gift to the MFA when he attended a house party at her new residence, completed in 1871, in her native Doylestown, Pennsylvania.

136. Suffolk County Probate Records, Docket Book 306, 183.

NOTES TO CHAPTER TWO

1. Harvard's Lawrence Scientific School was founded with a bequest of $50,000 from Abbott Lawrence. The Museum of Comparative Zoology was established with the $50,000 bequeathed by Francis Calley Gray to house the zoological collection amassed by Louis Agassiz. In 1866, when the Peabody Museum of

American Archaeology and Ethnology was established, the Athenæum deposited at the new museum more than 130 ethnological specimens.

2. The original idea for the conservatory was conceived when three existing organizations in cramped downtown quarters—the Massachusetts Horticultural Society, the Boston Society of Natural History, and the New England Historic Genealogical Society—considered merging into one institution in the Back Bay. Yet in the hands of its chief instigator, William Emerson Baker, a sewing machine entrepreneur, the proposed conservatory became a more comprehensive institution of learning, complete with a museum. The plan failed in 1859, when the state legislature banned the construction of any structures on the Public Garden site. "Memorial to the Legislature of Massachusetts in Relation to a Conservatory of Art and Science," March 9, 1859, quoted in [James Phinney Munroe], "The Conservatory Journal," *Technology Review* 4 (April 1902): 137–169; and Julius A. Stratton and Loretta H. Mannix, *Mind and Hand: The Birth of MIT* (Cambridge, MA: MIT Press, 2005), 141–168. See also the seven issues of *Conservatory Journal*, which Baker published from March to June 1859. Although the plan for the conservatory failed, many of its supporters later established MIT, embracing some of the aims of the proposed institution.

3. Ronald Story, *The Forging of an Aristocracy: Harvard and the Boston Upper Class, 1800–1870* (Middletown, CT: Wesleyan University Press, 1980).

4. See, for example, Robert F. Dalzell Jr., *Enterprising Elite: The Boston Associates and the World They Made* (Cambridge, MA: Harvard University Press, 1987); and Paul DiMaggio, "Cultural Entrepreneurship in Nineteenth-Century Boston: The Creation of an Organizational Base for High Culture in America," *Media, Culture, and Society* 4 (January 1982): 33–50.

5. Published sources about Charles Callahan Perkins include Samuel Eliot, "Memoir of Charles Callahan Perkins, A.M.," *Proceedings of the Massachusetts Historical Society*, 2nd ser., 3 (February 1888): 223–246; Martin Brimmer, "Charles Callahan Perkins," *Proceedings of the American Academy of Arts and Sciences* 22 (May–December 1886): 534–539; and Mark Anthony DeWolfe Howe, ed., *Later Years of the Saturday Club, 1870–1920* (Boston: Houghton Mifflin Company, 1927), 17–20. See also Cleveland-Perkins Family Papers and Ward-Perkins Family Papers.

6. Eliza Greene Callahan's father was John Callahan (1745–1806), an Irish sea captain who had gone to Boston in the 1760s, and her mother, Lucretia Greene (1748–after 1806), sister of Gardiner Greene (1753–1832). Charles's siblings were James Amory (1814–1824), Sarah Paine (1818–1893), Edward Newton, and James Henry (1826–1857).

7. Thomas Handasyd Perkins was entrusted, for example, with the care of Charles Perkins and his siblings while their parents traveled in Europe in 1825 and wrote a series of letters to the parents that were full of domestic news. Ward-Perkins Family Papers, box 8, folder 2.

8. James Elliot Cabot, *J. Elliot Cabot: I. Autobiographical Sketch, II. Family Reminiscences, III. Sedge Birds* (Boston: Geo. H. Ellis Company, 1904), 13. Cabot was the son of Samuel Cabot Jr. and Elizabeth Perkins, daughter of Thomas Handasyd Perkins. He was a brother of Edward Clarke Cabot, the architect of the Athenæum on Beacon Street, and a cousin of the Perkins children.

9. James Perkins Jr. died of apoplexy (a hemorrhagic stroke) in June 1828 in Lincoln, Massachusetts, on his way home from a trip to Lake George in New York State. *Salem Gazette*, June 27, 1828. Within a year, his widow married the Reverend George Washington Doane, who in 1830 became the rector of Trinity Church in downtown Boston. In 1832 Doane was elected the Episcopal bishop of New Jersey, and the couple moved to Burlington, New Jersey.

10. The Reverend and Mrs. Doane had two sons, both of whom became prominent religious figures. The first, George Hobart Doane, converted to Catholicism and rose to the rank of monsignor; the second, William Croswell Doane, became the first Episcopal bishop of Albany, New York, in 1869.

11. For Cleveland's life and writings, see George S. Hillard, *A Selection from the Writings of Henry R. Cleveland, with a Memoir* (Boston: privately printed, 1844). Cleveland, Longfellow, Sumner, with Cornelius Conway Felton, a Harvard professor who would become its president in 1860, and George Stillman Hillard, Sumner's law partner and future author of the widely admired *Six Months in Italy* (1853), were known as the

"Five of Clubs" and met regularly for convivial dinners and discussions on all matters of culture. Gertrude B. Diehl, "The Five of Clubs," *New England Galaxy* 12 (Summer 1970): 39–48.

12. Sarah and her daughter, Eliza Callahan Cleveland (1839–1914), who never married, lived at Pinebank, a summer residence built in the early nineteenth century by Sarah's grandfather James Perkins in Jamaica Plain, Massachusetts. After Edward's marriage in 1846, Sarah and Eliza moved out of Pinebank and thereafter divided their time between European travel and their two houses in America: Parva Domus (from the Latin *Parva domus, magna quies*, meaning "small house, great quiet") in Bethlehem, New Hampshire, and Nutwood, built in 1866 on a tract of land she purchased from Charles Perkins near Pinebank, at the corner of Perkins and Chestnut Streets.

13. Thomas Crawford to Charles Sumner, March 13, 1844. Robert L. Gale, *Thomas Crawford, American Sculptor* (Pittsburgh: University of Pittsburgh Press, 1964), 37–38.

14. Ibid.

15. Charles C. Perkins, unbound diary, October 30, 1847, Ward-Perkins Family Papers, box 8, folder 12.

16. Perkins deposited *Hebe and Ganymede* at the Athenæum when it arrived in Boston in 1855. In 1870 Perkins's gift of the sculpture to the MFA was one of the only two gifts the institution received in the year of its incorporation, but the statue remained at the Athenæum until 1876, when it was moved to the new museum. See Lauretta Dimmick, "A Catalogue of the Portrait Busts and Ideal Works of Thomas Crawford (1813?–1857), American Sculptor in Rome" (PhD diss., University of Pittsburgh, 1986), 479–491.

17. For the history of *Christian Pilgrim*, see ibid., 352–358.

18. Mary K. McGuigan, "'This Market of Physiognomy': American Artists and Rome's Art Academies, Life Schools, and Models, 1825–1870," in William L. Vance, McGuigan, and John F. McGuigan Jr., *America's Rome: Artists in the Eternal City, 1800–1900* (Cooperstown, NY: Fenimore Art Museum, 2009), 56.

19. Quoted in Henry James, *William Wetmore Story and His Friends from Letters, Diaries, and Recollections* (New York: Grove Press, 1903), 144–145.

20. Christopher Pearse Cranch to John S. Dwight, March 14, 1848, Letters to John S. Dwight, Department of Rare Books and Manuscripts, Boston Public Library. Courtesy of the Trustees of the Boston Public Library/Rare Books.

21. James, *William Wetmore Story*, 144–145.

22. On Ary Scheffer, see Marthe Kolb, *Ary Scheffer et son temps, 1795–1858* (Paris: Boivin, 1937); *Ary Scheffer, 1795–1858: Dessins, aquarelles, esquisses à l'huile* (Paris: L'Institute, 1980); and Edward Morris, "Ary Scheffer and His English Circle," *Oud Holland* 99 (1985): 294–323. Charles Perkins's great-uncle Thomas Handasyd Perkins had owned a painting by Scheffer, *Eberhard, Comte de Württemberg, Mourning over the Body of His Son* (ca. 1834; location unknown), depicting a scene from Friedrich Schiller's 1782 ballad "Count Eberhard, the Weeper of Württemberg," and presented it to the Athenæum in 1836. The Athenæum deposited the painting at the MFA in 1876 and sold it at an auction in 1980.

23. Charles Baudelaire, "On M. Ary Scheffer and the Apes of Sentiment," in *Art in Paris, 1845–1862: Salons and Other Exhibitions Reviewed by Charles Baudelaire*, trans. and ed. Jonathan Mayne (London: Phaidon Press, 1965), 99.

24. Perkins's sketches made in 1844 during his tour of Europe are preserved in the collection of the Boston Athenæum. For his post-Paris drawings (made into engravings), see, for example, the illustrations in his book *Tuscan Sculptors: Their Lives, Works, and Times; With Illustrations from Original Drawings and Photographs*, 2 vols. (London: Longman, Green, Longman, Roberts, and Green, 1864).

25. Quoted in Eliot, "Memoir of Charles Callahan Perkins," 226.

26. Charles C. Perkins, unbound diary, January 1, 1849, Ward-Perkins Family Papers, box 8, folder 12.

27. The concert took place on July 16, 1849. Charles C. Perkins, bound diary, July 15, 1849, Ward-Perkins Family Papers, box 8, folder 13.

28. Clipping from *L'Illustration* [1849], Ward-Perkins Family Papers, box 8, folder 13.

29. Charles C. Perkins, bound diary, July 15 and 16, 1849, Ward-Perkins Family Papers, box 8, folder 13.

30. Ibid., [September] 11 and n.d., 1849, Ward-Perkins Family Papers, box 8, folder 13.

31. Charles C. Perkins to Charles Amory [Fine Arts Committee chairman], May 21, 1850, BA Letters: "I have eight or ten pictures some of them quite large. . . . I had hoped that application would have been made to me in time to give them a good place [in the Athenæum gallery]. . . ."

32. Charles Perkins invited friends such as Longfellow to biweekly musical gatherings at his home, called the Quintette Club. Charles C. Perkins to Henry Wadsworth Longfellow, November 30, 1850, Letters to Henry Wadsworth Longfellow, MS AM 1340.2 (4344), Houghton Library, Harvard University. For descriptions of musical gatherings at Perkins's house, see Paul E. Paige, "Chamber Music in Boston: The Harvard Musical Association," *Journal of Research in Music Education* 18 (Summer 1970): 136; and Thomas Ryan, *Recollections of an Old Musician* (New York: E. P. Dutton and Company, 1899), 80–81. A concert of the Boston Musical Fund Society at the Tremont Temple on March 23, 1850, featured the Grand Symphony composed by Perkins; a chamber concert of the Mendelssohn Quintette Club at the Masonic Temple on April 13, 1850, included "Grand Septette, composed and dedicated to Samuel Eliot, Esq., by Charles C. Perkins," which made its debut under Perkins's direction; and a concert at the Melodeon (a performance space established in 1839) on April 19, 1851, premiered the Second Symphony composed for the occasion by Perkins and dedicated to the Boston Musical Fund Society. Ward-Perkins Family Papers, box 8, folder 13.

33. For the history of the Handel and Haydn Society, see Charles C. Perkins and John S. Dwight, *History of the Handel and Haydn Society, of Boston, Massachusetts*, vol. 1, *From the Foundation of the Society through Its Seventy-fifth Season, 1815–1890* (Boston: Alfred Mudge and Son, 1883–1893). On the relationship between the Harvard Musical Association and the Boston Music Hall, see Arthur W. Hepner, *Pro Bono Artium Musicarum: The Harvard Musical Association, 1837–1987* (Boston: Harvard Musical Association, 1987).

34. Earlier, public halls in the city had been venues for concerts, exhibitions, and theatricals, whereas the Boston Music Hall was dedicated exclusively to musical performance. It is today the Orpheum Theatre, near the Park Street subway station. For a history of theaters in Boston, see Donald C. King, *The Theatres of Boston: A Stage and Screen History* (Jefferson, NC: McFarland and Company, 2005).

35. Perkins's companion in Leipzig was the Bostonian James Cutler Dunn Parker (1828–1916), who later became a composer, organist, and instructor at the New England Conservatory of Music. Parker's recollections of their time in Leipzig are in the letter from Parker to Edward N. Perkins, September 7, 1887, Cleveland-Perkins Family Papers, box 9, folder 17.

36. Eliot, "Memoir of Charles Callahan Perkins," 228. Published musical scores by Perkins include *Eight Melodies Dedicated to My Sister* (Paris: Brandus et Cie, [ca. 1847]); *Eight Melodies (for Voice and Pianoforte)* (Paris: Brandus et Cie, [ca. 1860]); *Quartuor pour 2 violons, alto et violoncelle, Opus 8* (Leipzig: Breitkopf und Hartel, 1853); *Trio pour piano, violon et violoncelle, Opus 10* (Leipzig: Breitkopf und Hartel, [ca. 1854]); and *Pensées musicales pour piano et violon* (Leipzig: Breitkopf und Hartel, 1855), as listed in Donald Fitch, "The Ward-Perkins Papers," *Soundings* 16 (1985): 66–67.

37. Crawford and his wife attended the occasion in Munich. For details on the Beethoven statue, see Gale, *Thomas Crawford*, 101–102, 135, and 144.

38. Charles C. Perkins to Charles Folsom, May 1855, Charles Folsom Papers, Department of Rare Books and Manuscripts, Boston Public Library. Courtesy of the Trustees of the Boston Public Library/Rare Books. Deposited unofficially at the Athenæum, the Beethoven statue was not listed in the catalogue of the Athenæum's annual exhibition of 1855. Two other Beethoven-related sculptures were shown at the Athenæum gallery: *Cast of the Head of Beethoven*, shown by Perkins in 1855 and 1856, and *Cast of the Bust of Beethoven*, owned by the Athenæum and exhibited in 1857.

39. After the Music Hall Association dissolved in 1899, the statue reverted to the Handel and Haydn Society, which deposited it at the Boston Public Library. In 1903 the sculpture was moved to the new home of the New England Conservatory of Music on Huntington Avenue. In 1951 the ownership of the statue was officially transferred from the society to the conservatory, and *Beethoven* now stands in the lobby of Jordan Hall. The organ containing 5,474 pipes and 84 registers, the largest organ in the United States at the time, was built in Ludwigsburg, near Stuttgart, Germany, by Walcker Orgelbau and installed at the Music

Hall in 1863. In 1884 the organ was removed to make space on the stage for the growing orchestra and is now at the Methuen Memorial Music Hall in Methuen, Massachusetts. Louis C. Elson, *The History of American Music* (New York: Macmillan Company, 1904), 262–263.

40. In 1870 the conservatory moved to the former St. James Hotel in Franklin Square in the South End before settling, in 1903, into its current home on Huntington Avenue.

41. On Barnum's baby shows and their cultural implications, see Bluford Adams, *E Pluribus Barnum: The Great Showman and the Making of U.S. Popular Culture* (Minneapolis: University of Minnesota Press, 1997), 97–111.

42. Charles C. Perkins to John S. Dwight, August 12, 1855, Letters to John S. Dwight, Department of Rare Books and Manuscripts, Boston Public Library. Courtesy of the Trustees of the Boston Public Library/Rare Books.

43. Ibid. Perkins's protest was published in *Dwight's Journal of Music* 7 (September 1, 1855): 175.

44. Frances's father, Matthias Bruen, was a Presbyterian pastor in New York, and her grandfather by the same name, a judge in New York. In November 1847, when he returned to Rome from Paris, Perkins helped Crawford find an apartment for Crawford's friends the "Bruins" [*sic*]. Soon, Perkins befriended the two daughters, one of whom became his wife. Charles C. Perkins, unbound diary (1847–1849), Ward-Perkins Family Papers, box 8, folder 12. The Bruen family had known Crawford in Rome since the late 1830s and commissioned him to make busts of Frances's paternal grandfather, Matthias Bruen (1837; New Jersey Historical Society, Newark) and her father (before 1837; unlocated). Dimmick, "A Catalogue of the Portrait Busts and Ideal Works of Thomas Crawford," 121–125. Obituary for Frances Davenport Bruen Perkins, *New York Times*, March 28, 1909.

45. Perkins's mother-in-law, Mary Anne Devenport Bruen, had erected in 1851 a Gothic Revival stone cottage to the design by Seth C. Bradford (1801–1878), on Bellevue Avenue, which was significantly altered by the architect Richard Morris Hunt (1827–1895) in 1870–1872. In 1882–1883 Mrs. Bruen and her unmarried daughter, Mary Lundie Bruen, had another house built to the east of the stone cottage, designed by the architect William Ralph Emerson (1833–1917). Both houses still stand. James L. Yarnall, *Newport through Its Architecture: A History of Styles from Postmedieval to Postmodern* (Newport, RI: Salve Regina University Press, 2005), 204, 107–108, and 202. I thank Paul Miller, Curator, Newport Preservation Society, for clarifying these facts.

46. *Dictionary of American Biography* (New York: Charles Scribner's Sons, 1934), s.v. "Perkins, Charles Callahan."

47. On Villa Capponi, see Katie Campbell, *Paradise of Exiles: The Anglo-American Gardens of Florence* (London: Frances Lincoln, 2009), 147–154.

48. Brimmer, "Charles Callahan Perkins," 535.

49. Rio's treatise on the history of Italian art, *De la poésie chrétien* (Paris, 1836) was one of the first systematic studies on the subject. Alexis-François Rio, *The Poetry of Christian Art, Translated from the French of A. F. Rio* (London: T. Bosworth, 1854).

50. Samuel Eliot, Perkins's cousin and close friend, was the president of Trinity College. Eliot, "Memoir of Charles Callahan Perkins," 228.

51. Perkins, *Tuscan Sculptors*, 1:vii.

52. Ward-Perkins Family Papers, box 2, folder 36.

53. For Edward Newton Perkins's biography, see Howe, *Later Years of the Saturday Club*, 52–56.

54. Little is known of Mary Spring (1824–1882). Her father, Marshall Binney Spring, received from Harvard an A.B. in 1812 and an A.M. in 1825, and was a lawyer in Watertown, Massachusetts; her mother was Elizabeth Willing of Philadelphia.

55. Sarah Paine Cleveland to Louisa Terry, February 27, 1870, Cleveland-Perkins Family Papers, box 6, folder 12.

56. Quoted in Howe, *Later Years of the Saturday Club*, 56.

57. Edward N. Perkins to John Hubbard Sturgis, February 6, 1869, John Hubbard Sturgis Papers, BA Manuscript Collection: "When I built in 48 I began with our cos Edward [Clarke] Cabot and then not

being satisfied I left him & tried Lemoulnier, et then being perfect frankness, our pleasant relations were never disturbed. . . . "

58. On Lemoulnier, who was a *menuisier* (woodworker and interior decorator) by training but also worked as an architect, see Harold Kirker and David van Zanten, "Jean Lemoulnier in Boston, 1846–1851," *Journal of the Society of Architectural Historians* 31 (October 1972): 204–208. The sumptuous Rococo interior of the Deacon House on Washington Street that the Frenchman designed between 1846 and 1848 had catapulted Lemoulnier to the height of fashion in Boston society, and Edward Perkins eagerly became his second major client in this country.

59. Two excellent overviews of Boston's changing artistic taste in the second half of the nineteenth century are Alexandra R. Murphy, "French Paintings in Boston: 1800–1900," in Anne L. Poulet and Alexandra R. Murphy, *Corot to Braque: French Paintings from the Museum of Fine Arts, Boston* (Boston: Museum of Fine Arts, 1979), xvii–xlvi; and Carol Troyen, "The Boston Tradition: Painters and Patrons in Boston, 1720–1920," in her *The Boston Tradition: American Paintings from the Museum of Fine Arts, Boston* (New York: American Federation of Arts, 1980), 5–42.

60. Hunt's pupils included, among others, John La Farge (1835–1910), William Rimmer (1816–1879), Elihu Vedder (1836–1923), Thomas Robinson (1834–1888), George Fuller (1822–1884), Frank Duveneck (1848–1919), J. Foxcroft Cole (1837–1892), and Sarah Wyman Whitman (1842–1904).

61. Bainbridge Bunting, *Houses of Boston's Back Bay: An Architectural History, 1840–1917* (Cambridge, MA: Belknap Press of Harvard University Press, 1967), 82.

62. Murphy, "French Paintings in Boston," xxxv.

63. Troyen, "The Boston Tradition," 23.

64. After graduation from Harvard, in 1831, Appleton traveled in Europe with Charles Perkins and continued on to Greece and Constantinople with Hunt. Ibid., 21.

65. The Düsseldorf Gallery had been organized by the Prussian diplomat and dealer John G. Boker. Based in New York City, the exhibition toured several American cities. The presentation at the Athenæum opened in the spring, closed for the summer, and reopened in September with some changes to the selection. William H. Gerdts, "'Good Tidings to the Lovers of the Beautiful': New York's Düsseldorf Gallery, 1849–1862," *American Art Journal* 30 (1999): 64–65. The Athenæum's Fine Arts Committee rented one room of the picture gallery to Boker for $1,200. BA Proprietors Records, January 3, 1853.

66. The exact content of the Boston presentation is not known. Among the artists represented in the Düsseldorf Gallery in New York were Andreas Achenbach (1815–1910), Eduard Hildebrandt (1818–1868), Carl Wilhelm Hübner (1814–1879), Christian Koehler (1809–1861), Carl Friedrich Lessing (1808–1880), Emanuel Leutze (1816–1868), Johann Wilhelm Schirmer (1807–1863), and Eduard Steinbrück (1802–1882). *Catalogue of a Private Collection of Paintings and Original Drawings by Artists of the Düsseldorf Academy of Fine Arts* (New York: Wm. C. Bryant and Company, 1851).

67. Ruskin's two early publications exerted a particularly strong influence on both sides of the Atlantic: *Modern Painters by a Graduate of Oxford*, 5 vols. (London: Smith, Elder, and Company, 1843–1860), published in the United States beginning in 1847, and *The Seven Lamps of Architecture. By John Ruskin. With Illustrations, Drawn and Etched by the Author* (London: Smith, Elder, and Company, 1849).

68. For analyses of Ruskin's influence in the United States at midcentury, see Robert B. Stein, *John Ruskin and Aesthetic Thought in America, 1840–1900* (Cambridge, MA: Harvard University Press, 1967); and Linda S. Ferber and William H. Gerdts, *The New Path: Ruskin and the American Pre-Raphaelites* (Brooklyn, NY: Brooklyn Museum, 1985).

69. On Norton and other Ruskinians at Harvard, see Theodore E. Stebbins Jr. and Virginia Anderson, *The Last Ruskinians: Charles Eliot Norton, Charles Herbert Moore, and Their Circle* (Cambridge, MA: Harvard University Art Museums, 2007).

70. The *American Exhibition of British Art* had been organized by the retired British army officer Augustus A. Ruxton to tour in several American cities. The presentation in Boston, at the Athenæum from April 5 to June 19, comprised 200 objects, including 101 oils, 96 watercolors, and three medals. *Catalogue of the*

American Exhibition of British Art, at the Athenæum Gallery, Beacon Street, Boston. Oil Pictures and Water Colors (Boston: J. H. Eastburn's Press, 1858). For discussion of this traveling exhibition, see Susan P. Casteras, "The 1857–58 Exhibition of English Art in America and Critical Response to Pre-Raphaelitism," in Ferber and Gerdts, *The New Path*, 108–133; and Susan P. Casteras, *English Pre-Raphaelitism and Its Reception in America in the Nineteenth Century* (Rutherford, NJ: Fairleigh Dickinson University Press, 1990), 43–68.

71. The Massachusetts Academy of Fine Arts was founded in June 1852 by several Boston artists, including Chester Harding, Francis Alexander, Benjamin Champney (1817–1907), and Alfred Ordway (1821–1897), many of whom had participated in the Boston Artists' Association, founded in 1841. In 1853 the academy held an exhibition at 371–372 Tremont Row. See *Catalogue of the First Semi-Annual Exhibition of Paintings, in the Gallery of the Massachusetts Academy of Fine Arts, No. 371–2 Tremont Row, Boston* (Boston: Dutton and Wentworth, 1853).

72. The club's association with the Athenæum continued, however, in the person of Alfred Ordway, the club's secretary, treasurer, and president, who also served the Athenæum's Fine Arts Committee as the manager of its annual exhibitions from 1856 to 1863. The club became dormant in the mid-1860s but was revived in 1870 by Charles Perkins.

73. See Troyen, "The Boston Tradition," 25–27.

74. Some examples of Boston's commercial art galleries were Williams and Everett, originally established in 1810 as an art supplier; Doll and Richards, dating from the late 1830s or the mid-1840s; Vose Galleries under Seth Morton Vose, known for its radical embrace of Barbizon paintings in the 1850s; and, a little later, Elliott, Blakeslee & Noyes. Beth A. Treadway, "The Doll and Richards Gallery," *Archives of American Art Journal* 15 (1975): 12–14. In 1857 and 1859 the Belgian-English dealer Ernest Gambart brought to Boston an assortment of contemporary French paintings by Rosa Bonheur (1822–1899), Ernest Meissonier (1815–1891), Émile-Charles Lambinet (1813–1877), Constant Troyon, and Gustave Courbet (1819–1877); in 1866–1867 the French dealer and print publisher Alfred Cadart brought to Boston comparable offerings.

75. Murphy, "French Paintings in Boston," xxi.

76. Another painting by Scheffer, *Christ the Consolator* (1851; a replica of the original of 1837), was lent to the Athenæum gallery in 1863 for the special Sanitary Fair exhibition by William Story Bullard, brother-in-law of Charles Eliot Norton. (In 2007 this painting was discovered at the Gethsemane Lutheran Church in Dassel, Minnesota.) In his 1868 review of Philip Gilbert Hamerton's *Contemporary French Painters* (London, 1868), Henry James disapproved of the fact that the book again reproduced Scheffer's *Dante and Beatrice*: "Mr. Hamerton mentions Ary Scheffer, of whose too-familiar *Dante and Beatrice* he gives still another photograph." [Henry James], "Hamerton's Contemporary French Painters," *North American Review* 106 (April 1868): 721. In 1883 a critic who knew Scheffer in the 1840s gave a pathetic summary of Scheffer's career: "[Scheffer] was always a poor draughtsman. His 'Paolo and Francesca,' and many of his best-known religious pictures, are wretchedly drawn, but there is a pretension to purity of style about them which takes people in." Edward Armitage, *Lectures on Painting* (London: Trübner and Company, 1883), 82; quoted in Morris, "Ary Scheffer and His English Circle," 303.

77. *Boston Daily Evening Transcript*, April 21, 1869.

78. The committee's purchases during the 1850s and 1860s were Washington Allston's *Student* (ca. 1815; BA), in 1855 for $190; Albert Bierstadt's *Arch of Octavius* (1858; Fine Arts Museums of San Francisco), in 1858 for $400; Winckworth Allan Gay's (1821–1910) *Lake Champlain and Green Mountains, from Westport, N.Y.* (n.d.; unlocated), in 1859 for $300 (exchanged for *Mount Washington* [1861; BA], also by Gay, in 1862); Samuel F. B. Morse's (1791–1872) *James Monroe* (1819; BA), in 1863 for $40 (at the time thought to be of Lawrence Washington); and nine plaster casts of antique sculptures from William Wetmore Story, in 1858 for $1,000.

79. The Dowse watercolors had been made by a number of English artists in the early nineteenth century, and engravings made from them were published as *The British Gallery of Pictures* (London: Longman, Hurst, Rees, Orme, and Brown, 1818) by the engraver Peltro William Tomkins. When the volume brought financial losses, however, Tomkins disposed of the original watercolors and the engravings by lottery, in 1821. Dowse won the second and third prizes, of watercolors and two full sets of engravings. For more information on the

Dowse collection at the Athenæum, see Harry L. Katz, "The Thomas Dowse Collection of Watercolors," in Jonathan P. Harding, *The Boston Athenæum Collection: Pre-Twentieth Century American and European Painting and Sculpture* (Boston: Boston Athenæum, 1984), 93–109.

80. *Boston Daily Evening Transcript*, April 21, 1869. James Jackson Jarves, "Museums of Art, Artists, and Amateurs in America," *Galaxy* 10 (July–December 1870): 58.

81. For details of Jarves's travails from 1859 to 1861, see Francis Steegmuller, *The Two Lives of James Jackson Jarves* (New Haven: Yale University Press, 1951), 164–195. Stein, *John Ruskin and Aesthetic Thought in America*, 139–146, discusses the American reception of the Jarves collection.

82. For example, the city had just raised $18,000 for the controversial statue of Daniel Webster (1858) by Hiram Powers for the Massachusetts State House, and Norton himself was collecting subscriptions for the statue of the Harvard president Josiah Quincy (1860) by William Wetmore Story.

83. In 1855 Jarves exhibited at the Athenæum gallery (under his father's name) *Roman Campagna before Sunrise* by Claude Lorraine (1604 or 1605–1682) and *Danäe* attributed to Titian (ca. 1488–1576). John Neal of Portland, Maine, quickly purchased both. While the paintings were on view, however, the editors of the *Crayon* declared the Titian attribution erroneous. Jarves's letter to the *Crayon* in the summer of 1855, asserting the authenticity of the Titian, led to a rebuttal by the journal, and the Titian attribution was eventually denounced by all. Neal exhibited the two paintings again at the Athenæum in 1856 and 1857, but thereafter they disappeared into obscurity. Steegmuller, *The Two Lives of James Jackson Jarves*, 147–153.

84. Jarves's book came two decades after William Dunlap's *History of the Rise and Progress of the Arts of Design in America* (1834).

85. Edward, who had gone to see the paintings, cited an English artist—John Hadwen Wheelwright (active 1834–1849)—who thought little of the collection. Wheelwright lived in Italy, where he produced watercolor copies of Old Master paintings, some of which were reproduced in George Redford and J. Hadwen Wheelwright, *Studies of Italian Art: Descriptive Catalogue of a Series of Paintings in Water-colour by J. Hadwen Wheelwright, Taken from Pictures in . . . the Various Churches [and Galleries] of Italy and the Gallery of the Louvre* (London, 1866).

86. Edward Perkins to Charles Eliot Norton, in Steegmuller, *The Two Lives of James Jackson Jarves*, 189–190. According to Edward, Charles had earlier persuaded, at Jarves's request, his mentor Rio to write a recommendation for Jarves's collection.

87. According to Charles Perkins's daughter-in-law, Elizabeth Ward Perkins (Mrs. Charles Bruen Perkins), Charles purchased the triptych (and other works) in Rome during the 1850s "through the advice of Mr. [Otto] Mündler," a German connoisseur and dealer who served, between 1855 and 1858, as the purchasing agent for the National Gallery of London. Elizabeth Ward Perkins to Edward Waldo Forbes, April 27, 1918, object file, 1918.33, Paintings Department, Fogg Art Museum, Harvard University. For Mündler's activities, see Carol Tognari Dowd, ed., "The Travel Diaries of Otto Mündler: 1855–1858," *Walpole Society* 51 (1985).

88. For details of Yale's purchase of the Jarves collection, see Susan B. Matheson, *Art for Yale: A History of the Yale University Art Gallery* (New Haven: Yale University Art Gallery, 2001), 45–54.

89. Perkins, *Art Education in America*, 20.

90. Ibid.

91. Henry James to Charles Eliot Norton, February 4 and 5, 1872, *The Complete Letters of Henry James, 1855–1872*, 2 vols. (Lincoln: University of Nebraska Press, 2006), 2:438.

92. After Perkins received the *Légion d'honneur* in July 1867, his friend George Bancroft, then the American ambassador to Berlin, invited Perkins to serve as his secretary. (Bancroft's second wife was Elizabeth David Bliss Bancroft, who was a longtime friend of the Bruens, Charles Perkins's wife's family.) But despite Bancroft's repeated overtures, Perkins finally declined the offer in June 1868. For letters among Perkins, Mrs. Perkins, and Bancroft, see Ward-Perkins Family Papers, box 2, folder 2.

93. Eliza Callahan Cleveland to an unknown recipient, [summer 1869], Cleveland-Perkins Family Papers, box 6, folder 12. The three children were Mary Eleanor, born in Boston or Newport in 1856; Edward Clifford, born in Florence in 1858; and Charles Bruen, also born in Florence in 1860.

94. Perkins was a university lecturer on art history at Harvard University from 1869 to 1875. He also gave several lecture series at the Lowell Institute: in 1869–1870, the first of twelve lectures presented by the American Social Science Association, titled "Art Education in the United States"; in 1870–1871, twelve lectures on "Grecian" art, on which his publication *Italian Art* (Boston: Little, Brown and Company, 1875), was based; in 1873–1874, another twelve on Italian art; and in 1877–1878, twelve on the history of the art of engraving. Harriette Knight Smith, *The History of the Lowell Institute* (Boston: Lamson, Wolffe and Company, 1898). Perkins also provided notes to the American edition, published in 1872, of Charles Eastlake's *Hints on Household Taste*.

95. For a discussion of the "South Kensington idea," see Anthony Burton, *Vision and Accident: The Story of the Victoria and Albert Museum* (London: V&A Publications, 1999).

96. William B. Rogers, president, "Address of the Executive Committee of the American Social Science Association," November 22, 1865, ASSA Records, box 1, folder 2.

97. The other three departments were Public Health; Jurisprudence; and Economy, Trade, and Finance.

98. Samuel Eliot declared in 1878 that the Education Department of the association "had been dead for several years." Samuel Eliot to Frank Sanborn, [n.d.] 1878, ASSA Records, box 4, folder 68.

99. A somewhat mysterious figure, James M. Bernard had had a hand in 1850 in the handover of the casts belonging to the family of the late sculptor Shobal Vail Clevenger (1812–1843) from the Athenæum (James M. Bernard to Charles Folsom, November 25, 1850, BA Letters) and presented a cast of *Venus with the Apple* by Bertel Thorvaldsen (1770–1844) to the Athenæum in 1864. The progressively minded Barnard recommended to William Endicott Jr., the MFA's president pro tempore in 1900, that the museum admit women to its board of trustees. James M. Bernard to William Endicott Jr., April 12, 1900, MFA Director's Correspondence. For biographical information on Barnard, see William Robert Ware, "James Munson Barnard," *Proceedings of the American Academy of Arts and Sciences* 41 (May 1905–May 1906): 837–841. Ware was appointed professor of architecture at MIT in 1865 but delayed founding the architecture department until 1868 in order to travel to Europe to study existing architecture schools there. After graduating from Harvard, Ware had worked in the office of Edward Clarke Cabot in the 1850s. J. A. Chewning, "William Robert Ware at MIT and Columbia," *Journal of Architectural Education* 33 (November 1979): 25–29.

100. Records of the Sub Committee on Art in Education, July 7, 1869, ASSA Records.

101. Perkins, *Art in Education*, 1–2.

102. This "new body" was probably MIT, specifically Ware's department of architecture.

103. Records of the Sub Committee on Art in Education, November 22, 1869, ASSA Records.

104. "Mr. Perkins read the statement of our plan & Mr. Cabot exhibited & explained our plan of building [of the proposed art gallery]." Ibid., November 24, 1869. These drawings by Cabot are unlocated.

105. Ibid.

106. Ibid.

107. Almost certainly, Perkins's writing at this time became the basis of the article on the proposed museum, *Boston Daily Evening Transcript*, November 29, 1869.

108. Records of the Sub Committee on Art in Education, November 29, 1869, ASSA Records.

109. In attendance at the meeting of December 3, 1869, were John Amory Lowell (Athenæum president; Lowell Institute director), Benjamin Smith Rotch (Athenæum trustee, Fine Arts Committee, Harvard overseer, and son-in-law of Abbott Lawrence), Edward N. Perkins, Abbott Lawrence Jr. (brother of the late Timothy Bigelow Lawrence, donor of the Lawrence collection), George Washington Wales (Athenæum trustee, Fine Arts Committee), Charles Shimmin (lawyer), Martin Brimmer, Theodore Lyman (Harvard overseer), Charles William Eliot (Harvard president), Thomas Gold Appleton (Harvard overseer), William Whitwell Greenough (Boston Public Library president), Edward Atkinson (Harvard overseer, MIT corporation member, head of the Boston Insurance Company), Henry Sayles (stockbroker), J. S. Blatchford (ASSA treasurer), Henry Villard (ASSA secretary, journalist, financier, and son-in-law of William Lloyd Garrison), Edward Clarke Cabot, William Robert Ware, James M. Barnard, and Charles C. Perkins.

110. Records of the Sub Committee on Art in Education, November 24, 1869, ASSA Records.

111. Ibid., November 29, 1869.

112. MFA General Organizational Material, December 21, 1869.

113. Otis Norcross, John Tisdale Bradlee, and Benjamin Smith Rotch, all prosperous merchants with strong political ties, were added separately at the bottom of the handwritten list of fourteen applicants. Ibid.

114. Ware, "James Munson Barnard," 840. After 1870 Barnard clearly continued to take pride in his role in creating the museum. Three decades later, in 1900, Barnard wrote to the museum's president pro tempore, William Endicott Jr.: "As I was present at the first meeting for the establishment of a Museum of Fine Arts in Boston, in fact was chairman of the committee, it is pleasant for me to see its present very prosperous condition." James M. Barnard to William Endicott Jr., April 12, 1900, MFA Director's Correspondence.

NOTES TO CHAPTER THREE

1. "Notice of first meeting of Board of Trustees, [March 1870]," MFA Early Organizational Material, 1869–1870.

2. To this day, the composition of the museum's board has changed only slightly: the number of representatives from the Athenæum, Harvard, and MIT has each been reduced from three to one, and one from the museum's Ladies' Committee has been added; the ex officii appointments are essentially the same as they were in 1870, except that what was in 1870 "the Secretary of Boston's Board of Education" is now "the Massachusetts Commissioner of Education," and the representative from the Boston Public Library is currently an individual appointed by the library's board, not necessarily the president of the trustees.

3. The museum's first woman trustee was appointed in 1954.

4. Martin Brimmer to Charles Eliot Norton, December 3, 1882. Quoted in Neil Harris, "The Gilded Age Revisited: Boston and the Museum Movement," *American Quarterly* 14 (Winter 1962): 551.

5. For a history of the company, see Gerald Taylor White, *A History of the Massachusetts Hospital Life Insurance Company* (Cambridge, MA: Harvard University Press, 1955); and Robert F. Dalzell Jr., *Enterprising Elite: The Boston Associates and the World They Made* (Cambridge, MA: Harvard University Press, 1987), 134–137.

6. The Lowell Institute, founded in 1836 by John Lowell as a forum for public lectures, relegated the entire authority over the institution to a single trustee, preferably a male Lowell descendant, who served as the director and reported annually to the trustees of the Athenæum.

7. These drafts are in MFA Early Organizational Material, 1869–1870.

8. MFA Trustees Minutes, March 17, 1870.

9. The Athenæum was to deposit a portion of its art collection as well as the Lawrence collection of arms and armor; Harvard University, the Gray collection of engravings; and the Boston Public Library, the Tosti collection of engravings, a recent gift of Thomas Gold Appleton. The Tosti collection, however, never went to the museum.

10. MFA Trustees Minutes, March 17, 1870.

11. At Brimmer's and Loring's deaths, in 1896 and 1902, respectively, the museum printed long tributes in its annual reports and acquired works of art in their memory; Perkins's death in 1886 was mentioned only briefly in the annual report.

12. Perkins, *Art Education in America*, 21, 3, and 4. Perkins delivered the lecture titled "Art Education in America" at a meeting of the American Social Science Association, which later printed it. He repeated most of his recommendations in another article, "American Art Museums," published in July of the same year in the *North American Review*.

13. Ibid., 8.

14. "A Museum of Art," *Boston Daily Evening Transcript*, November 29, 1869.

15. MFA Trustees Minutes, March 17, 1870.

16. "The Art Museum: The Formal Opening Today—the Addresses," *Boston Evening Transcript*, July 5, 1876.

17. Ibid.

18. For the history of the museum, see Anthony Burton, *Vision and Accident: The Story of the Victoria and Albert Museum* (London: V&A Publications, 1999); and Malcolm Baker and Brenda Richardson, eds., *A Grand Design: The Art of the Victoria and Albert Museum* (New York: Harry N. Abrams; Baltimore: Baltimore Museum of Art, 1997).

19. Quoted in Margaret Henderson Floyd, "A Terra-Cotta Cornerstone for Copley Square: Museum of Fine Arts, Boston, 1870–1876, by Sturgis and Brigham," *Journal of the Society of Architectural Historians* 32 (May 1973): 83.

20. Perkins, *Art Education in America*, 14.

21. Burton, *Vision and Accident*, 18.

22. *Report of a Special Committee of the Council of the Government School of Design. . . .* (London: HMSO, 1847), 25. Quoted in Burton, *Vision and Accident*, 23.

23. MFA Trustees Minutes, March 17, 1870.

24. *Newton's London Journal of Arts and Sciences* 10 (1859): 321. Quoted in Burton, *Vision and Accident*, 54.

25. Burton, *Vision and Accident*, 36. On the museum's contradictory educational aspirations, see, esp. Rafael Cardoso Denis, "Teaching by Example: Education and the Formation of South Kensington's Museum," in Baker and Richardson, *A Grand Design*, 107–116.

26. *Addresses of the Superintendents of the Department of Practical Art, Delivered in the Theatre at Marlborough House, I. On the Facilities Afforded to All Classes of the Community for Obtaining Education in Art. By Henry Cole. . . .* (London: Chapman and Hall, 1853), 33. Quoted in Burton, *Vision and Accident*, 29.

27. Perkins, "American Art Museums," 15.

28. The Metropolitan Museum of Art's twenty-seven founding trustees were elected on January 31, the state legislature passed the act of incorporation for the museum on April 13, and the first meeting of the founding trustees took place on May 24, 1870. Calvin Tomkins, *Merchants and Masterpieces: The Story of the Metropolitan Museum of Art* (New York: E. P. Dutton and Company, 1970), 35.

29. http://www.philamuseum.org/information/45-19.

30. The eight required subjects were orthography, reading, writing, English grammar, geography, arithmetic, the history of the United States, and good behavior.

31. Quoted in Paul E. Bolin, "The Massachusetts Drawing Act of 1870: Industrial Mandate or Democratic Maneuver?" in *Framing the Past: Essays on Art Education*, ed. Donald Soucy and Mary Ann Stankiewicz (Reston, VA: National Art Education Association, 1990), 66.

32. Arthur D. Efland, *A History of Art Education: Intellectual and Social Currents in Teaching the Visual Arts* (New York: Teachers College Press, 1990), 100.

33. Manufacturing industries were defined as "manufacturing, mechanical, and mining industries." Charles B. Stetson, introduction to Joseph Langl, *Modern Art Education: Its Practical and Aesthetic Character Educationally Considered* (Boston: L. Prang and Company, 1875), xix.

34. Quoted in Bolin, "The Massachusetts Drawing Act of 1870," 60.

35. The subcommittee on drawing requested Perkins's opinion on how to implement the Drawing Act, and Perkins wrote on September 6, 1870, to William T. Brigham, committee chairman. In the letter, Perkins revealed that he had already consulted Henry Cole, a friend and the director of the South Kensington Museum, on salary requirements for an English instructor who might come to Boston. Perkins enclosed a prospectus, sent by Cole, of the South Kensington School of Design with the letter. *Annual Report of the School Committee of the City of Boston, 1870* (Boston: Alfred Mudge and Son, 1871), 326–327. Cole recommended Walter Smith. Diana Korzenik, *Drawn to Art: A Nineteenth-Century American Dream* (Hanover, NH: University Press of New England, 1985), 154–155.

36. Walter Smith, *Art Education, Scholastic and Industrial* (Boston: James R. Osgood and Company, 1872), 36–39.

37. Charles C. Perkins, "Report," in *First Annual Report of the Committee on the Museum of Fine Arts, March 20, 1873* (Boston: Alfred Mudge and Son, 1873), 9.

38. Smith, *Art Education*, 44.

39. Within the Boston School Committee, internal strife culminated in March 1878 when a new, reformist faction critical of the entrenched bureaucracy dismissed Philbrick from the position of superintendent. See Michael B. Katz, *Class, Bureaucracy, and Schools: The Illusion of Educational Change in America* (New York: Praeger, 1971), 73–97; see also Katrina L. Billings, "Sophisticated Proselytizing: Charles Callahan Perkins and the Boston School Committee" (master's thesis, Massachusetts College of Art, 1987). In his 1879 report to the Boston School Committee, Perkins wrote "With Music all goes harmoniously. . . . With Drawing, on the contrary, there is no peace," and described the criticisms faced by the Committee on Music and Drawing (committees on music and drawing had merged in 1878 with Perkins as chairman). *Annual Report of the School Committee of the City of Boston, 1879* (Boston: Rockwell and Churchill, 1879), 3.

40. The 1875 debate between Hunt and Moore originated as a critical dialogue about Hunt's recent work and his book, *Talks on Art* (1875), but it quickly turned into a public argument about art education in general. For details of the controversy, see Sally Webster, *William Morris Hunt, 1824–1879* (Cambridge: Cambridge University Press, 1991), 111–115; and Theodore E. Stebbins Jr. and Virginia Anderson, *The Last Ruskinians: Charles Eliot Norton, Charles Herbert Moore, and Their Circle* (Cambridge, MA: Harvard University Art Museums, 2007), 23.

41. The dramatic events leading up to Smith's dismissal and Perkins's effort to save Smith in 1881 are described in Efland, *A History of Art Education*, 111–113.

42. Perkins, "American Art Museums," 14.

43. Carol Duncan, "From the Princely Gallery to the Public Art Museum: The Louvre Museum and the National Gallery, London," in *Grasping the World: The Idea of the Museum*, ed. Donald Preziozi and Claire Farago (Aldershot, UK; Burlington, VT: Ashgate Publishing, 2004), 255.

44. Ibid.

45. James Jackson Jarves, "Museums of Art, Artists, and Amateurs in America," *Galaxy* 10 (July–December 1870): 50.

47. Circular issued on August 25, 1876, reproduced in *Museum of Fine Arts: School of Drawing and Painting; First Annual Report of the Permanent Committee in Charge of the School* (Boston: Alfred Mudge and Son, 1877), 13.

48. Ibid., 9. William Morris Hunt criticized what he viewed as the school's amateurish tendencies: "This plan of the Art-Museum School will produce teachers and people skilled in academical drawing—not painters." Hunt, *On Painting and Drawing* (1875; New York: Dover Publications, 1976), 136.

49. The School of Carving and Modelling and the School of Art Needlework were administered by the Women's Educational Association, and the School of Pottery and Painting of Porcelain under the auspices of the Society of Decorative Arts. In 1884 the museum school established the Department of Decorative Design. The department separated from the school in 1903 to merge with the Massachusetts School of Design (founded by the Lowell Institute in 1872 as the Lowell School of Practical Design). *Trustees of the Museum of Fine Arts: Twenty-Eighth Annual Report, for the Year Ending Dec. 31, 1903* (Boston: Alfred Mudge and Son, 1904), 39.

50. Charles C. Perkins, "Report of the Committee on the Museum," in *Trustees of the Museum of Fine Arts: Second Annual Report, for the Year Ending Dec. 31, 1877* (Boston: Alfred Mudge and Son, 1878), 8.

51. The architects were Edward Clarke Cabot, Robert S. Peabody (1845–1917), and William R. Ware; the painters were William Morris Hunt, John La Farge, Francis William Loring (1838–1905), Francis D. Millet (1846–1912), and Frank Hill Smith (1842–1904); in addition, Edward W. Hooper, treasurer of Harvard University, was also on the founding Permanent Committee. Among the artists, Millet was the most closely involved with the committee and the school, and he was instrumental in bringing his erstwhile Saxon classmate in Antwerp, Otto Grundmann (1848–1890), to the school as its first instructor.

52. In 1901 the museum trustees assumed control of the school after two recent bequests to the school

had made it possible to create an endowment. *School of the Museum of Fine Arts: Twenty-Sixth Annual Report, for the Year Ending June 1, 1902* (Boston: Alfred Mudge and Son, 1902), 6–8.

53. Perkins, "American Art Museums," 15.

54. Perkins, *Art Education in America*, 4–5. A very similar argument was advanced even before the museum's incorporation, in the fall of 1869: "Casts of more than six hundred objects of art, great and small, from the British Museum could be bought, transported from England and set up in Boston, for less than $10,000. Double or triple that sum and we should approach completeness." "A Museum of Art," *Boston Daily Evening Transcript*, November 29, 1869.

55. Perkins, *Art Education in America*, 4.

56. MFA Trustees Minutes, March 17, 1870.

57. Francis Haskell and Nicholas Penny, *Taste and the Antique: The Lure of Classical Sculpture, 1500–1900* (New Haven: Yale University Press, 1981), 122.

58. Perkins, *Art Education in America*, 8.

59. In 1867, at the instigation of Henry Cole, fifteen European princes signed an agreement ("The International Convention for Promoting Universal Reproductions of Works of Art") that promised mutual exchange of plaster copies of objects across Europe. Diane Bilbey and Marjorie Trusted, "'The Question of Casts'—Collecting and Later Reassessment of the Cast Collections at South Kensington," in *Plaster Casts: Making, Collecting, and Displaying from Classical Antiquity to the Present*, ed. Rune Frederiksen and Eckart Marchand (Berlin: De Gruyter, 2010), 466.

60. Committee on the Museum, "Special Report on the Increase of the Collections," in *Trustees of the Museum of Fine Arts: Eighth Annual Report, for the Year Ending Dec. 31, 1883* (Boston: Alfred Mudge and Son, 1884), 10.

61. George Fiske Comfort, "Art Museums in America," *Old and New* 1 (April 1870): 506.

62. James Elliot Cabot to Charles Eliot Norton, May 10, 1875, Charles Eliot Norton Papers, MS AM 1088 (947). Houghton Library, Harvard University. Quoted in Harris, "The Gilded Age Revisited," 553.

63. The much maligned sale of the Sumner bequest was proposed by Perkins and supported by the rest of the board. The preface to the catalogue of the Sumner exhibition in 1874, reportedly excerpted from the *Daily Advertiser* (n.d.), stated that in bequeathing his collection to the museum, Sumner "did not pretend that all were worthy of a place in it, and showed that he did not, by leaving the Trustees at liberty to dispose of them as they might see fit." *Catalogue of Pictures Exhibited by the Athenæum: Pictures and Engravings Bequeathed to the Museum of Fine Arts by the Hon. Charles Sumner* (Boston: Rockwell and Churchill, 1874), 3–4.

64. The large purchase had been ordered from London in December 1875, but on February 12, 1876, the ship carrying the casts put in to the harbor of St. Thomas "dismasted and leaky." The casts were safe, but the ship underwent extensive repairs at the Caribbean port, unable to embark for Boston in time to reach it by May 1. Charles C. Perkins, "Report of the Committee on the Museum," in *Proceedings*, 18.

65. Perkins, *Art Education in America*, 8.

66. Ibid., 14.

67. The full board voted on February 6, 1871, to "request the Committee on the Museum to consider and report a design for the seal of the Corporation"; the committee made its proposal for the design on May 27, 1871. MFA Trustees Minutes, February 6 and May 27, 1871.

68. It is not known who executed the seal.

69. Charles G. Loring, *Twenty-Five Years of the Museum's Growth: A Historical Sketch* (Boston: Museum of Fine Arts, Boston, 1901), 4.

70. The Smithsonian Institution, founded in 1846 from the unexpected bequest of the Englishman James Smithson (d. 1829), was one potential exception. The institution did not have a full-fledged museum (except for the small display at the Castle that opened in 1855) until 1876, when it purchased a large number of objects from the Centennial Exhibition and established the United States National Museum (now the Arts and Industries Building).

71. Perkins, "American Art Museums," 28.

72. Sarah Paine [Perkins] Cleveland to Louisa Terry, September 20, 1870, Cleveland-Perkins Family Papers, box 6, folder 12.

73. Appointed to this committee were Charles C. Perkins and Samuel Eliot. MFA Trustees Minutes, November 29, 1870. Allston's painting was a gift of Mrs. Samuel Hooper and Miss Alice Hooper.

74. MFA Trustees Minutes, March 10, 1871.

NOTES TO CHAPTER FOUR

1. BA Trustees Records, January 17, 1870.

2. The founding members of the Committee on the Museum, in 1870, were Charles Callahan Perkins (chairman), Henry Jacob Bigelow, James Elliot Cabot, Benjamin Smith Rotch, and George Washington Wales. Of the five members, Cabot, Rotch, and Wales were Athenæum trustees and members of the Fine Arts Committee; Perkins and Bigelow were Athenæum proprietors.

3. The painting by Gustave Courbet had been brought to the United States in 1866 by Alfred Cadart and purchased by the Allston Club.

4. *Boston Daily Evening Transcript*, January 10, 1871.

5. On February 20, 1871, the Athenæum's board approved the Fine Arts Committee chairman Edward Perkins's request to hold a charity exhibition for the cause. BA Trustees Records, February 20, 1871.

6. "Report of the Fine Arts Committee," January 8, 1872, BA Proprietors Records. The French Fair featured works donated by artists and poets, handicrafts made by ladies, and goods and services provided by businesses for sale and raffles, and the visitors enjoyed the emporium with band music and refreshments, taking the specially run trains home late into the night. *Boston Daily Evening Transcript*, April 15 and 18, 1871.

7. It is not known how much money the Athenæum's special French exhibition raised. Profit from gallery exhibitions for the entire year of 1871 was $543.29. BA Proprietors Records, January 8, 1872.

8. The special French exhibition of 1871 included *Landscape with Figures* by Constant Troyon, lent by Thomas Gold Appleton; *Harvesting* by Émile Charles Lambinet; *Zouaves in Africa* by Isidore Pils; and *Reverie* by Charles Baugniet, all lent by Thomas Wigglesworth.

9. The catalogue also listed a miniature portrait of John Harris by Allston as belonging to the museum, but Miss Charlotte Harris did not bequeath the miniature until 1873.

10. The Deacon House had been built in 1846–1848 on Washington Street for Edward Preble Deacon by his father-in-law, Peter Parker, to the design by the French architect Jean F. Lemoulnier. Deacon died in 1851, his widow left the house ten years later, and in February 1871 the house was sold and its contents put up for auction. There, the heirs of Peter Parker bought the two Boucher paintings, and Miss Deacon, daughter of Edward Preble Deacon, purchased the Flemish tapestry, and all were given to the museum in March. At the same auction, Harleston Parker, brother-in-law of Edward Preble Deacon, purchased the eight eighteenth-century carved panels from Claude-Nicolas Ledoux's Hôtel de Montmorency in Paris that had been installed in the Deacon House. Harleston Parker exhibited the panels in the Athenæum's exhibition beginning in 1871. In 1879 the museum and the Athenæum jointly purchased the eight Montmorency panels.

11. The Arundel Society prints were considered reference materials rather than works of art, for they were catalogued by the librarian, Charles Ammi Cutter, before they joined the Athenæum's exhibition in the winter of 1871–1872.

12. Abraham O. Bigelow, one of the owners of the jewelry firm, had succeeded Charles Perkins as the president of the Handel and Haydn Society, in 1851, and likely knew Perkins well.

13. For Cesnola's life and collection, see, among others, Sir John Linton Myers, *Handbook of the Cesnola Collection of Antiquities from Cyprus* (New York: Metropolitan Museum of Art, 1914); Elizabeth McFadden, *The Glitter and the Gold: A Spirited Account of the Metropolitan Museum of Art's First Director, the Audacious*

and *High-Handed Luigi Palma di Cesnola* (New York: Dial Press, 1971); and Vassos Karageorghis, in collaboration with Joan R. Mertens and Marice E. Rose, *Ancient Art from Cyprus: The Cesnola Collection in the Metropolitan Museum of Art* (New York: Metropolitan Museum of Art, 2000).

14. Hiram Hitchcock, a New York hotelier and Cesnola's foremost American promoter, called the Cypriot antiquities "Sepulchres of the ages" and believed that they could "unfold the history of ancient civilization to one who searches the dark recesses with a heart for classic memory and who can read their language of death." Hitchcock, "The Explorations of Di Cesnola in Cyprus," *Harper's New Monthly Magazine* 45 (July 1872): 192. Hitchcock did not mention Boston in this article, possibly to preserve the impression that the entire Cesnola collection was being offered for sale to the Metropolitan Museum of Art.

15. *Proceedings*, 11.

16. MFA Trustees Minutes, June 9, 1870.

17. Charles C. Perkins to Hiram Hitchcock, March 10, 1872, Papers of Luigi Palma di Cesnola, Rauner Special Collections Library, Dartmouth College (hereafter cited as Cesnola Papers).

18. Ibid. In an undated letter in the archives of the Hermitage, Friederichs told Cesnola that Friederichs had told Perkins that he "cannot recommend the acquisition." Quoted in McFadden, *The Glitter and the Gold*, 108.

19. Cesnola to Hiram Hitchcock, March 14, 1872, Cesnola Papers.

20. The collection was "about to be shipped to Boston" from New York on February 12, 1872. John Augustus Johnson to Hiram Hitchcock, February 12, 1872, Cesnola Papers.

21. MFA Trustees Minutes, April 25, 1872. The exhibition likely ran from late February to late April, but the exact dates are not known. The expense book of the Bigelow, Kennard, and Company, covering the spring of 1872 in the collection of the Baker Library, Harvard University, may provide more clues, but, as of March 2010, the book could not be located.

22. According to the MFA Register of Purchases, 1870–1906, the MFA purchased more than five hundred objects from the Cesnola collection on May 16, 1872. The cost is listed as $1,500 in gold, $1,704.39 in currency, and $111.79 for expenses, for a total of $3,316.18. Thanks to Julia A. McCarthy, Manager of Collections Documentation at the MFA, for this information.

23. Cesnola to Hiram Hitchcock, July 2, 1872, Cesnola Papers.

24. Objects sold by Cesnola are now among the holdings of numerous American museums, some of which acquired the pieces from the Metropolitan Museum of Art in the 1920s: the Ringling Museum, Sarasota, FL; the Semitic Museum at Harvard University; and the Hood Museum of Art, Dartmouth College, Hanover, NH, among others.

25. Quoted in McFadden, *The Glitter and the Gold*, 190.

26. MFA Trustees Minutes, April 25, 1872.

27. The museum paid $7 for the tablet. MFA Trustees Minutes, June 28, 1872.

28. MFA Trustees Minutes, May 16, 1872.

29. In 1873, for example, the museum's *Hebe and Ganymede* by Thomas Crawford was placed in the first-floor reading room, and *The First Inspirations of Columbus*, by Giulio Monteverde, in the vestibule, at the Athenæum. *Second Catalogue of the Collection of Ancient and Modern Works of Art Given or Loaned to the Trustees of the Museum of Fine Arts, at Boston, Now on Exhibition in the Picture Gallery of the Athenæum* (Boston: Alfred Mudge and Son, 1873), 66.

30. The collection was formed by the Scotsman Robert Hay in Egypt during the 1820s and 1830s and purchased by the Bostonian Samuel A. Way in London in 1868–1872. By one account, Way wished to present the collection to the MFA but withheld the gift when his name was not added to the list of incorporators in 1870. *Boston Evening Transcript*, June 11, 1872. Way died on June 4, 1872, and his son C. Granville Way gave the collection to the museum on June 28, 1872.

31. MFA Trustees Minutes, June 28, 1872.

32. *Catalogue of the Collection of Ancient and Modern Works of Art Given or Loaned to the Trustees of the Museum of Fine Arts, at Boston* (Boston: Alfred Mudge and Son, 1872), 43.

33. Charles C. Perkins, preface to ibid., 3.

34. Charles C. Perkins, preface to *Second Catalogue of the Collection of Ancient and Modern Works of Art Given or Loaned to the Trustees of the Museum of Fine Arts, at Boston, Now on Exhibition in the Picture Gallery of the Athenæum* (Boston: Alfred Mudge and Son, 1873), 18–19. The same paragraph was also printed at the end of the preface for the 1874 and 1875 catalogues.

35. MFA Trustees Minutes, May 16 and June 28, 1872.

36. Ibid., June 28, 1872.

37. *First Annual Report of the Committee on the Museum of Fine Arts, March 20, 1873* (Boston: Alfred Mudge and Son, 1873), 8.

38. MFA Trustees Minutes, June 28, 1872.

39. BA Proprietors Records, January 12, 1874.

40. MFA Trustees Minutes, May 26, 1870. The order from the city, included in this record, was dated May 16, 1870.

41. *Proceedings*, 13.

42. After the museum opened, the area to its north—cut across diagonally by Huntington Avenue—was known popularly as Art Square, a designation that continued to be in use even after the space was named Copley Square in 1883.

43. Printed circular, Committee on Finance, May 26, 1870, MFA Building Records.

44. "Art in America: The Proposed Museum on the Site of the Coliseum in Boston," *New York Times*, February 6, 1871.

45. The speakers also included Phillips Brooks, the rector of the Trinity Church since 1869; William Gray, a civic leader and a museum trustee; and E. R. Mudge, a businessman who would become a museum trustee in March of that year.

46. Quoted in *Boston Daily Evening Transcript*, February 4, 1871.

47. "Special Notice," *Boston Daily Evening Transcript*, April 11, 1871. See also a printed circular dated March 21, 1871, MFA Building Records.

48. "Special Notice," *Boston Daily Evening Transcript*, April 11, 1871.

49. *Boston Daily Evening Transcript*, April 17, 1871.

50. Albert J. Wright to William Gray, February 10, 1871, MFA Building Records.

51. Greenough's exhibition took place at the gallery of Elliot, Blakeslee, and Noyes on Tremont Street, March 30–April 12, 1871. *Boston Daily Evening Transcript*, March 27, 1871. MFA Trustees Minutes, March 10, 1871. Greenough's statue is undocumented and unlocated. It may have been related to, or a version of, the sculptor's 1869 work, *Mary Magdalene*, now at the Brooklyn Museum.

52. MFA Trustees Minutes, March 10 and 16, 1871.

53. MFA Trustees Minutes, May 27, 1871.

54. *Proceedings*, 13.

55. MFA Trustees Minutes, June 9, 1870.

56. *Proposals for Designs for Museum of Fine Arts (June 15, 1870)*, MFA Building Records. This was to be an open competition, not requiring an invitation for architects to participate, as was often the case with nineteenth-century architectural contests.

57. Ibid.

58. Charles Brigham to John H. Sturgis, March 8, 1870, John Hubbard Sturgis Papers, BA Manuscript Collection.

59. *Proposals for Designs for Museum of Fine Arts (June 15, 1870)*.

60. Perkins, "American Art Museums," 28 and 29.

61. *Proceedings*, 9.

62. Peabody and Stearns (two designs), W. G. Preston, Sturgis and Brigham, S. J. F. Thayer, and Ware and Van Brunt.

63. To examine the architectural drawings, the trustees had to borrow rooms at the Boston Society of Natural History and the Boston Art Club. MFA Trustees Minutes, November 29, 1870. Martin Brimmer, handwritten report of the Building Committee, February 6, 1871, MFA Building Records.

64. MFA Trustees Minutes, February 6, 1871. Most of the large-size architectural drawings submitted to the competition are in off-site storage of the MFA.

65. Sturgis and Brigham designed, after the MFA, the High Anglican Church of the Advent on Beacon Hill (1875–1888). After Sturgis's death in 1888, Brigham went on to design, most notably, the annex to the Massachusetts State House (1898) and the First Church of Christ, Scientist (1906). The 1906 church by Brigham adjoined the smaller Mother Church edifice built in 1894. In the 1960s the church building became part of the larger and current Christian Science Plaza, designed by I. M. Pei.

66. *Specifications of the Materials to Be Provided and Labor to Be Performed in the Construction of a Portion of a Building . . . for the Museum of Fine Arts. Boston. . . .* (Boston: printed by T. W. Ripley, 1874), 2.

67. "Report of the Committee on Building," February 6, 1871, MFA Building Records.

68. Copy of a letter to Martin Brimmer, n.d., John H. Sturgis journal, February 4, 1870, John Hubbard Sturgis Papers, BA Manuscript Collection.

69. Sturgis discovered that "on a cubic foot basis the South Kensington buildings had cost but half (9 1/2d. per cubic foot) of Robert Smirke's British Museum (1847) (1/6d. [18d] per cubic foot)." Margaret Henderson Floyd, "A Terra-Cotta Cornerstone for Copley Square: Museum of Fine Arts, Boston, 1870–1876, by Sturgis and Brigham," *Journal of the Society of Architectural Historians* 32 (May 1973): 92 and 94.

70. Charles Brigham to John Hubbard Sturgis in London, March 8, 1870: "[Edward Perkins] says that he has written you fully on the subject . . . [of] terracotta design 'Art Museum.'" John Hubbard Sturgis Papers, BA Manuscript Collection.

71. Charles C. Perkins to Martin Brimmer, September 11, [1871], MFA Building Records. In this letter, Perkins wrote that he "had always been in favor of" such decorative scheme.

72. "Report of the Committee on Building," February 6, 1871, MFA Building Records.

73. John Hubbard Sturgis's paternal grandmother, Elizabeth Perkins Sturgis, was a sister of James Perkins, Edward Perkins's grandfather.

74. Charles Brigham to John H. Sturgis, August 18, 1869, John Hubbard Sturgis Papers, BA Manuscript Collection.

75. Charles Brigham to John H. Sturgis, October 18, 1869, John Hubbard Sturgis Papers, BA Manuscript Collection. On Pinebank II, see Floyd, "A Terra-Cotta Cornerstone for Copley Square." After Edward Perkins moved out of Pinebank III in the 1890s (to live with his niece Eliza Callahan Cleveland at her nearby Nutwood), Pinebank III housed the headquarters for the city's Park Department until 1913, and the Children's Museum from 1913 to 1936. Thereafter, the house suffered neglect and was demolished in February 2007. For a concise history of the three Pinebanks, see Cynthia Zaitzevsky, *Frederick Law Olmsted and the Boston Park System* (Cambridge, MA: Belknap Press of Harvard University Press, 1982), 88–91.

76. The Building Committee was authorized, however, on September 21, to hire a company to drive piles into the ground to support the entire northern flank of the building facing St. James Avenue. MFA Trustees Minutes, September 21 and 28, 1871.

77. *Specifications of the Materials to Be Provided*, 2.

78. On the museum's site, a large wooden edifice popularly known as the Coliseum had been erected in 1869, to house the National Peace Jubilee, a musical extravaganza held to commemorate the end of the Civil War. After the first Coliseum suffered wind damage, the second Coliseum reappeared in 1872 on the same spot, in which the International Peace Jubilee was held until July of that year.

79. *Specifications of the Materials to Be Provided*, 2–6.

80. Martin Brimmer lamented in 1876, "since the Chicago fire there has been no time when it was thought expedient to renew and appeal for funds [for the building]." *Proceedings*, 13.

81. MFA Trustees Minutes, January 14, 1874.

82. Ibid., January 24, 1873.

83. Along the southern edge of the vacant portion of the lot, two small structures appeared in the late 1880s and were used by the School of Drawing and Painting. One of them was known as the Crowninshield Studio after Frederic Crowninshield (1845–1918), an artist and a popular instructor at the school. In 1886, when he left Boston for New York, the MFA purchased the building and the school paid for its short transport onto the MFA's land. H. Winthrop Peirce, *The History of the School of the Museum of Fine Arts, Boston, 1877–1927* (Boston: T. O. Metcalf, 1930), 40. For descriptions of the events of 1886 and 1887, see *Museum of Fine Arts. School of Drawing and Painting. Tenth Annual Report of the Permanent Committee in Charge of the School* (Boston: Alfred Mudge and Son, 1886), 8; and *Museum of Fine Arts. School of Drawing and Painting. Eleventh Annual Report of the Permanent Committee in Charge of the School* (Boston: Alfred Mudge and Son, 1887), 4 and 5.

84. The committee members were Charles C. Perkins (chairman), Martin Brimmer, Thomas Gold Appleton, George Washington Wales, Charles G. Loring, and Edward N. Perkins (secretary). In a sign of closeness, the joint Montpensier committee's meeting minutes were entered in the same bound notebook used by the Athenæum's Fine Arts Committee.

85. The Galerie Espagnole at the Louvre closed on January 1, 1849. The collection was sold at Christie's in London in 1853, from which the duc de Montpensier purchased a number of important works. On the Galerie Espagnole, see Jeannine Baticle and Cristina Marinas, *La Galerie espagnole de Louis-Philippe au Louvre, 1838–1848* (Paris: Ministère de la Culture, Éditions de la Réunion des Musées Nationaux, 1981); and Jeannine Baticle, "The Galerie Espagnole of Louis-Philippe," in Gary Tinterow and Geneviève Lacambre, *Manet/Velázquez: The French Taste for Spanish Painting* (New York: Metropolitan Museum of Art, 2003), 174–189.

86. *Catalogue of Pictures Belonging to His Royal Highness the Duke de Montpensier, and of Other Pictures, Also Loaned to the Museum of Fine Arts* (Boston: Alfred Mudge and Son, 1874), 24–25; "Fine Arts. The Montpensier Collection of Paintings," *Appleton's Journal* 12 (September 26, 1874): 412–413; and "The Montpensier Pictures," *Dwight's Journal of Music* 34 (October 3, 1874): 309.

87. *Proceedings*, 14.

88. BA Fine Arts Committee Records, March 9, 16, and October 19, 1874.

89. At the meeting on March 9, 1874, Charles Loring read "a letter from Hon Charles Sumner congratulating the Trustees on the prospect of receiving such a valuable collection in Boston & its influence on the cultivation of a sound Artistic Taste in the United States." "Record of the Committee of the Museum of Fine Arts on the Montpensier Exhibition (1874–1876) (March 9, 1874)," BA Fine Arts Committee Records.

90. "Record of the Committee . . . on the Montpensier Exhibition (March 2, 9, and 16, 1874)," BA Fine Arts Committee Records.

91. The Sumner staircase, rising from the vestibule up to the third floor, was named after Senator Charles Sumner, who had helped to design it. Finished in the early 1850s, the marble staircase had been admired for its majestic grandeur until it was dismantled in 1889 to make space for books.

92. *Catalogue of Pictures Exhibited by the Athenæum; of Pictures and Engravings Bequeathed to the Museum of Fine Arts by the Hon. Charles Sumner, and of Works of Art Lately Added to the Collections of the Museum* (Boston: Press of Rockwell and Churchill, 1874), n.p.

93. BA Proprietors Records, January 1, 1875.

94. Ibid.

95. BA Fine Arts Committee Records, September 19 or 21, 1874. The Montpensier pictures appear to have been packed and left Boston by November 1876, when "the Curator was directed to have the bill of Messrs Doll & Richards divided to see that the charges for packing the Spanish pictures be charged to their account." MFA Committee on the Museum Records, November 13, 1876.

96. BA Fine Arts Committee Records, September 26, 1874.

97. The number of weekly visitors during the thirteen months is calculated from the total of 10,601. Charles C. Perkins, "Report of the Committee on the Museum," in *Proceedings*, 19.

98. The quote is from *Appleton's Journal* 12 (September 26, 1874): 412.

99. Quoted in "The Montpensier Pictures," *Dwight's Journal of Music* 34 (October 3, 1874): 309. Perkins's text was reprinted from the *Boston Daily Advertiser*, September 1, 1874.

100. "The Montpensier Pictures in Boston," *Scribner's Monthly* 9 (December 1874): 257. For additional coverage of the exhibition, see *Boston Daily Advertiser*, September 1, 22, 23, 24, and 25, 1874; *Springfield (MA) Republican*, September 23, 1874; *San Francisco Bulletin*, October 6, 1874; *Chicago Daily Inter Ocean*, October 10, 1874; *Every Saturday: A Journal of Choice Reading* 2 (October 10, 1874): 416; and *Appleton's Journal* 12 (October 17, 1874): 508.

101. Henry James, "The Duke of Montpensier's Pictures in Boston" (originally published in the *Atlantic Monthly* in November 1874), in *The Painter's Eye: Notes and Essays on the Pictorial Arts by Henry James*, ed. John L. Sweeney (Cambridge, MA: Harvard University Press, 1956), 86.

102. In Baticle and Marinas, *La Galerie espagnole*, the five paintings by Zurbarán are numbers 335, 337, 338, 339, and 375; one by Murillo is number 160; and one by Ribera (now attributed to Giordano) is number 249. See also for the four by Zurbarán, Baticle, "The Galerie Espagnole," 179–180; for the Murillo, see Suzanne L. Stratton-Pruitt, "Murillo in America," in her *Bartolomé Esteban Murillo (1617–1682): Paintings from American Collections* (New York: Harry N. Abrams, 2002), 97; and for the Giordano, Tinterow and Lacambre, *Manet/Velázquez*, 445. The Montpensier exhibition also included three works attributed to Velázquez (and two of them, *Equestrian Portrait of Philip IV, King of Spain* and *Equestrian Portrait of the Count Duke d'Olivares, Prime Minister of Philip IV*, both related to the larger paintings of the same subjects at the Museo del Prado, Madrid, have been included in multiple catalogues raisonnés of the artist's oeuvre), but their present whereabouts are unknown.

103. In 1886 Murillo's biographer Luis Alfonso attributed to the artist only eight paintings in American collections. Stratton-Pruitt, "Murillo in America," 96.

104. For a list of the works in the exhibition, see "Pictures Loaned to the Museum of Fine Arts by Mr. Q. A. Shaw," dated "April, 1875," in *Fifth Catalogue of the Collection of Ancient and Modern Works of Art, Given or Loaned to the Trustees of the Museum of Fine Arts, at Boston, Now on Exhibition in the Picture Gallery of the Athenæum* (Boston: Alfred Mudge and Son, 1875), n.p.

105. It is not known how Shaw came to display his collection at the Athenæum in 1875. Shaw was supremely well connected in Brahmin Boston and also a neighbor of Edward Perkins in Jamaica Plain, having built a house in 1862 across a cove from Perkins's Pinebank. It was by Perkins's nomination that Shaw became a museum trustee in 1877. MFA Trustees Minutes, January 18, 1877.

106. Susan Fleming, "The Boston Patrons of Jean-François Millet," in Alexandra R. Murphy, *Jean-François Millet* (Boston: Museum of Fine Arts, Boston, 1984), xii.

107. Ibid.

108. *Quincy Adams Shaw Collection: Italian Renaissance Sculpture; Paintings and Pastels by Jean François Millet. Exhibition Opening April 18, 1918* (Boston: Museum of Fine Arts, Boston, 1918).

109. For example, after 1876 Hollis Hunnewell exhibited at the museum his Rousseau, Daubigny, Fromentin, Corot, and Delacroix, and Joshua M. Sears his Dupré, Troyon, Corot, and Hunt. Martin Brimmer lent to the Museum his Millets (oils and pastels), Hunt, and Vedder; Henry P. Kidder his Frère, Troyon, and Dupré (he had previously shown only a Bonnat and a Diaz); and Thomas Gold Appleton his Vedder, Hunt, and Kensett (none of which he had shown before). Still, some notable collectors remained distant from the early museum: Henry C. Angell, a friend of Hunt, who had by 1870 begun to form one of Boston's largest collections of French paintings (including works by Boudin, Daubigny, and Bonheur), began showing only in 1880. Likewise, Henry Sayles, who purchased mainly in the 1860s and the 1870s, showed only Courbet's *The Quarry* (which he had bought from the defunct Allston Club about 1873) at the museum's opening in 1876, before he began to lend more works in the late 1870s.

110. Only two works of art joined the Athenæum's collection in 1870: a plaster cast of the statue of *Inopus* at the Louvre, by gift, and a large cartoon by Paul Delaroche, *Christ, the Hope and Support of the Afflicted* (n.d.; BA), by purchase.

111. BA Fine Arts Committee Records, February 16 and May 18, 1874. The French sculptor Henri-Joseph-François de Triqueti was popular in both France and England and is best known for his Gothic Revival cenotaph of *Prince Albert* (after 1865) in the Albert Memorial Chapel, Windsor Castle. Triqueti was also a friend of Ary Scheffer, Charles Perkins's painting teacher, and to Scheffer's design Triqueti carved the cenotaph of Ferdinand Philippe, duc d'Orléans (1842–1843) at the Chapelle St.-Ferdinand in Neuilly-sur-Seine. Perkins acknowledged his gratitude to Triqueti in the preface of his book *Italian Sculptors: Being a History of Sculpture in Northern, Southern, and Eastern Italy* (London: Longmans, Green, and Company, 1868).

112. The company was that of Augustine Heard, formerly of Ipswich, Massachusetts, and Canton, China. For a history of the company, see Stephen Chapman Lockwood, *Augustine Heard and Company, 1858–1862: American Merchants in China* (Cambridge, MA: East Asian Research Center, Harvard University, 1971).

113. In 1876 the Athenæum deposited at the museum 51 Arundel Society prints and 552 Braun photographs. In the ensuing years, the Athenæum added more to these loans.

114. Augustus Thorndike Perkins, *Losses to Literature and the Fine Arts by the Great Fire in Boston* (Boston: Press of David Clapp and Son, 1873), 10; Thomas Gold Appleton, *Boston Museum of the Fine Arts: A Companion to the Catalogue* (Boston: Roberts Brothers, 1877), 72.

115. BA Trustees Records, December 16, 1872.

116. BA Fine Arts Committee Records, October 18, 1875.

117. For a history of the Lawrence Room, see John Harris, *Moving Rooms: The Trade in Architectural Salvages* (New Haven: Yale University Press for the Paul Mellon Centre for Studies in British Art, 2007), 146–158.

118. Ibid.

119. Ibid.

120. For the Castellani family and their work, see Susan Weber Soros and Stefanie Walker, eds., *Castellani and Italian Archaeological Jewelry* (New Haven: Yale University Press for Bard Graduate Center for Studies in the Decorative Arts, Design, and Culture, New York, 2004); and Geoffrey C. Munn, *Castellani and Giuliano: Revivalist Jewellers of the 19th Century* (New York: Rizzoli, 1984).

121. Michael Tyskiewicz, *Memories of An Old Collector* (London: Longmans, Green, 1898), 71; and Margherita Barnabei and Filippo Delpino, eds., *Le "Memorie di un archeologo" di Felice Barnabei* (Rome: De Luca Edizioni d'Arte, 1991), 119. Both quoted in Soros and Walker, *Castellani and Italian Archaeological Jewelry*, 63–64.

122. BA Fine Arts Committee Records, October 13, 1875. This record mentions letters from Castellani to Charles Perkins, [1875], Martin Brimmer to Castellani, July 24, 1875, and Castellani to Brimmer, n.d. [1875], all of which probably initiated the negotiation, but the letters are unlocated.

123. *Catalogue of the Collection of Ancient and Modern Works of Art Given or Loaned to the Trustees of the Museum of Fine Arts, at Boston* (Boston: Alfred Mudge and Son, 1872), 32.

124. Soros and Walker, *Castellani and Italian Archaeological Jewelry*, 293.

125. Charles C. Perkins, "Report of the Committee on the Museum," in *Proceedings*, 18.

126. Alessandro Castellani to Edward N. Perkins, May 2, 1876, Cleveland-Perkins Family Papers, box 9, folder 14.

127. *Boston Evening Transcript*, June 19, 1876. This article reported Castellani's arrival in Boston two days earlier.

128. BA Fine Arts Committee Records, June 23 and July 3, 1876.

129. The large assortment of carved oak paneling, then purported to be English and Flemish work of the sixteenth century, had been purchased by Mrs. Lawrence in 1871 in London. These additional objects from Mrs. Lawrence had appeared in the museum's exhibitions at the Athenæum since 1872, without clear indication of their ownership. The exact dates when Mrs. Lawrence gave them to the Athenæum are not known. When placed on deposit at the MFA in 1876, they were considered the Athenæum's property.

130. BA Fine Arts Committee Records, November 1, 1876. The inscribed copy, in the Athenæum's collection, is *Special Catalogue of the Collection of Antiquities, Exhibited by Alessandro Castellani, of Rome, in Rooms U, V, W, Memorial Hall* (Philadelphia: Press of Edward Stern and Company, 1876).

131. Appleton, *A Companion*, 73. Arthur Rotch, "The Museum Building," in Museum of Fine Arts, Boston, "The Museum of Fine Arts, Boston," *American Architect and Building News* 8 (October 30, 1880): 207.

132. MFA Committee on the Museum Records, January 5, 10, 20, February 4 and 7, 1876.

133. Ibid., June 12, 1876.

134. Ibid., January 10, 1876.

135. MFA Trustees Minutes, April 20, 1876.

136. MFA Committee on the Museum Records, May 29, 1876.

137. MFA Trustees Minutes, January 25, 1876.

138. Memorandum by James Elliot Cabot, March 27, [1876], Department of Conservation and Collections Management, MFA.

139. The loan of much of the Athenæum's art collection to the MFA was simply reported verbally, without a written document: "verbal report was made by Mr. Wales that the Trustees of the Athenæum had granted the request of the Trustees of the Art Museum in reference to the loan of pictures and other works of art." MFA Committee on the Museum Records, March 13, 1876.

140. For a detailed study of Gray and his collection, see Marjorie B. Cohn, *Francis Calley Gray and Art Collecting for America* (Cambridge, MA: Harvard University Art Museums, 1986).

141. The agreement is reproduced in *Proceedings*, 20–22. According to this agreement, the museum appointed, in May 1876, Erastus Brainerd [or Brainard], an employee of the printer James R. Osgood, as the Curator of Gray Engravings. The loan was renewed in 1884 for two more seven-year terms before the collection returned to Harvard in 1897, to be placed at the newly founded Fogg Art Museum.

142. Details of Ware's European sojourn, especially the serendipitous circumstances under which he stumbled on the Lincoln Cathedral casts, are in the William Robert Ware Papers, Institute Archives and Special Collections, Massachusetts Institute of Technology.

143. Appleton had purchased the collection in early 1869 and gave it to the library later that year. See Boston Public Library, *The Tosti Engravings: The Gift of Thomas G. Appleton, Esq. Received Oct. 1869* (Boston: issued by the Library, 1873).

144. This final decision was recorded in June 1877: "The Chairman [of the Committee on the Museum] reported that the Trustees of the Public Library were unwilling to transfer any of the Engravings given by Mr. Appleton." MFA Committee on the Museum Records, June 4, 1877.

145. A notice announced the closing of the museum's exhibition at the Athenæum "on Saturday," the following day. *Boston Evening Transcript*, [Friday] June 2, 1876.

146. MFA Committee on the Museum Records, May 29, 1876. Little is known of the logistics of the move. A. E. Steele, a carpenter who had been helping the Athenæum gallery for some years, moved sculptures and paintings for the Athenæum in 1876 from February through the fall, and the Athenæum made payments of $33 for "carpentry" and of $52.19 for "removing pictures, etc." *BA Treasurer's Report for the Year 1876* (Boston, 1877). Invoices from Steele are in "Fine Arts Committee Accounts, box 4," BA Archive.

147. *Proceedings*, 9. For descriptions of the opening ceremony, see also *Boston Evening Transcript*, July 5, 1876. As of July 1876, the Boston Public Library was still expected to deposit its Tosti collection of prints.

148. *Proceedings*, 11.

149. Ibid., 8.

150. Ibid., 9.

151. These archaeological objects comprised a large portion of the more than 5,400 objects that the museum owned when it opened in 1876. The figure 5,400 is from Maureen Melton, *Invitation to Art: A History of the Museum of Fine Arts, Boston* (Boston: MFA Publications, 2009), 9.

152. The handwritten list, "Works of Art Deposited at the Museum of Fine Arts by the Boston Athenæum, Jan. 1, 1877," is signed by the museum's curator, Charles G. Loring, on December 30, 1876, and by the Athenæum's Fine Arts Committee on January 1, 1877. The list is in a manuscript volume entitled "Boston Athenæum: Records and letters of Fine Arts Committee, 1860–69; also, lists of purchases and deposits, 1860–80." An abbreviated version of the list was printed in *Proceedings*, 36–37.

153. *Museum of Fine Arts: Third Catalogue of the Collection of Ancient and Modern Works of Art Given or Loaned to the Trustees* (Boston: Alfred Mudge and Son, 1876), 53. The other three marble sculptures in the hall belonged to the museum: *Hebe and Ganymede* by Thomas Crawford, gift of Charles C. Perkins; *Bust of Charles Sumner* (1842; MFA), also by Crawford, bequest of Charles Sumner; and *The First Inspirations of Columbus* (1871; MFA) by Giulio Monteverde (1837–1917), gift of A. P. Chamberlain. The undated third and last edition of the 1876 catalogue was published in November or later since it recorded the five paintings Faneuil Hall had deposited at the Museum "for safe-keeping, Nov., 1876."

154. Appleton, *A Companion*, 7.

155. During that period, the museum admitted 5,551 visitors on weekdays and 33,147 on "free" Saturdays. *Trustees of the Museum of Fine Arts: First Annual Report, for the Year Ending Dec. 31, 1876* (Boston: Alfred Mudge and Son, 1877), 5.

156. Slautterback, *Designing the BA*, 63.

157. BA Proprietors Records, January 8, 1877.

158. A copy of this agreement, signed on March 19, 1877, by Charles Francis Adams (BA president) and Martin Brimmer (MFA president), is in the BA Archive.

NOTES TO CHAPTER FIVE

1. Martin Brimmer, "Report of the Executive Committee," in *Trustees of the Museum of Fine Arts: First Annual Report, for the Year Ending Dec. 31, 1876* (Boston: Alfred Mudge and Son, 1877), 6.

2. The number of visitors to the museum (15,013 paid and 141,015 free in 1877) is from *Trustees of the Museum of Fine Arts: Second Annual Report, for the Year Ending Dec. 31, 1877* (Boston: Alfred Mudge and Son, 1878), 6.

3. Martin Brimmer, "Report of the Executive Committee," in *Trustees of the Museum of Fine Arts: Second Annual Report*, 7.

4. The five special exhibitions of 1880 featured Gilbert Stuart; living American artists; the late William Rimmer; William Blake (1757–1827) (with loans from the widow of Alexander Gilchrist, Blake's biographer); and John Ruskin (with loans chiefly from Charles Eliot Norton). For the Stuart exhibition, for example, the museum appropriated only $500. MFA Trustees Minutes, April 15, 1880.

5. Whitehill, *MFA*, 60.

6. Ibid., 43.

7. Martin Brimmer, "Report of the Executive Committee," in *Trustees of the Museum of Fine Arts: Fifth Annual Report, for the Year Ending Dec. 31, 1880* (Boston: Alfred Mudge and Son, 1881), 4.

8. Charles C. Perkins to Charles G. Loring, June 17, 1881, MFA General Correspondence.

9. Clipping (probably *Boston Evening Transcript*), August 4, 1888, AAA, Reel 2496, MFA Archives.

10. "Report of the Committee on the Museum," in *Trustees of the Museum of Fine Arts: First Annual Report, for the Year Ending Dec. 31, 1876* (Boston: Alfred Mudge and Son, 1877), 10.

11. "The Museum of Fine Arts, Boston," *American Architect and Building News* 8 (October 30, 1880): 206.

12. "Special Report on the Increase of the Collections," in *Trustees of the Museum of Fine Arts: Eighth Annual Report, for the Year Ending Dec. 31, 1883* (Boston: Alfred Mudge and Son, 1884), 9.

13. Ibid.

14. Ibid., 12.

15. Ibid., 10.

16. Ibid., 11–12.

17. Charles C. Perkins, "Report of the Committee on the Museum," in *Trustees of the Museum of*

Fine Arts: Fourth Annual Report, for the Year Ending Dec. 31, 1879 (Boston: Alfred Mudge and Son, 1880), 7, 8.

18. MFA Register of Casts, 156–157.

19. For a description of the Olympia excavation, see Stephen L. Dyson, *In Pursuit of Ancient Pasts: A History of Classical Archaeology in the Nineteenth and Twentieth Centuries* (New Haven: Yale University Press, 2006), 82–84. For the pieces from Olympia that came to the museum, see Edward Robinson, *Museum of Fine Arts, Boston. Catalogue of Casts: Parts I, II, and III; Ancient Sculpture* (Boston: Houghton, Mifflin and Company, 1892), 86–96. In Boston, the Olympia excavation inspired Charles Eliot Norton to establish, in 1879, the Archaeological Institute of America. In 1881–1883 the institute undertook the Assos excavation (in present-day Turkey), the first archaeological dig sponsored by Americans, with partial funding from the Museum of Fine Arts. For the history of the institute and its close ties to the museum, see Archaeological Institute of America, *First Annual Report of the Executive Committee, with Accompanying Papers, 1879–1880* (Cambridge, MA: John Wilson and Son, 1880).

20. In addition to the plaster casts, the Fine Arts Committee purchased some didactic materials from the Berlin Museum: "a book of Photographs of the sculptures & inscriptions with descriptive letter press published at Berlin showing how the fragments may be properly arranged." BA Fine Arts Committee Records, February 19, 1877.

21. For the extensive list of the museum's purchases in plaster casts from this period, see MFA Register of Casts.

22. The committee voted that "all letters written in behalf of the Comtee be sent to the Museum to be copied before transmission." MFA Committee on the Museum Records, February 4, 1879.

23. Whitehill, *MFA*, 76.

24. The Fine Arts Committee paid $208.00 for the twelve Whistler prints and thirteen other etchings. BA Fine Arts Committee Records, January 13, February 22, and September 29, 1879; January 21, 1884; BA Proprietors Records, February 9, 1885.

25. MFA Trustees Minutes, October 16, 1879.

26. The British Museum had produced for sale electrotype copies of ancient coins in its collection, using the new technology of electrodeposition process.

27. The Fine Arts Committee gave Perkins £100 for the purpose. BA Fine Arts Committee Records, February [n.d.], 1881. Perkins had mentioned the electrotype coins the Fine Arts Committee as early as November 1878, when the British Museum announced its plan to make the reproductions. BA Fine Arts Committee Records, November [n.d.], 1878. For detailed communications about the electrotype coins, see Charles C. Perkins to Charles G. Loring, August 10 and 12, 1880, April 30 and June 17, 1881, MFA General Correspondence; BA Fine Arts Committee Records, February [n.d.] and May 3, 1881; and "Report of the Fine Arts Committee for 1881," BA Proprietors Records, February 13, 1882. For Perkins's statement in 1881 about coins in the museum's collection, see Charles C. Perkins, "Report of the Committee on the Museum," in *Trustees of the Museum of Fine Arts: Fifth Annual Report, for the Year Ending Dec. 31, 1880* (Boston: Alfred Mudge and Son, 1881), 9.

28. Edward N. Perkins to Charles G. Loring, February 17, 1883, MFA General Correspondence.

29. See, for example, Edward N. Perkins to Charles G. Loring, July 17, 1881; Edward N. Perkins to Edward H. Greenleaf, July 26, 1881; and Edward N. Perkins to Edward H. Greenleaf, August 10, 1881, MFA General Correspondence; MFA Committee on the Museum Records, February 7, 1882, November 6, 1883, and December 2, 1884; Charles G. Loring to Edward N. Perkins, n.d. (but presumably between January 21 and 22, 1885), MFA Director's Correspondence.

30. For descriptions of the sarcophagi, see James Jackson Jarves, *Handbook for Visitors to the Collections of Old Art of the Foreign Art Exhibition* (Boston: Mills, Knight and Company, 1883), 30–33; Charles Benjamin Norton, *Official Catalogue Foreign Exhibition, Boston, 1883* (Boston: George Coolidge, 1883), 45–46; and Mary B. Comstock and Cornelius C. Vermeule, *Sculpture in Stone: The Greek, Roman and Etruscan Collections of the Museum of Fine Arts, Boston* (Boston: Museum of Fine Arts, Boston, 1976), 244, 247. The pair of sarcophagi was appraised by Castellani at 200,000 francs, according to Jarves. The official name of the 1883 fair was the

American Exhibition of Foreign Products, Arts and Manufactures, and it was held at the Mechanics Hall on Huntington Avenue, just a few blocks west of the museum.

31. Whitehill, *MFA*, 65.

32. BA Fine Arts Committee Records, May 25, 1885; MFA Committee on the Museum Records, October 19, 1886.

33. MFA Committee on the Museum Records, April 6, 1886.

34. During these months, the ownership of the sarcophagi came into question—they now belonged to Jarves as well as to his partner George Maquay of Florence—and all necessary forms had to cross the Atlantic several times for signatures. MFA Committee on the Museum Records, October 19, 1886.

35. Whitehill, *MFA*, 65.

36. MFA Committee on the Museum Records, October 19 and December 7, 1886.

37. Receipt for the Athenæum's sarcophagus, dated January 18, 1887, is in the Department of Conservation and Collections Management, MFA.

38. For a history of the San Donato collection, see *Anatole Demidoff, Prince of San Donato (1812–70)* (London: Trustees of the Wallace Collection, 1994).

39. For a list of the San Donato objects deposited by Blake, with descriptions, see *Museum of Fine Arts: Catalogue of Works of Art Exhibited; Part II, Paintings, Drawings, Engravings, and Decorative Art, July 23, 1881* (Boston: Alfred Mudge and Son, 1881), 4–8; and subsequent catalogues. Of these objects, the following remain in the museum's collection: in painting, Simon Peeterz Verelst (1644–1721), *Still Life with Dead Partridge and Kingfisher*, n.d.; Frans Snyders (attributed to Willem Kalf in the 1881 catalogue), *Vegetables and a Basket of Fruit on a Table*, n.d.; Nicolaes Maes (1634–1693), *The Eavesdropper*, 1655–1656; Matthijs Naiveu (1647–1721; attributed to Gaspard Netscher in 1881), *Boy and Girl Blowing Soap Bubbles*, n.d.; David Teniers the Younger, *Butcher Shop*, 1642; Gabriel Metsu, *Usurer with a Tearful Woman*, 1654; Jan van Huysum II, *Vase of Flowers in a Niche*, ca. 1715; in sculpture, unidentified artist (attributed to Bernini in 1881), *Christ at the Column*, ca. 1700; and Théodore Joseph Napoléon Jacques (1804–1876), *Bust of Peter the Great*, n.d. The following two landscapes have left the museum's collection: *Skirt of the Forest*, attributed to Jacob van Ruisdael (1628 or 1629–1682) in 1881; and *The Ruined Cottage*, attributed to Ruisdael and Philips Wouwerman (1619–1668). One landscape, *Dordrecht*, then attributed to Aelbert Cuyp, was assigned to the Athenæum in 1889.

40. BA Fine Arts Committee Records, February [n.d.], 1881.

41. MFA Trustees Minutes, July 15, 1880.

42. Francis Bartlett gave the museum $10,000 "from the amount left by his father, Sydney Bartlett [d. 1889] for charitable purposes—expressing a wish that the amount should be appropriated to the purchase of the San Donato pictures." MFA Committee on the Museum Records, October 1, 1889.

43. For records of the purchase of the San Donato collection, see MFA Committee on the Museum Records, May 7, June 7, and July 7, 1889, and MFA Trustees Minutes, July 15, 1880. The Athenæum's painting, later attributed to Jacob van Strij, was sold in 1977 to Rosenberg and Stiebell, New York.

44. MFA Committee on the Museum Records, January 7, 1879. The Fine Arts Committee had first voted to allot only $1,500 for the four panels but increased the sum to $2,000 at the museum's request. MFA Committee on the Museum Records, October 6, 1879. Edward N. Perkins to Charles G. Loring, September 30, 1879, MFA Director's Correspondence.

45. The Athenæum deposited at the museum 547 Braun photographs in 1876 and an additional 204 in 1884. Most of the second batch was returned to the Athenæum in 1885 (and the last eight in 1953), and all of the first batch, in 1895. MFA Register of BA Loans.

46. MFA Committee on the Museum Records, May 5, 1885.

47. For records and correspondence on the issues of access, from 1885, see MFA Committee on the Museum Records, May 5 and June 2, 1885; Charles G. Loring to Edward N. Perkins, n.d. [presumably between June 22 and July 1885]; Charles G. Loring to Charles A. Cutter, June 22, 1885, MFA Director's Correspondence.

48. BA Fine Arts Committee Records, April 5, 1886.

49. Charles G. Loring to Charles A. Cutter, November 16, 1882, MFA Director's Correspondence. The letter from Cutter to Loring that had inspired the above letter is unlocated. The Athenæum deposited at the museum, in 1876, fifty-one Arundel Society prints (the same selection that it had exhibited in its gallery since the winter of 1871–1872), and thirty more in 1882. All eighty-one prints were returned to the Athenæum "by order of the Fine Arts Comtee" in 1886. MFA Register of BA Loans.

50. BA Fine Arts Committee Records, June 1, 1885.

51. For records and correspondence on the issue of the return of the Braun photographs, from 1885, see BA Fine Arts Committee Records, June 1, 1885; MFA Committee on the Museum Records, October 3, 1885; Charles G. Loring to Charles A. Cutter, July [before 10], 1885; Charles G. Loring to Edward N. Perkins, December 21, 1885, MFA Director's Correspondence; BA Fine Arts Committee Records, April 5, 1886.

52. Windsor was home to a large estate belonging to Senator Evarts. Edward Clarke Cabot also had a summer house in the town.

53. For Charles Perkins's obituaries, see the *New York Times*, August 26, 1886, and a number of clippings inserted in the Athenæum's copy of Samuel Eliot, "Memoir of Charles Callahan Perkins, A.M.," *Proceedings of the Massachusetts Historical Society*, 2nd ser., 3 (February 1888): 223–246. Chester L. Barrows, *William M. Evarts: Lawyer, Diplomat, Statesman* (Chapel Hill: University of North Carolina Press, 1941), 442.

54. "A Rare American," n.d. [probably 1886], Cleveland-Perkins Family Papers, box 11, folder 4.

55. Handwritten note, October 4, 1886, Cleveland-Perkins Family Papers, box 11, folder 4.

56. Sarah [Perkins] Cleveland to H. W. S. Cleveland, September 21, 1886, Cleveland-Perkins Family Papers, box 6, folder 13.

57. "Charles C. Perkins," in *Trustees of the Museum of Fine Arts: Eleventh Annual Report, for the Year Ending Dec. 31, 1886* (Boston: Alfred Mudge and Son, 1887), 6.

58. Henry Lee to Edward N. Perkins, August 17, 1886, Cleveland-Perkins Family Papers, box 9, folder 16.

59. Henry James, *William Wetmore Story and His Friends from Letters, Diaries, and Recollections* (New York: Grove Press, 1903), 144.

60. Perkins, *Art in Education*, 2.

61. Ibid.

62. Thomas L. Haskell, *The Emergence of Professional Social Science: The American Social Science Association and the Nineteenth-Century Crisis of Authority* (Urbana: University of Illinois Press, 1977), 49.

63. For tributes by the museum for Brimmer and Loring, respectively, see *Trustees of the Museum of Fine Arts: Twentieth Annual Report, for the Year Ending Dec. 31, 1895* (Boston: Alfred Mudge and Son, 1896), 3–7; and *Museum of Fine Arts, Boston: Twenty-Seventh Annual Report for the Year 1902* (Cambridge, MA: University Press, 1903), 1–10.

64. MFA Committee on the Museum Records, October 19, 1886.

65. The Athenæum's purchase of the Etruscan sarcophagus was concluded in late 1886 and that of the San Donato collection in 1889, but for both, preliminary arrangements had been made before Perkins's death.

66. MFA Committee on the Museum Records, January 4, 1887.

67. MFA Trustees Minutes, April 19 and May 24, 1877, and April 15, 1880.

68. MFA Committee on the Museum Records, July 2, 1887. The museum's annual report for 1886 included for the first time a separate, departmental account, prepared by Robinson; the following year, a report of the Print Department, by Koehler, also appeared for the first time.

69. The German-born Koehler had worked for Boston's foremost chromolithographer, Louis Prang, and launched, in 1879, a scholarly (if short-lived) journal, the *American Art Review*, with Charles C. Perkins. Robinson was one of the earliest American classical archaeologists with university training, first at Harvard under Charles Eliot Norton and then in Germany.

70. See the report by the keeper of paintings in *Museum of Fine Arts, Boston: Twenty-Seventh Annual Report for the Year 1902*, 97–101.

71. Ibid., 23.

72. *Trustees of the Museum of Fine Arts: Nineteenth Annual Report, for the Year Ending December 31, 1894* (Boston: Alfred Mudge and Son, 1895), 4.

73. Some sizable bequests received by the museum during the 1880s included $10,000 from Nathaniel C. Nash in 1880, $20,000 from John Lowell Gardner in 1881, $100,000 from Harvey D. Parker in 1884, and $50,000 from Richard Perkins in 1886, to name a few. Whitehill, *MFA*, 50.

74. Charles G. Loring, "Twenty-Five Years of the Museum's Growth," in *Trustees of the Museum of Fine Arts: Twenty-Sixth Annual Report, for the Year Ending December 31, 1901* (Boston: Alfred Mudge and Son, 1902), 23.

75. For detailed discussions of this "battle," see Whitehill, *MFA*, 172–217; and Alan Wallach, "The American Cast Museum: An Episode in the History of the Institutional Definition of Art," in his *Exhibiting Contradiction: Essays on the Art Museum in the United States* (Amherst: University of Massachusetts Press, 1998), 38–56. For an international context of this shift, see Rune Frederiksen and Eckart Marchand, eds., *Plaster Casts: Making, Collecting, and Displaying from Classical Antiquity to the Present* (Berlin: De Gruyter, 2010).

76. Arthur Fairbanks, "The Museum of Fine Arts," *Boston Sun*, September 14, 1912. Quoted in Neil Harris, "The Gilded Age Revisited: Boston and the Museum Movement," *American Quarterly* 14 (Winter 1962): 560.

77. Whitehill, *MFA*, 156.

78. The first two gifts in classical antiquities from the Warren brothers were the 1887 gifts of Samuel D. Warren of a Greek terra-cotta figurine of Helios and a bronze statuette, also Greek, of Athena. On the Warren brothers, see Osbert Burdett and E. H. Goddard, *Edward Perry Warren: The Biography of a Connoisseur* (London: Christophers, 1941); Martin Green, *The Mount Vernon Street Warrens: A Boston Story, 1860–1910* (New York: Charles Scribner's Sons, 1989); and David Sox, *Bachelors of Art: Edward Perry Warren and the Lewes House Brotherhood* (London: Fourth Estate, 1991).

79. In 1902 Gilman was also made secretary of the board and librarian.

80. By 1904 Gilman's title had changed to secretary of the museum and Prichard's to assistant director.

81. Matthew S. Prichard, "The Museum and Education," n.d., in a folder titled "Casts—Reports and Correspondence, 1899–1905," in a box titled "Casts," MFA Archives.

82. Matthew S. Prichard, "The Utility and Futility of Casts," November 1, 1904, in a folder titled "Casts—Reports and Correspondence, 1899–1905." Also Matthew S. Prichard, "Letter from the Assistant Director," in *Communication to the Trustees II. The Collection of Casts in the New Museum. Recent European Opinion on Museum Methods* (Boston: privately printed by authority of the Committee on the Museum, [December] 1904), 24.

83. Within days, Robinson accepted the position of assistant director at New York's Metropolitan Museum of Art, where he would be promoted, in 1910, to director.

84. Matthew S. Prichard, "The Utility and Futility of Casts," November 1, 1904, in a folder titled "Casts—Reports and Correspondence, 1899–1905." Also Matthew S. Prichard, "Letter from the Assistant Director," in *Communication to the Trustees II* (Boston: privately printed by authority of the Committee on the Museum, [December] 1904), 24.

85. Ibid.

86. Perkins, *Art in Education*, 2.

87. Loring, "Twenty-Five Years of the Museum's Growth," 23.

88. The bylaws issued in 1876 had charged the Committee on the Museum with "supervision and control of all the collections . . . and of the arrangement and exhibition thereof," while also assigning to the curator (changed to director in 1887) "the general charge and management of the Museum." *Museum of Fine Arts Bulletin* 4 (February 1906): 2.

89. The bylaw change created a new, single executive committee from two former standing committees, the Executive Committee and the Committee on the Museum. This new executive committee was called, somewhat confusingly, the Committee on the Museum, even though its function had been revised. Ibid., 3.

90. Ibid.

91. Prichard was demoted to the position of burser in January 1906 and resigned in July of the same year. Thereafter, he was secretary of the Committee on the Utilization of the Museum by Schools and Colleges, a committee founded in 1904 under the auspices of Simmons College, and soon returned to England. Samuel Warren, the board president, was also relieved of his duties in 1906, his fellow trustees clearly disapproving of his too-close alliance with the aesthetic camp personified by Prichard.

92. As of 1907 the collections were divided into seven sections: Chinese and Japanese Art, Classical Art, Egyptian Art, Pictures (including Prints), Western Art (other than pictures), Library and Photograph Collection, and Collections of Casts. *Museum of Fine Arts Bulletin* 4 (June 1907): 28; *Handbook of the Museum of Fine Arts* (Boston, 1907), 316. Gilman presented his theory at the founding meeting of the Association of American Museums in 1906. See also Benjamin I. Gilman and Matthew S. Prichard, "Aims and Principles of the Construction and Management of Museums of Fine Art: A Syllabus," reprinted from the *Museums Journal* 9 (July 1909), in Gilman, *Museum Ideals of Purpose and Method* (Cambridge, MA: Trustees of the Museum, at Riverside Press, 1918), 401.

93. Benjamin I. Gilman to S. Warren, September 28, 1904, in a folder titled "Casts—Reports and Correspondence, 1899–1905."

94. Benjamin I. Gilman, "On the Distinctive Purpose of Museums of Art," *Museums Journal* 3 (January 1904): 213.

95. *Handbook of the Museum of Fine Arts* (Boston, 1907), 317; and *Museum of Fine Arts Bulletin* 4 (June 1907): 47.

96. E. Robinson to Thornton K. Lothrop, September 9, 1904 (about sculptures) and January 5, 1905 (about paintings), BA Letters. The plaster casts were stored at the Boston Storage Warehouse, either at the corner of Massachusetts and Westland Avenues or at the corner of Huntington Avenue and Bryant Street. Charles K. Bolton to Edward Robinson, September 22, 1904 (photocopy), BA Art Department file.

97. Edward Robinson to Thornton K. Lothrop, January 5, 1905, BA Letters; Thornton K. Lothrop to Edward Robinson, February 15, 1905 (photocopy), Department of Conservation and Collections Management, MFA.

98. Interestingly, the soon-to-be-empty museum building in Copley Square was one of the possible locations that the trustees considered for the Athenæum, but they decided against it because of the building's flammability. Slautterback, *Designing the BA*, 67.

99. For example, the Athenæum offered six paintings of "religious character" to Boston College in 1905: *The Flight into Egypt* (then attributed to Annibale Caracci); *St. John the Baptist* after Leonardo da Vinci (1452–1519); *Madonna* after Carlo Dolci (1616–1686), *Holy Family* and *Rebecca at the Well*, both after Murillo; and *Christ Healing the Blind* after Guercino (1591–1666). Charles K. Bolton to the Reverend John J. Williams, December 12, 1905, BA Letters.

100. For example, the Athenæum consigned five paintings to the auctioneer Leonard and Company in 1905, with the stipulation that the Athenæum's name not be mentioned in connection with them: *The Cottage Grandfather* by John Russell (1745–1806); *The Bishop* by Gottfried Bernhard Göz (1708–1774); *Sunset on the Campagna* by George L. Brown (1814–1889); *Landscape, New York Scenery*, by Alvan Fisher; and *Judith* after Guido Reni (1575–1642). Charles K. Bolton to Leonard and Company, December 20, 1905, BA Letters.

101. The marble statue had been at the Athenæum, albeit with indeterminate ownership, since its deposit there by the artist in the 1850s. In 1902 the Athenæum granted the sculptor's family official title to the work, and in 1904 the artist removed it from the Athenæum to transport it to the Worcester Art Museum. E. A. Brackett to Charles K. Bolton, October 14, 1904, BA Letters. Charles K. Bolton, "Report of the Librarian for the Year 1904," dated December 31, 1904, BA Proprietors Records.

102. Already in 1883 the Library Committee had the authority to spend half of the income of the Fine Art Fund on art books. BA Fine Arts Committee Records, January 4, 1883; and BA Proprietors Records, n.d., 1902.

103. BA Proprietors Records, February 1911.

104. BA Proprietors Records, n.d., 1912.

105. Ibid.

106. Committee on the Museum, "Special Report on the Increase of the Collections," in *Trustees of the Museum of Fine Arts: Eighth Annual Report, for the Year Ending Dec. 31, 1883* (Boston: Alfred Mudge and Son, 1884), 10, 12.

107. Benjamin I. Gilman to S. Warren, October 22, 1904, in a folder titled "Casts—Reports and Correspondence, 1899–1905." Also, Matthew S. Prichard, "Letter from the Assistant Director," in *Communication to the Trustees II*, 24.

108. Typewritten response to William Robert Ware's letter to S. Warren, May 12, 1905, by Benjamin I. Gilman and Matthew S. Prichard, n.d., in a folder titled "Casts—Reports and Correspondence, 1899–1905."

109. Ibid.; and Benjamin I. Gilman to S. Warren, October 22, 1904, in a folder titled "Casts—Reports and Correspondence, 1899–1905."

NOTES TO EPILOGUE

1. This number included the more than 500 Adolphe Braun photographs, more than eighty Arundel Society prints, and fifty-two watercolors from the Dowse Collection. Appleton Prentiss Clark Griffin, "Property of the Athenæum at the Museum of Fine Arts, 1895. A List," BA Archive.

2. *BA Report for the Year 1933*, 2.

3. While many of the museum's plaster casts were destroyed in the early 1930s, some were sent to museums and schools throughout the country, and some as far as Tokyo. At the request of Professor Yukio Yashiro of Tokyo Fine Arts School (now Tokyo University of the Arts), who was a visiting lecturer on Japanese art at Harvard University, the museum sent in 1933 and 1934 thirty-four plaster casts, including at least one that had been deposited by the Athenæum (Michelangelo's *Day* and *Night*), to the school in Tokyo, where some of them still remain. For more information on this transaction, see two folders, respectively titled "Casts—Tokyo" and "Casts—Correspondence & Shipping," in a box titled "Casts," MFA Archives; "Boston Museum Disposed of Casts," *Art and Archaeology* 34 (May–June 1933): 162; "At the Museum, the Casts Lose Caste and, Accordingly, Are Cast out [of] Its Halls," clipping, n.d. [1933 or 1934], BA Art Department file; and *Tokyo geijutsu daigaku hyakunenshi: Tokyo bijutsu gakko hen, dai 3 kan* [A hundred-year history of Tokyo University of the Arts: Tokyo Fine Arts School, vol. 3] (Tokyo: Gyousei, 1997), 682–683. The author thanks Shinya Araki of the University of Tokyo for bringing the last item to her attention. In the folder "Casts—Correspondence & Shipping," in the MFA Archives, two photographs of the museum's Renaissance Court are marked by hand to indicate the destination of each cast; the initial "Y" stood for Yashiro.

4. Emphasis mine. The oft-quoted sentence is from the two brass tablets installed in the Athenæum's vestibule in 1928. In 1927 the Athenæum authorized a trustee, Charles K. Cummings, chairman of the Fine Arts Committee, to compose (or, possibly, to have someone compose) the text, which was then engraved on the tablets by the Birmingham Guild, England, according to the design by Daniel Berkeley Updike of the Merrymount Press. *BA Report for the Year 1928*, 1–2. The use of the word "nucleus" may have come from an earlier text, written in 1888 by the museum's Edward H. Greenleaf: "the collections both of Casts and paintings belonging to the Athenæum thus became the nucleus of the new galleries." Greenleaf, "The Museum of Fine Arts, Boston," *Art Review* 3 (July–August 1888): 2.

5. Held from March 21 to April 27, 1947, the museum's exhibition marked the centennial of the laying of the cornerstone for the Athenæum's Beacon Street building.

BIBLIOGRAPHY

This bibliography lists the major manuscript collections and printed sources that were consulted or cited. Full citations for newspapers and the following publications are found in the notes:

BA annual reports

BA exhibition catalogues

MFA annual reports

MFA bulletins

MFA exhibition catalogues

MFA handbooks

School of the MFA annual reports

MANUSCRIPT COLLECTIONS

Boston Athenæum, Boston
> BA Fine Arts Committee Records, Archive
> BA Letters, Archive
> BA Proprietors Records, Archive
> BA Trustees Records, Archive
> John Hubbard Sturgis Papers, Manuscript Collection

Boston Public Library, Boston
> Charles Folsom Papers, Department of Rare Books and Manuscripts
> Letters to John S. Dwight, Department of Rare Books and Manuscripts

Dartmouth College, Hanover, NH
> Papers of Luigi Palma di Cesnola, Rauner Special Collections Library

Massachusetts Institute of Technology, Cambridge, MA
> William Robert Ware Papers, MIT Institute Archives and Special Collections

Museum of Fine Arts, Boston
        MFA Building Records, Archives
        MFA Committee on the Museum Records, Archives
        MFA Director's Correspondence, Archives
        MFA Early Organizational Material, 1869–1870, Archives
        MFA General Correspondence, Archives
        MFA General Organizational Material, Archives
        MFA Register of BA Loans, Department of Conservation and Collections Management
        MFA Register of Casts, Department of Conservation and Collections Management
        MFA Register of Purchases, 1876–1906, Department of Conservation and Collections Management
        MFA Trustees Minutes, Archives

New York Public Library. Astor, Lenox and Tilden Foundations
        Cleveland-Perkins Family Papers, Manuscripts and Archives Division

University of California, Santa Barbara
        Ward-Perkins Family Papers, Mss 129, Department of Special Collections, Davidson Library

Yale University, New Haven
        American Social Science Association Records, Manuscripts and Archives, Yale University Library

PRINTED SOURCES

Abbott, Richard H. *Cotton and Capital: Boston Businessmen and Antislavery Reform, 1854–1868.* Amherst: University of Massachusetts Press, 1991.

Adams, Bluford. *E Pluribus Barnum: The Great Showman and the Making of U.S. Popular Culture.* Minneapolis: University of Minnesota Press, 1997.

Addison, Julia de Wolfe. *The Boston Museum of Fine Arts.* Boston: L. C. Page, 1910.

Amory, Cleveland. *The Proper Bostonians.* New York: E. P. Dutton and Company, 1947.

Anatole Demidoff, Prince of San Donato (1812–70). London: Trustees of the Wallace Collection, 1994.

Angulo, A. J. *William Barton Rogers and the Idea of MIT.* Baltimore: Johns Hopkins University Press, 2009.

Annual Report of the School Committee of the City of Boston, 1870. Boston: Alfred Mudge and Son, 1871.

Annual Report of the School Committee of the City of Boston, 1879. Boston: Rockwell and Churchill, 1879.

Anthology Society: Journal of the Proceedings of the Society Which Conducts the Monthly Anthology and Boston Review, October 3, 1805, to July 2, 1811. Boston: Boston Athenæum, 1910.

Appleton, Thomas Gold. *Boston Museum of the Fine Arts: A Companion to the Catalogue.* Boston: Roberts Brothers, 1877.

Archaeological Institute of America. *First Annual Report of the Executive Committee, with Accompanying Papers. 1879–80.* Cambridge, MA: John Wilson and Son, 1880.

Ary Scheffer, 1795–1858: Dessins, aquarelles, esquisses à l'huile. Paris: L'Institut, 1980.

The Athenæum Centenary: The Influence and History of the Boston Athenæum from 1807 to 1907. Boston: Boston Athenæum, 1907.

Baker, Malcolm, and Brenda Richardson, eds. *A Grand Design: The Art of the Victoria and Albert Museum.* New York: Harry N. Abrams; Baltimore: Baltimore Museum of Art, 1997.

Barrows, Chester L. *William M. Evarts: Lawyer, Diplomat, Statesman.* Chapel Hill: University of North Carolina Press, 1941.

Baticle, Jeannine. "The Galerie Espagnole of Louis-Philippe." In *Manet/Velázquez: The French Taste for Spanish Painting*, by Gary Tinterow and Geneviève Lacambre, 174–189. New York: Metropolitan Museum of Art, 2003.

———, and Cristina Marinas. *La Galerie espagnole de Louis-Philippe au Louvre, 1838–1848.* Paris: Ministère de la Culture, Éditions de la Réunion des Musées Nationaux, 1981.

Baudelaire, Charles. "On M. Ary Scheffer and the Apes of Sentiment." In *Art in Paris, 1845–1862: Salons and Other Exhibitions Reviewed by Charles Baudelaire*, translated and edited by Jonathan Mayne, 98–101. London: Phaidon Press, 1965.

Bennett, Tony. *The Birth of the Museum: History, Theory, Politics.* London: Routledge, 1995.

———. *Pasts beyond Memory: Evolution, Museums, Colonialism.* London: Routledge, 2004.

Benson, Eugene. "Museums of Art as a Means of Instruction." *Appleton's Journal* 3 (January 15, 1870): 80–81.

Bilbey, Diane, and Marjorie Trusted. "'The Question of Casts'—Collecting and Later Reassessment of the Cast Collections at South Kensington." In *Plaster Casts: Making, Collecting, and Displaying from Classical Antiquity to the Present*, edited by Rune Frederiksen and Eckart Marchand, 465–483. Berlin: De Gruyter, 2010.

Billings, Katrina L. "Sophisticated Proselytizing: Charles Callahan Perkins and the Boston School Committee." Master's thesis, Massachusetts College of Art, 1987.

Black, Barbara J. *On Exhibit: Victorians and Their Museums.* Charlottesville: University Press of Virginia, 2000.

Bolin, Paul E. "The Massachusetts Drawing Act of 1870: Industrial Mandate or Democratic Maneuver?" In *Framing the Past: Essays on Art Education*, edited by Donald Soucy and Mary Ann Stankiewicz, 58–68. Reston, VA: National Art Education Association, 1990.

———. "Overlooked and Obscured through History: The Legislative Bill Proposed to Amend the Massachusetts Drawing Act of 1870." *Studies in Art Education* 37 (Autumn 1995): 55–64.

Boston Athenæum. *Catalogue of the American Exhibition of British Art, at the Athenæum Gallery, Beacon Street, Boston. Oil Pictures and Water Colors.* Boston: J. H. Eastburn's Press, 1858.

———. *Change and Continuity: A Pictorial History of the Boston Athenæum.* Boston: Boston Athenæum, 1985.

"Boston Museum Disposed of Casts." *Art and Archaeology* 34 (May–June 1933): 162.

Boston Public Library. *The Tosti Engravings. The Gift of Thomas G. Appleton, Esq. Received Oct. 1869.* Boston: issued by the Library, 1873.

Bowen, Abel. *Bowen's Picture of Boston.* Boston: Otis, Broaders and Company, 1838.

Brimmer, Martin. "Charles Callahan Perkins, A.M." *Proceedings of the American Academy of Arts and Sciences* 22 (May–December 1886): 534–539.

———. *Egypt: Three Essays on the History, Religion and Art of Ancient Egypt*. Cambridge, MA: Riverside Press; Houghton, Mifflin and Company, 1892.

Brooks, Van Wyck. *The Dream of Arcadia: American Writers and Artists in Italy, 1760–1915*. New York: E. P. Dutton and Company, 1958.

Bunting, Bainbridge. *Houses of Boston's Back Bay: An Architectural History, 1840–1917*. Cambridge, MA: Belknap Press of Harvard University Press, 1967.

Burckhardt, Jacob. *The Cicerone; or, Art Guide to Painting in Italy: For the Use of Travellers*. London: J. Murray, 1873.

Burdett, Osbert, and E. H. Goddard. *Edward Perry Warren: The Biography of a Connoisseur*. London: Christophers, 1941.

Burt, Nathaniel. *Palaces for the People: A Social History of the American Art Museum*. Boston: Little, Brown, 1977.

Burton, Anthony. *Vision and Accident: The Story of the Victoria and Albert Museum*. London: V&A Publications, 1999.

Cabot, James Elliot. *J. Elliot Cabot: I. Autobiographical Sketch, II. Family Reminiscences, III. Sedge Birds*. Boston: Geo. H. Ellis Company, 1904.

Campbell, Katie. *Paradise of Exiles: The Anglo-American Gardens of Florence*. London: Frances Lincoln, 2009.

Carbonell, Bettina Messias, ed. *Museum Studies: An Anthology of Contexts*. Malden, MA: Blackwell Publishers, 2004.

Carpenter, Kenneth E. "America's Most Influential Library?" In *The Boston Athenæum Bicentennial Essays*, edited by Richard Wendorf, 33–68. Boston: Boston Athenæum, 2009.

Cary, Thomas Greaves. *Memoir of Thomas Handasyd Perkins*. Boston: Little, Brown, 1856.

Casteras, Susan P. "The 1857–58 Exhibition of English Art in America and Critical Response to Pre-Raphaelitism." In *The New Path: Ruskin and the American Pre-Raphaelites*, by Linda S. Ferber and William H. Gerdts, 109–133. Brooklyn, NY: Brooklyn Museum, 1985.

———. *English Pre-Raphaelitism and Its Reception in America in the Nineteenth Century*. Rutherford, NJ: Fairleigh Dickinson University Press, 1990.

Catalogue of a Private Collection of Paintings and Original Drawings by Artists of the Düsseldorf Academy of Fine Arts. New York: Wm. C. Bryant and Company, 1851.

Catalogue of the First Semi-Annual Exhibition of Paintings, in the Gallery of the Massachusetts Academy of Fine Arts, No. 371–2 Tremont Row, Boston. Boston: Dutton and Wentworth, 1853.

Cesnola, Luigi Palma di. *The Antiquities of Cyprus Discovered (Principally on the Sites of the Ancient Golgoi and Idalium) by General Luigi Palma di Cesnola*. London: W. A. Mansell and Company, 1873.

———. *Cyprus: Its Ancient Cities, Tombs, and Temples*. New York: Harper and Brothers, 1878.

Chewning, J. A. "William Robert Ware at MIT and Columbia." *Journal of Architectural Education* 33 (November 1979): 25–29.

———. "William Robert Ware and the Beginnings of Architectural Education in the United States, 1861–1881." PhD diss., Massachusetts Institute of Technology, 1986.

Clapper, Michael. "Popularizing Art in Boston, 1865–1910: L. Prang & Co. and the Museum of Fine Arts." PhD diss., Northwestern University, 1997.

Cohn, Marjorie B. *Francis Calley Gray and Art Collecting for America*. Cambridge, MA: Harvard University Art Museums, 1986.

Comfort, George Fiske. "Art Museums in America." *Old and New* 1 (April 1870): 503–512.

Comstock, Mary B., and Cornelius C. Vermeule. *Sculpture in Stone: The Greek, Roman and Etruscan Collections of the Museum of Fine Arts, Boston*. Boston: Museum of Fine Arts, Boston, 1976.

Conn, Steven. *Museums and American Intellectual Life, 1876–1926*. Chicago: University of Chicago Press, 1998.

Connor, Peter. "Cast-Collecting in the Nineteenth Century: Scholarship, Aesthetics, Connoisseurship." In *Rediscovering Hellenism: The Hellenic Inheritance and the English Imagination*, edited by G. W. Clarke, 187–235. Cambridge: Cambridge University Press, 1989.

Cushing, Stanley Ellis, and David B. Dearinger. *Acquired Tastes: 200 Years of Collecting for the Boston Athenæum*. Boston: Boston Athenæum, 2006.

Dalzell, Robert F., Jr. *Enterprising Elite: The Boston Associates and the World They Made*. Cambridge, MA: Harvard University Press, 1987.

Dana, John Cotton. *The Gloom of the Museum*. Woodstock, VT: Elm Tree Press, 1917.

Denis, Rafael Cardoso. "Teaching by Example: Education and the Formation of South Kensington's Museum." In *A Grand Design: The Art of the Victoria and Albert Museum*, edited by Malcolm Baker and Brenda Richardson, 107–116. New York: Harry N. Abrams; Baltimore: Baltimore Museum of Art, 1997.

Dictionary of American Biography. 20 vols. New York: Charles Scribner's Sons, 1928–1936.

Diehl, Gertrude B. "The Five of Clubs." *New England Galaxy* 12 (Summer 1970): 39–48.

DiMaggio, Paul. "Cultural Entrepreneurship in Nineteenth-Century Boston: The Creation of an Organizational Base for High Culture in America." *Media, Culture, and Society* 4 (January 1982): 33–50.

Dimmick, Lauretta. "A Catalogue of the Portrait Busts and Ideal Works of Thomas Crawford (1813?–1857), American Sculptor in Rome." PhD diss., University of Pittsburgh, 1986.

Dinsmoor, William B. "Early American Studies of Mediterranean Archaeology." *Proceedings of the American Philosophical Society* 87 (1943): 70–104.

Doggett's Repository. *Descriptive Catalogue of Original Cabinet Paintings, Now Arranged in the Gallery, Doggett's Repository of Arts. . . .* Boston, 1821.

Dowd, Carol Tognari, ed. "The Travel Diaries of Otto Mündler: 1855–1858." *Walpole Society* 51 (1985).

Duncan, Carol. *Civilizing Rituals: Inside Public Art Museums*. London: Routledge, 1995.

———. "From the Princely Gallery to the Public Art Museum: The Louvre Museum and the National Gallery, London." In *Grasping the World: The Idea of the Museum*, edited by Donald Preziozi and Claire Farago, 250–278. Aldershot, UK; Burlington, VT: Ashgate Publishing, 2004.

Dyson, Stephen L. *Ancient Marbles to American Shores: Classical Archaeology in the United States*. Philadelphia: University of Pennsylvania Press, 1998.

———. *In Pursuit of Ancient Pasts: A History of Classical Archaeology in the Nineteenth and Twentieth Centuries*. New Haven: Yale University Press, 2006.

Eastlake, Charles L. *Hints on Household Taste in Furniture, Upholstery, and Other Details*. Boston: James R. Osgood and Company, Late Ticknor and Fields, and Fields, Osgood, and Company, 1872.

Efland, Arthur D. *A History of Art Education: Intellectual and Social Currents in Teaching the Visual Arts*. New York: Teachers College Press, 1990.

Eliot, Samuel. *The Liberty of Rome: A History; With an Historical Account of the Liberty of Ancient Nations*. 2 vols. New York: G. P. Putnam; London: R. Bentley, 1849.

——. *History of Liberty: Part I, The Ancient Romans*. 2 vols. Boston: Little, Brown and Company, 1853.

——. *History of Liberty: Part II, The Early Christians*. 2 vols. Boston: Little, Brown and Company, 1853.

——. *Manual of United States History: From 1492 to 1850*. Boston: Hickling, Swan, and Brown, 1856.

——. "Memoir of Charles Callahan Perkins, A.M." *Proceedings of the Massachusetts Historical Society*, 2nd ser., 3 (February 1888): 223–246.

——. "Memoir of Martin Brimmer." *Proceedings of the Massachusetts Historical Society*, 2nd ser., 10 (April 1896): 586–595.

"Eliot's *Sketch of Harvard College*." *North American Review* 68 (January 1849): 99–128.

Elson, Louis C. *The History of American Music*. New York: Macmillan Company, 1904.

Emerson, Edward Waldo, ed. *The Early Years of the Saturday Club, 1855–1870*. Boston: Houghton Mifflin Company, 1918.

Fairbrother, Trevor J. *The Bostonians: Painters of an Elegant Age, 1870–1930*. Boston: Museum of Fine Arts, Boston, 1986.

Farrell, Betty G. *Elite Families: Class and Power in Nineteenth-Century Boston*. Albany: State University of New York Press, 1993.

Ferber, Linda S., and William H. Gerdts. *The New Path: Ruskin and the American Pre-Raphaelites*. Brooklyn, NY: Brooklyn Museum, 1985.

"Fine Arts." *Appleton's Journal* 12 (October 19, 1874): 508–509.

"Fine Arts. The Athenæum Exhibition, I." *Dwight's Journal of Music* 13 (April 24, 1858): 26–27.

"Fine Arts. The Athenæum Exhibition, II. Oil Pictures." *Dwight's Journal of Music* 13 (May 8, 1858): 46–47.

"Fine Arts. The Athenæum Exhibition, III. Oil Pictures (Continued)." *Dwight's Journal of Music* 13 (May 15, 1858): 55–56.

"Fine Arts. The Athenæum Exhibition, IV. Oil Pictures (Continued)." *Dwight's Journal of Music* 13 (May 22, 1858): 61.

"Fine Arts. The Athenæum Exhibition, V. Oil Pictures (Continued)." *Dwight's Journal of Music* 13 (June 5, 1858): 79–80.

"Fine Arts. The Athenæum Exhibition, VI. Oil Pictures (Continued)." *Dwight's Journal of Music* 13 (June 12, 1858): 87–88.

"Fine Arts. The Athenæum Exhibition, VII. Oil Pictures (Continued)." *Dwight's Journal of Music* 13 (June 19, 1858): 92–93.

"Fine Arts. The Athenæum Exhibition, VIII. Oil Pictures (Continued)." *Dwight's Journal of Music* 13 (July 10, 1858): 120.

"Fine Arts. The Athenæum Exhibition, IX. Watercolors." *Dwight's Journal of Music* 13 (July 13, 1858): 127–128.

"Fine Arts. Athenæum Gallery of Fine Arts." *Dwight's Journal of Music* 19 (May 4, 1861): 38–39.

"Fine Arts. The Montpensier Collection of Paintings." *Appleton's Journal* 12 (September 26, 1874): 412–413.

Fink, Lois Marie. "French Art in the United States, 1850–1870: Three Dealers and Collectors." *Gazette des beaux-arts* 6 (September 1978): 87–100.

———. *A History of the Smithsonian American Art Museum: The Intersection of Art, Science, and Bureaucracy.* Amherst: University of Massachusetts Press, 2007.

First Annual Report of the Trustees of the Peabody Museum of American Archaeology and Ethnology. Cambridge, MA: John Wilson and Son, 1868.

Fitch, Donald. "The Ward-Perkins Papers." *Soundings* 16 (1985): 18–77.

Fleming, Susan. "The Boston Patron of Jean-François Millet." In *Jean-François Millet*, by Alexandra R. Murphy, ix–xviii. Boston: Museum of Fine Arts, Boston, 1984.

Fletcher, William I. "Some Recollections of the Boston Athenæum, 1861–1866." *Library Journal* 39 (August 1914): 579–583.

Floyd, Margaret Henderson. "A Terra-Cotta Cornerstone for Copley Square: Museum of Fine Arts, Boston, 1870–1876, by Sturgis and Brigham." *Journal of the Society of Architectural Historians* 32 (May 1973): 83–103.

———. "A Terra Cotta Cornerstone for Copley Square: An Assessment of the Museum of Fine Arts, Boston, by Sturgis and Brigham (1870–1876), in the Context of Its English Technological and Stylistic Origins." PhD diss., Boston University, 1974.

Fox, Celina. *The Arts of Industry in the Age of Enlightenment.* New Haven: Yale University Press, 2009.

Frederiksen, Rune, and Eckart Marchand, eds. *Plaster Casts: Making, Collecting, and Displaying from Classical Antiquity to the Present.* Berlin: De Gruyter, 2010.

Gale, Robert L. *Thomas Crawford, American Sculptor.* Pittsburgh: University of Pittsburgh Press, 1964.

Gemmill, Helen Hartman. *The Bread Box Papers: A Biography of Elizabeth Chapman Lawrence.* Bryn Mawr, PA: Dorrance and Company; Doylestown, PA: Bucks County Historical Society, 1983.

Gerdts, William H. "'Good Tidings to the Lovers of the Beautiful': New York's Düsseldorf Gallery, 1849–1862." *American Art Journal* 30 (1999): 50–81.

Gilman, Benjamin Ives. "On the Distinctive Purpose of Museums of Art." *Museums Journal* 3 (January 1904): 213–224.

———. "Docent Service at the Boston Art Museum." *Nation* 91 (September 1, 1910): 197–198.

———. *Museum Ideals of Purpose and Method.* Cambridge, MA: Trustees of the Museum, at Riverside Press, 1918.

———. *Museum of Fine Arts, Boston, 1870–1920.* Boston: [Museum of Fine Arts, Boston], 1921.

Green, Martin. *The Problem of Boston: Some Readings in Cultural History.* New York: W. W. Norton, 1966.

———. *The Mount Vernon Street Warrens: A Boston Story, 1860–1910.* New York: Charles Scribner's Sons, 1989.

Greenleaf, Edward H. "The Museum of Fine Arts, Boston." *Art Review* 3 (July–August 1888): 1–8.

Hale, Philip L. "The Boston Art Museum." *Scribner's Magazine* 47 (February 1910): 253–256.

Hall, Peter Dobkin. *The Organization of American Culture, 1700–1900: Private Institutions, Elites, and the Origins of American Nationality*. New York: New York University Press, 1982.

Hamerton, Philip Gilbert. *Contemporary French Painters: An Essay*. London: Seeley, Jackson, and Halliday, 1868.

Handlin, Oscar. *Boston's Immigrants, 1790–1865: A Study in Acculturation*. Cambridge, MA: Belknap Press of Harvard University Press, 1959.

Harding, Jonathan P. "The Painting Gallery." In *A Climate for Art: The History of the Boston Athenæum Gallery, 1827–1873*, by Pamela Hoyle, 9–22. Boston: Boston Athenæum, 1980.

———. *The Boston Athenæum Collection: Pre-Twentieth Century American and European Painting and Sculpture*. Boston: Boston Athenæum, 1984.

Harris, John. *Moving Rooms: The Trade in Architectural Salvages*. New Haven: Yale University Press for the Paul Mellon Centre for Studies in British Art, 2007.

Harris, Neil. "The Gilded Age Revisited: Boston and the Museum Movement." *American Quarterly* 14 (Winter 1962): 545–566.

Hartford, William F. *Money, Morals, and Politics: Massachusetts in the Age of the Boston Associates*. Boston: Northeastern University Press, 2001.

Haskell, Francis. *Rediscoveries in Art: Some Aspects of Taste, Fashion and Collecting in England and France*. London: Phaidon Press, 1976.

———. *The Ephemeral Museum: Old Master Paintings and the Rise of the Art Exhibition*. New Haven: Yale University Press, 2000.

———, and Nicholas Penny. *Taste and the Antique: The Lure of Classical Sculpture, 1500–1900*. New Haven: Yale University Press, 1981.

Haskell, Thomas L. *The Emergence of Professional Social Science: The American Social Science Association and the Nineteenth-Century Crisis of Authority*. Urbana: University of Illinois Press, 1977.

Henry de Triqueti, 1803–1874: Le sculpteur des princes. Paris: Éditions Hazan, 2007.

Hepner, Arthur W. *Pro Bono Atrium Musicarum: The Harvard Musical Association, 1837–1987*. Boston: Harvard Musical Association, 1987.

Hill, Kate. *Culture and Class in English Public Museums, 1850–1914*. Burlington, VT: Ashgate, 2005.

Hillard, George S. *A Selection from the Writings of Henry R. Cleveland: With a Memoir*. Boston: privately printed, 1844.

———. *Six Months in Italy*. Boston: Ticknor, Reed, and Fields, 1853.

Hirayama, Hina. "*Interior of St. Peter's, Rome*." In *Acquired Tastes: 200 Years of Collecting for the Boston Athenæum*, by Stanley Ellis Cushing and David B. Dearinger, 194–197. Boston: Boston Athenæum, 2006.

———. "The Boston Athenæum and the Creation of Boston's Museum of Fine Arts." In *The Boston Athenæum Bicentennial Essays*, edited by Richard Wendorf, 231–271. Boston: Boston Athenæum, 2009.

Hitchcock, Hiram. "The Explorations of Di Cesnola in Cyprus." *Harper's New Monthly Magazine* 45 (July 1872): 188–208.

Holmes, Oliver Wendell. *Elsie Venner: A Romance of Destiny*. Boston: Houghton, Mifflin and Company, 1861.

Howe, Mark Antony DeWolfe, ed. *Later Years of the Saturday Club, 1870–1920*. Boston: Houghton Mifflin Company, 1927.

Hoyle, Pamela. *A Climate for Art: The History of the Boston Athenæum Gallery, 1827–1873*. Boston: Boston Athenæum, 1980.

Hunt, William Morris. *On Painting and Drawing*. 1875. Reprint, New York: Dover Publications, 1976.

Jaher, Frederic Cople. "The Politics of the Boston Brahmins, 1800–1860." In *Boston, 1700–1980: The Evolution of Urban Politics*, edited by Ronald P. Formisano and Constance K. Burns, 59–86. Westport, CT: Greenwood Press, 1984.

[James, Henry]. "Hamerton's Contemporary French Painters." *North American Review* 106 (April 1868): 716–723.

James, Henry. *William Wetmore Story and His Friends from Letters, Diaries, and Recollections*. New York: Grove Press, 1903.

———. "The Duke of Montpensier's Pictures in Boston." In *The Painter's Eye: Notes and Essays on the Pictorial Arts by Henry James*, edited by John L. Sweeney, 79–87. Cambridge, MA: Harvard University Press, 1956.

———. *The Complete Letters of Henry James, 1855–1872*. 2 vols. Lincoln: University of Nebraska Press, 2006.

Jarves, James Jackson. *Art-Hints: Architecture, Sculpture, and Painting*. New York: Harper and Brothers, 1855.

———. *Art Thoughts: The Experiences and Observations of an American Amateur in Europe*. New York: Hurd and Houghton; Cambridge, MA: Riverside Press, 1869.

———. "Museums of Art, Artists, and Amateurs in America." *Galaxy* 10 (July–December 1870): 50–59.

———. *Handbook for Visitors to the Collections of Old Art of the Foreign Art Exhibition*. Boston: Mills, Knight and Company, 1883.

Jarzombek, Nancy Allyn. *Boston Art Club: 1855–1950*. Boston: Vose Galleries of Boston, 2000.

Johnson, Richard I. "The Rise and Fall of the Boston Society of Natural History." *Northeastern Naturalist* 11 (1994): 81–108.

Jordy, William H. "The Beaux-Arts Renaissance: Charles McKim's Boston Public Library." In *American Buildings and Their Architects: Progressive and Academic Ideals at the Turn of the Twentieth Century*, 314–396. Garden City, NY: Anchor Press/Doubleday, 1976.

Karageorghis, Vassos, in collaboration with Joan R. Mertens and Marice E. Rose. *Ancient Art from Cyprus: The Cesnola Collection in the Metropolitan Museum of Art*. New York: Metropolitan Museum of Art, 2000.

Katz, Harry L. "The Thomas Dowse Collection of Watercolors." In *The Boston Athenæum Collection: Pre-Twentieth Century American and European Painting and Sculpture*, by Jonathan P. Harding, 93–109. Boston: Boston Athenæum, 1984.

———. *A Continental Eye: The Art and Architecture of Arthur Rotch*. Boston: Boston Athenæum, 1985.

Katz, Michael B. *Class, Bureaucracy, and Schools: The Illusion of Educational Change in America*. New York, Praeger, 1971.

Kellogg, Augusta W. "The Boston Athenæum." *Public Library Monthly* 1 (October 1903): 35–39.

King, Donald C. *The Theatres of Boston: A Stage and Screen History*. Jefferson, NC: McFarland and Company, 2005.

Kirker, Harold, and David van Zanten. "Jean Lemoulnier in Boston, 1846–1851." *Journal of the Society of Architectural Historians* 31 (October 1972): 204–208.

Kirkland, John T. "Memoir of the Boston Athenæum, with the Act of Incorporation, and Organization of the Institution." In *The History of the Boston Athenæum, with Biographical Notices of Its Deceased Founders*, by Josiah Quincy, 25–43. Cambridge, MA: Metcalf and Company, 1851.

Koehler, Sylvester Rosa. *American Art*. New York: Cassell and Company, 1886.

Kolb, Marthe. *Ary Scheffer et son temps, 1795–1858*. Paris: Boivin, 1937.

Korzenik, Diana. *Drawn to Art: A Nineteenth-Century American Dream*. Hanover, NH: University Press of New England, 1985.

Kouwenhoven, John. *Made in America: The Arts in Modern Civilization*. Garden City, NY: Doubleday, 1948.

Kriegel, Lara. *Grand Designs: Labor, Empire, and the Museum in Victorian Culture*. Durham, NC: Duke University Press, 2007.

Langl, Joseph. *Modern Art Education: Its Practical and Aesthetic Character Educationally Considered*. Boston: L. Prang and Company, 1875.

Lawrence, Abbott. *T. Bigelow Lawrence*. Boston: privately printed, 1869.

Lerman, Leo. *The Museum: One Hundred Years and the Metropolitan Museum of Art*. New York: Viking Press, 1969.

Lipton, Leah. "The Boston Artists' Association, 1841–1851." *American Art Journal* 15 (Autumn 1983): 45–57.

Lockwood, Stephen Chapman. *Augustine Heard and Company, 1858–1862: American Merchants in China*. Cambridge, MA: East Asian Research Center, Harvard University, 1971.

Loring, Charles G. *Twenty-Five Years of the Museum's Growth: A Historical Sketch*. Boston: Museum of Fine Arts, Boston, 1901.

Low, Theodore Lewis. *The Educational Philosophy and Practice of Art Museums in the United States*. New York: Teachers College, Columbia University, 1948.

MacGregor, Arthur. *Curiosity and Enlightenment: Collectors and Collections from the Sixteenth to the Nineteenth Century*. New Haven: Yale University Press, 2007.

Mancini, JoAnne Marie. *Pre-Modernism: Art-World Change and American Culture from the Civil War to the Armory Show*. Princeton: Princeton University Press, 2005.

Marquand, John P. *The Late George Apley*. Boston: Little, Brown, and Company, 1937.

Marrinan, Michael. *Painting Politics for Louis-Philippe: Art and Ideology in Orléanist France, 1830–1848*. New Haven: Yale University Press, 1988.

Massachusetts Institute of Technology. *Report of the President . . . Massachusetts Institute of Technology, 1871–1872*. Boston: A. A. Kingman, 1872.

Mather, Frank Jewett. "An Art Museum for the People." *Atlantic Monthly* 100 (December 1907): 729–740.

Matheson, Susan B. *Art for Yale: A History of the Yale University Art Gallery*. New Haven: Yale University Art Gallery, 2001.

Mayne, Jonathan, trans. and ed. *Art in Paris, 1845–1862: Salons and Other Exhibitions Reviewed by Charles Baudelaire*. London: Phaidon Press, 1965.

McCaughey, Robert A. "From Town to City: Boston in the 1820s." *Political Science Quarterly* 88 (June 1973): 191–213.

McFadden, Elizabeth. *The Glitter and the Gold: A Spirited Account of the Metropolitan Museum of Art's First Director, the Audacious and High-Handed Luigi Palma di Cesnola*. New York: Dial Press, 1971.

McGuigan, Mary K. "'This Market of Physiognomy': American Artists and Rome's Art Academies, Life Schools, and Models, 1825–1870." In *America's Rome: Artists in the Eternal City, 1800–1900*, by William L. Vance, McGuigan, and John F. McGuigan Jr., 39–71. Cooperstown, NY: Fenimore Art Museum, 2009.

Melton, Maureen. *Invitation to Art: A History of the Museum of Fine Arts, Boston*. Boston: MFA Publications, 2009.

Miller, Lillian B. *Patrons and Patriotism, The Encouragement of the Fine Arts in the United States, 1790–1860*. Chicago: University of Chicago Press, 1966.

"The Montpensier Pictures." *Dwight's Journal of Music* 34 (October 3, 1874): 309.

"The Montpensier Pictures in Boston." *Scribner's Monthly* 9 (December 1874): 256–257.

Morris, Edward. "Ary Scheffer and His English Circle." *Oud Holland* 99 (1985): 294–323.

Munn, Geoffrey C. *Castellani and Giuliano: Revivalist Jewellers of the 19th Century*. New York: Rizzoli, 1984.

[Munroe, James Phinney]. "The Conservatory Journal." *Technology Review* 4 (April 1902): 137–169.

Murphy, Alexandra R. "French Paintings in Boston: 1800–1900." In *Corot to Braque: French Paintings from the Museum of Fine Arts, Boston*, by Anne L. Poulet and Murphy, xvii–xlvi. Boston: Museum of Fine Arts, Boston, 1979.

——. *Jean-François Millet*. Boston: Museum of Fine Arts, Boston, 1984.

——. *European Paintings in the Museum of Fine Arts, Boston: An Illustrated Summary Catalogue*. Boston: Museum of Fine Arts, Boston, 1985.

Museum of Fine Arts, Boston. *The Act of Incorporation, By-laws, etc. of the Museum of Fine Arts*. Boston: Alfred Mudge and Son, 1870.

——. *First Annual Report of the Committee on the Museum of Fine Arts, March 20, 1873*. Boston: Alfred Mudge and Son, 1873.

——. *Catalogue of Pictures Belonging to His Royal Highness the Duke de Montpensier, and of Other Pictures, Also Loaned to the Museum of Fine Arts*. Boston: Alfred Mudge and Son, 1874.

——. *Catalogue of Pictures Exhibited by the Athenæum; of Pictures and Engravings Bequeathed to the Museum of Fine Arts by the Hon. Charles Sumner, and of Works of Art Lately Added to the Collections of the Museum*. Boston: Press of Rockwell and Churchill, 1874.

——. *Specifications of the Materials to Be Provided and Labor to Be Performed in the Construction of a Portion of a Building on the Corner of St. James Avenue and Dartmouth Street, Boston, for the Museum of Fine Arts, in Accordance with Plans and Working Drawings Made by and under the Superintendence of John H. Sturgis and Charles Brigham, Architects, 7 Pemberton Square, Boston*. Boston: T. W. Ripley, 1874.

——. *Proceedings at the Opening of the Museum of Fine Arts: With the Reports for 1876, a List of Donations, the Act of Incorporation, By-Laws, etc.* Boston: Alfred Mudge and Son, 1876.

——. "The Museum of Fine Arts, Boston." *American Architect and Building News* 8 (October 30, 1880): 205–215.

——. *Communications to the Trustees Regarding the New Building.* Boston: privately printed by authority of the Committee on the Museum, [March] 1904.

——. *Communications to the Trustees II: The Collection of Casts in the New Museum; Recent European Opinion on Museum Methods.* Boston: privately printed by authority of the Committee on the Museum, [December] 1904.

——. *Communications to the Trustees III: The Museum Commission in Europe.* Boston: privately printed by authority of the Committee on the Museum, [January] 1905.

——. *Communications to the Trustees IV: The Experimental Gallery.* Boston: privately printed by authority of the Committee on the Museum, [January] 1906.

——. *Quincy Adams Shaw Collection: Italian Renaissance Sculpture; Paintings and Pastels by Jean François Millet, Exhibition Opening April 18, 1918.* Boston: Museum of Fine Arts, Boston, 1918.

Museum of Fine Arts, School of Drawing and Painting: First Annual Report of the Permanent Committee in Charge of the School. Boston: Alfred Mudge and Son, 1877.

Myers, Sir John Linton. *Handbook of the Cesnola Collection of Antiquities from Cyprus.* New York: Metropolitan Museum of Art, 1914.

Newman, William A., and Wilfred E. Holton. *Boston's Back Bay: The Story of America's Greatest Nineteenth-Century Landfill Project.* Boston: Northeastern University Press; Hanover, NH: University Press of New England, 2006.

Norton, Charles Benjamin. *Official Catalogue Foreign Exhibition, Boston, 1883.* Boston: George Coolidge, 1883.

"Notes." *Every Saturday: A Journal of Choice Reading* 2 (October 10, 1874): 416.

Nutter, Charles Read. *Harvard Musical Association, History from 1837–1937.* Boston, [1937].

Objects and Plan of an Institute of Technology: Including a Society of Arts, a Museum of Arts, and a School of Industrial Science; Proposed to Be Established in Boston. Boston: John Wilson and Son, 1861.

O'Brien, Maureen C., and Mary Bergstein, eds. *Image and Enterprise: The Photographs of Adolphe Braun.* Providence: Museum of Art, Rhode Island School of Design; London: Thames and Hudson, 2000.

O'Connor, Thomas H. *The Athens of America: Boston, 1825–1845.* Amherst: University of Massachusetts Press, 2006.

Oleson, Alexandra, and John Voss, eds. *The Organization of Knowledge in Modern America, 1860–1920.* Baltimore: Johns Hopkins University Press, 1979.

Oliver, Jean N. "The Copley Society of Boston." *New England Magazine* 31 (January 1905): 605–617.

Orosz, Joel J. *Curators and Culture: The Museum Movement in American, 1740–1870.* Tuscaloosa: University of Alabama Press, 1990.

Paige, Paul E. "Chamber Music in Boston: The Harvard Musical Association." *Journal of Research in Music Education* 18 (Summer 1970): 134–142.

Peirce, H. Winthrop. *The History of the School of the Museum of Fine Arts, Boston, 1877–1927*. Boston: T. O. Metcalf, 1930.

Perkins, Augustus Thorndike. *Losses to Literature and the Fine Arts by the Great Fire in Boston*. Boston: Press of David Clapp and Son, 1873.

Perkins, Charles Callahan. *Tuscan Sculptors: Their Lives, Works and Times; With Illustrations from Original Drawings and Photographs*. 2 vols. London: Longman, Green, Longman, Roberts, and Green, 1864.

———. *Italian Sculptors: Being a History of Sculpture in Northern, Southern, and Eastern Italy*. London: Longmans, Green, and Company, 1868.

———. *Art Education in America: Read before the American Social Science Association at the Lowell Institute, Boston, Feb. 22, 1870*. Cambridge, MA: Riverside Press, 1870.

———. "American Art Museums." *North American Review* 111 (July 1870): 1–29.

———. *Art in Education: Reprinted from the Second Volume of the Journal of the American Social Science Association*. New York: Nation Press, 1870.

———. *The Antefix Papers: Papers on Art Educational Subjects, Read at the Weekly Meetings of the Massachusetts Art Teachers' Association, by Members and Others Connected with the Massachusetts Normal Art School*. Boston: privately printed, 1875.

———. *Italian Art*. Boston: Little, Brown and Company, 1875.

———. *Raphael and Michelangelo: A Critical and Biographical Essay*. Boston: J. R. Osgood and Company, 1878.

———. "The Relation of the Artist to His Times." In *Proceedings at the Opening of the New Club House of the Boston Art Club, March 4, 1882*, 29–43. Boston: Milles, Knight and Company, 1882.

———. *Historical Handbook of Italian Sculpture*. New York: Scribner, 1883.

———. *Ghiberti et son école*. Paris: G. Pierson, n.d.

———, and John S. Dwight. *History of the Handel and Haydn Society, of Boston, Massachusetts*. Vol. 1, *From the Foundation of the Society through Its Seventy-fifth Season, 1815–1890*. Boston: Alfred Mudge and Son, 1883–1893.

Perkins, Robert F., Jr., and William J. Gavin III. *The Boston Athenæum Art Exhibition Index, 1827–1874*. Boston: Boston Athenæum, 1980.

Poulet, Anne L., and Alexandra R. Murphy. *Corot to Braque: French Paintings from the Museum of Fine Arts, Boston*. Boston: Museum of Fine Arts, Boston, 1979.

Preziozi, Donald, and Claire Farago, eds. *Grasping the World: The Idea of the Museum*. Aldershot, UK; Burlington, VT: Ashgate Publishing, 2004.

Quincy, Josiah. *The History of the Boston Athenæum, with Biographical Notices of Its Deceased Founders*. Cambridge, MA: Metcalf and Company, 1851.

———. *An Appeal in Behalf of the Boston Athenæum, Addressed to the Proprietors*. Boston: John Wilson and Son, 1853.

Redford, George, and J. Hadwen Wheelwright. *Studies of Italian Art: Descriptive Catalogue of a Series of Paintings in Water-colour by J. Hadwen Wheelwright, Taken from Pictures in . . . the Various Churches [and Galleries] of Italy and the Gallery of the Louvre*. London, 1866.

Rio, Alexis-François. *The Poetry of Christian Art. Translated from the French of A. F. Rio*. London: T. Bosworth, 1854.

Robinson, Edward. *Descriptive Catalogue of the Casts from Greek and Roman Sculpture: Boston Museum of Fine Arts*. Boston: Alfred Mudge and Son, 1887.

——. *The Hermes of Praxiteles and the Venus Genetrix: Experiments in Restoring the Color of Greek Sculpture by Joseph Lindon Smith*. Boston: Alfred Mudge and Son, 1892.

——. *Museum of Fine Arts, Boston. Catalogue of Casts: Parts I, II, and III; Ancient Sculpture*. Boston: Houghton, Mifflin and Company, 1892.

Robinson, John Charles. *Italian Sculptures of the Middle Ages and Period of the Revival of Art: A Descriptive Catalogue of the Works Forming the Above Section of the Museum, with Additional Illustrative Notices*. London: Chapman and Hall, 1862.

Rusk, Ralph L., ed. *The Letters of Ralph Waldo Emerson*. 6 vols. New York: Columbia University Press, 1939.

Ruskin, John. *Modern Painters by a Graduate of Oxford*. 5 vols. London: Smith, Elder, and Company, 1843–1860.

——. *The Seven Lamps of Architecture. By John Ruskin. With Illustrations, Drawn and Etched by the Author*. London: Smith, Elder, and Company, 1849.

Ryan, Thomas. *Recollections of an Old Musician*. New York: E. P. Dutton and Company, 1899.

Seaburg, Carl, and Stanley Paterson. *Merchant Prince of Boston: Colonel T. H. Perkins, 1764–1854*. Cambridge, MA: Harvard University Press, 1971.

Seasholes, Nancy S. *Gaining Ground: A History of Landmaking in Boston*. Cambridge, MA: MIT Press, 2003.

Sheehan, Roberta A. "Boston Museum School: A Centennial History, 1876–1976." PhD diss., Boston College, 1983.

Simpson, Lewis P., ed. *The Federalist Literary Mind; Selections from the Monthly Anthology, and Boston Review, 1803–1811, Including Documents Relating to the Boston Athenæum*. [Baton Rouge]: Louisiana State University Press, 1962.

Slautterback, Catharina. *Designing the Boston Athenæum: 10½ at 150*. Boston: Boston Athenæum, 1999.

Smith, Harriette Knight. *The History of the Lowell Institute*. Boston: Lamson, Wolffe and Company, 1898.

Smith, Walter. *Art Education, Scholastic and Industrial*. Boston: James R. Osgood and Company, 1872.

——. *Popular Industrial Art Education*. Boston: Rand, Avery, and Company, 1882.

Soros, Susan Weber, and Stefanie Walker, eds. *Castellani and Italian Archaeological Jewelry*. New Haven: Yale University Press for Bard Graduate Center for Studies in the Decorative Arts, Design, and Culture, New York, 2004.

Soucy, Donald, and Mary Ann Stankiewicz, eds. *Framing the Past: Essays on Art Education*. Reston, VA: National Art Education Association, 1990.

Sox, David. *Bachelors of Art: Edward Perry Warren and the Lewes House Brotherhood*. London: Fourth Estate Press, 1991.

"Spanish Painting." *Dwight's Journal of Music* 34 (October 3, 1874): 309–310.

Special Catalogue of the Collection of Antiquities, Exhibited by Alessandro Castellani, of Rome, in Rooms U, V, W, Memorial Hall. Philadelphia: Press of Edward Stern and Company, 1876.

Stebbins, Theodore E., Jr., and Virginia Anderson. *The Last Ruskinians: Charles Eliot Norton, Charles Herbert Moore, and Their Circle*. Cambridge, MA: Harvard University Art Museums, 2007.

Steegmuller, Francis. *The Two Lives of James Jackson Jarves*. New Haven: Yale University Press, 1951.

Stein, Robert B. *John Ruskin and Aesthetic Thought in America, 1840–1900*. Cambridge, MA: Harvard University Press, 1967.

Stetson, Charles B. Introduction to Joseph Langl, *Modern Art Education: Its Practical and Aesthetic Character Educationally Considered*, 5–7. Boston: L. Prang and Company, 1875.

Story, Ronald. "Class and Culture in Boston: The Athenæum, 1807–1860." *American Quarterly* 27 (May 1975): 178–199.

———. *The Forging of an Aristocracy: Harvard and the Boston Upper Class, 1800–1870*. Middletown, CT: Wesleyan University Press, 1980.

Stratton, Julius A., and Loretta H. Mannix. *Mind and Hand: The Birth of MIT*. Cambridge, MA: MIT Press, 2005.

Stratton-Pruitt, Suzanne L. *Bartolomé Esteban Murillo (1617–1682): Paintings from American Collections*. New York: Harry N. Abrams, 2002.

Struik, Dirk J. *Yankee Science in the Making*. Boston: Little, Brown and Company, 1948.

Sturgis, Russell. "Fine Arts. The Boston Museum's Enlargement. I." *Nation* 50 (March 27, 1890): 266–267.

———. "Fine Arts. The Boston Museum's Enlargement. II." *Nation* 50 (April 3, 1890): 285–286.

Swan, Mabel Munson. *The Athenæum Gallery, 1827–1873: The Boston Athenæum as an Early Patron of Art*. Boston: Boston Athenæum, 1940.

Sweeney, John L., ed. *The Painter's Eye: Notes and Essays on the Pictorial Arts by Henry James*. Cambridge, MA: Harvard University Press, 1956.

Ticknor, George. *Union of the Boston Athenæum and the Public Library*. Boston: Dutton and Wentworth, 1853.

Tokyo geijutsu daigaku hyakunenshi: Tokyo bijutsu gakkoh hen, dai 3 kan [A hundred-year history of Tokyo University of the Arts: Tokyo Fine Arts School, vol. 3]. Tokyo: Gyousei, 1997.

Tomkins, Calvin. *Merchants and Masterpieces: The Story of the Metropolitan Museum of Art*. New York: E. P. Dutton and Company, 1970.

Tomkins, Peltro William. *The British Gallery of Pictures*. London: Longman, Hurst, Rees, Orme, and Brown, 1818.

Treadway, Beth A. "The Doll and Richards Gallery." *Archives of American Art Journal* 15 (1975): 12–14.

Troyen, Carol. *The Boston Tradition: American Paintings from the Museum of Fine Arts, Boston*. New York: American Federation of Arts, 1980.

[Tudor, William]. "An Institution for the Fine Arts." *North American Review* 2 (January 1816): 153–164.

Vance, William L., Mary K. McGuigan, and John F. McGuigan Jr. *America's Rome: Artists in the Eternal City, 1800–1900*. Cooperstown, NY: Fenimore Art Museum, 2009.

Wallach, Alan. *Exhibiting Contradiction: Essays on the Art Museum in the United States*. Amherst: University of Massachusetts Press, 1998.

———. "The Birth of the American Art Museum." In *The American Bourgeoisie: Distinction and Identity in the Nineteenth Century*, edited by Sven Beckert and Julia B. Rosenbaum, 247–256. New York: Palgrave Macmillan, 2010.

Ware, William Robert. *An Outline of A Course of Architectural Instruction*. Boston: Press of John Wilson and Sons, 1866.

———. "James Munson Barnard." *Proceedings of the American Academy of Arts and Sciences* 41 (May 1905–May 1906): 837–841.

Watkins, Walter K. "The New England Museum and the Home of Art in Boston." *Bostonian Society Publications*, 2nd ser., 2 (1917): 101–130.

Webster, Sally. *William Morris Hunt, 1824–1879*. Cambridge: Cambridge University Press, 1991.

Wendorf, Richard. "Athenæum Origins." In *The Boston Athenæum Bicentennial Essays*, edited by Wendorf, 3–32. Boston: Boston Athenæum, 2009.

———, ed. *The Boston Athenæum Bicentennial Essays*. Boston: Boston Athenæum, 2009.

Wentworth, Michael. *Look Again: Essays on the Boston Athenæum's Art Collections*. Boston: Boston Athenæum, 2003.

White, Gerald Taylor. *A History of the Massachusetts Hospital Life Insurance Company*. Cambridge, MA: Harvard University Press, 1955.

Whitehill, Walter Muir. *Boston Public Library: A Centennial History*. Cambridge, MA: Harvard University Press, 1956.

———. *Boston: A Topographical History*. 2nd ed. Cambridge, MA: Belknap Press of Harvard University Press, 1968.

———. *Museum of Fine Arts, Boston: A Centennial History*. Cambridge, MA: Harvard University Press, 1970.

Williamson, William Landram. *William Frederick Poole and the Modern Library Movement*. New York: Columbia University Press, 1963.

Wolff, Katherine Frances. *Culture Club: The Curious History of the Boston Athenæum*. Amherst: University of Massachusetts Press, 2009.

———. "Whose Library?" In *The Boston Athenæum Bicentennial Essays*, edited by Richard Wendorf, 123–148. Boston: Boston Athenæum, 2009.

Yarnall, James L. *Newport through Its Architecture: A History of Styles from Postmedieval to Postmodern*. Newport, RI: Salve Regina University Press, 2005.

Zaitzevsky, Cynthia. *Frederick Law Olmsted and the Boston Park System*. Cambridge, MA: Belknap Press of Harvard University Press, 1982.

INDEX